A REPORTER IN SEARCH OF GOD

Books by Howard Whitman

A REPORTER IN SEARCH OF GOD

TERROR IN THE STREETS

LET'S TELL THE TRUTH ABOUT SEX

A REPORTER IN SEARCH OF GOD

BY HOWARD WHITMAN

1953

Doubleday & Company, Inc.
Garden City, New York

231
W59
a

Library of Congress Catalog Card Number 52–13387

Copyright, 1951, 1952, 1953, by Howard Whitman
All Rights Reserved
Printed in the United States at
The Country Life Press, Garden City, N.Y.

To Sue,
Constance, and Kenneth

The world of matter or even of atoms
is somehow too narrow for any one of us.

SIDNEY LOVETT

FOREWORD

As a journalist, I have done my exploring in the past mainly in two fields, psychiatry and sociology. I have not used these labels very much, because the traditions of journalism roll over in their graves at the sound of long-hair terms. But that was it nonetheless. My books and articles have dealt with mental health and with social problems because I felt that therein were the two great relationships of life: man's relationship to himself and man's relationship to others. Psychiatry seemed to take pretty good care of the first relationship, and sociology the second.

Then, I don't know just when, but I think perhaps one day when I was pruning apple trees or perhaps running a wheel cultivator along some rows of corn, I began to get interested in a third relationship. It seemed, actually, to be a cut above the other two and perhaps even to embrace them. It was man's relationship to his universe. This implied, of course, man's relationship to the infinite, or, if you please, to God.

This was a field which the journalist very rarely looked into.

In fact he shied away from it. It was imagined to be full of taboos and sacred cows and hypersensitivity. Better leave it to the long-hairs and the sermonizers, many a reporter figured.

In the past this was not only good sense but good journalism. Religion was like some antique vase on the shelves of people's minds; acquired at some half-forgotten time in the past, it was acknowledged to have some value or other, but was best left undisturbed on the shelf and put to no real use.

But in recent years one could hardly have been a reporter of the American scene and not sensed a great change. It was a new mood. It was not disillusionment, as in the wake of World War I. For the disillusioned man simply says, "The hell with it," and goes out to raise Cain as he did in the Roaring Twenties. This new mood was something different. It was a mood of confusion. More people were admitting they were mixed up, or secretly suspecting they were mixed up, than ever in the varied crises of the past. Our culture seemed to have come to the end of something.

It was a time for digging and exploration. It was a time to probe and ask questions. Here was an assignment to go on and a story to be told. And this is what a reporter is born to do.

HOWARD WHITMAN

CONTENTS

A REPORTER IN SEARCH OF GOD

1

THE SEARCH

People want to believe

I know the perfect solution to the world's problems," the mechanic said. The scene was a small New England garage. The mechanic, greasy-handed, was working with his head cocked upward at an odd angle under a car on a hydraulic lift.

"The perfect solution?" I queried.

"Yup," he snapped, shooting a blob of grease into a spring knuckle. Then he came out from under the car, straightened up his head, and said, "Man ought to abdicate and let God take over."

I set those words down in my notebook. They took their place beside so many similar words I had heard from the lips of Americans everywhere. A woman sitting next to me on a cable car in San Francisco said, "Human beings have made such a mess of this world. I wish God would take it back and run it Himself." A businessman in little Kutztown, Pennsylvania, remarked, "Mankind's had his chance—and muffed it." An old farmer near Ashtabula, Ohio, tersely crackled, "Only God can save the world now."

Any observer of the American scene knows how disoriented, how bewildered, how lost many people are. A New York publisher remarked, "People's nerves have never been closer to the surface." A social scientist observed, "People are reaching out in all directions for something to hold on to." Probably never before has there been so crying a need for faith. And no wonder. We have come through the pagan twenties, the depressing thirties, the warring forties, and on into the A-bomb fifties.

"Is this our forty years in the wilderness?" an old storekeeper in Louisville, Kentucky, wanted to know.

Americans everywhere are turning to God as they never have before. Some, like the mechanic, want to throw in the chips and let God take over. Some just want God to pull their chestnuts out of the fire. Some, badly frightened, are rushing to the security of God's apron string. Some sincerely want to find God and abide with Him.

Whatever the shades of motive, millions of Americans who previously may never have been sure, or even cared, whether God was in His heaven, are turning to Him now.

Churches are filling up. They are dusting off pews they haven't used in years. Memberships are zooming. The Oak Park Christian Church in Kansas City, Missouri—like many others—has had to hold duplicate services to accommodate the crowds. Evangelists, from Billy Graham to comely Kathryn Kuhlman, are packing 'em in. People are gobbling up religious books as though they were spiritual headache tablets. And one earthy metropolitan newspaper featured the story of Jesus in the very same big, black type it customarily reserved for dope rings, murders, and Hollywood divorces.

Reverend George W. Lucas, of the Bethel Baptist Church in Dayton, Ohio, described the feeling which people have nowadays as a "heart hunger." He said to me, "Everybody is feeling for something, listening for something. People are hoping that they can catch a bit of that *something* as the rush goes by."

At a medical school in the Middle West, I met a young man

who was dropping out in his final year. He had decided not to be a doctor. He was going to be a minister instead.

"Why?" I asked.

The youth, tall, Lincolnesque, with heavy black eyebrows, replied, "I've been cutting man apart for several years now. But I've never found what I've been looking for. The *soul* never showed up under my microscope."

A businessman in Lebanon, Pennsylvania, Harold U. Landis, head of the Penn Oil and Penn Lumber Companies, crisply remarked, "More and more people are willing to sit down and listen. They are realizing that there is more to life than meets the eye."

Undoubtedly you too have seen or sensed this "reaching out," this search for God. As a reporter I joined it. I went out on safari to the small towns and the big cities, to the factories and the farms, to the big crossroads and the obscure corners of America —to wherever the search led me.

This is the report of what I found. You will see in it not only a great many facts, but also, undoubtedly, some evidence of what those facts meant to me and what they did to me and *for* me. Perhaps they will mean something to you too—and do something to you too and *for* you.

My search took me over thousands of miles, to the corners of the continent. It took me to the inner sanctums of the Protestants, the Catholics, and the Jews. I probed the faiths of scientists, of nature lovers, and intellectuals—even atheists. The urgent questions of everyday religion and the personal relationship to God were ever upon the path. And tangled byways of the trail were strewn with such questions as the value of prayer, the problem of fate, and the existence of life after death.

But in this report I want to set down first things first. *Why* are people turning to God? What do they mean by "God"? In plain language, what *is* God? What are they searching for?

For the feeling I found in America was more than disillusionment. If we simply felt we were at the end of our rope, we'd hang ourselves. Period. Instead, our eyes are shifting upward and our spirits grope and we feel deep in our mysterious essence a "heart hunger."

"People are turning to God," said Bishop Henry Knox Sherrill, "because they've learned something from history. They've learned that mankind cannot save himself by himself."

We sat in the bishop's study on Fourth Avenue, New York, and saw out the window some of the wondrous towers of steel and stone which man had built. I remembered how that morning, in one of the wondrous towers, I had seen a busy little man tacking up notices about where to run in case it should come toppling down.

Bishop Sherrill continued, "Until now people felt that man himself could work out everything. 'Progress' was the answer to all his problems. He thought he was going up an escalator. All he had to do was learn more, invent more, progress more—and the world would get better and better. Now people can see that something has been left out of the picture. What has been left out—is God."

Something deep inside of people seems to tell them that. That's why they're reaching out. Bishop Sherrill, then presiding bishop of the Protestant Episcopal Church and president of the National Council of the Churches of Christ in the U.S.A., summed up the mood of the times—"Man's necessity is God's opportunity."

But certainly man has found himself in a spot before. He's been bogged down so many times. What's different about this time?

The difference, as I found it, is that now—for the *first time*—people feel *really* helpless. They've never felt *really* helpless before. They've always had some ace up their sleeve: science, technology, mass production, medicine, psychiatry, education, government, League of Nations, United Nations.

Do they *really* think such things can save them now?

"Naw," said a man I met. "We've exhausted the tangibles!"

So people are turning to God.

It's not just a "save me, save my skin" kind of turning. It is not all foxhole religion. Much of it is the sincere "heart hunger" Reverend Lucas of Dayton talked about. People are not merely quaking; they are searching.

When the National Council of Churches was being formed in 1950, Reverend Ralph W. Sockman, of Christ Church in New York, declared, "Never since the first century have conditions been so ripe for a new Apostolic Age. The dangers which threaten the world, the longings for peace and brotherhood in the hearts of common men, the visions of unity caught by church leaders, all furnish a striking parallel to the conditions confronting Christ's first disciples."

But if people are reaching out for God, just what is it they're reaching for? People I talked to everywhere, in country stores, along busy thoroughfares, on farms, and in skyscrapers—all of them used the word "God" without hesitation. But just what did they mean by "God"? In the language of grass-roots reporting, "Who, what, where, when, and why—is God?"

In Rochester, New York, I heard these questions batted back and forth between a minister and a biochemist. The minister, Reverend Murray Alexander Cayley, of the First Presbyterian Church of Rochester, had taken me to the home of the biochemist. I was an extra man on a pastoral visit. We had eaten a fine dinner of roast beef. Now the biochemist, the minister, their wives, and I sat about in the living room—and the question of God came up.

THE BIOCHEMIST: To me, God is intelligence. God is the sum-total of intelligence in the universe—the *supreme intelligence.*

THE MINISTER: I'd say God is *infinite spirit.*

THE BIOCHEMIST'S WIFE: Just what do you mean by that?

THE MINISTER: That's always the trouble when we use words. Words are finite. How can we use them to describe the infinite? Anyway, I'll try. I'd say God is a *spiritual reality, an intelligent personality, best described as infinite wisdom, love, and power.*

THE BIOCHEMIST'S WIFE: It's hard to picture anything like that.

THE MINISTER: Of course. A student of mine had the same trouble. He finally described God as an "oblong blur."

THE BIOCHEMIST: Why be so mysterious? I can observe God every day—in terms of supreme intelligence—right on my laboratory table. I put two chemicals together, they act upon each other, and there you have it. They act upon each other in accordance with absolute natural laws. There is intelligence, sense, rhyme, reason to the way they act upon each other. That intelligence, that *power* behind the immutable law and design of the universe, is my concept of God.

THE MINISTER: That *power,* you say?

THE BIOCHEMIST: Yes.

THE MINISTER: Well, you're a scientist. Have you ever *seen* power?

THE BIOCHEMIST: Certainly.

THE MINISTER: No, you haven't. All you've seen are the results of power—the manifestations of power. Can you see electricity? Oh, you can see molecular and electronic activity *caused by* electricity. You can see a bulb light, a spark jump. But can you see the essence—the power itself?

THE BIOCHEMIST: Well, we know it's there.

THE MINISTER: Precisely. *We know God is there.*

THE BIOCHEMIST'S WIFE: Isn't it easier just to think of God as a person? I don't mean any special person. That is, He wouldn't look like anybody in particular. But He would be, well, more or less in the shape of a person.

THE BIOCHEMIST: You mean an old man with a white beard sitting on the edge of a cloud?

THE BIOCHEMIST'S WIFE: Oh, I know it sounds childish. But when I pray to God, I like to think of Him as being something definite, not a particular person, but—in the general shape of a person.

THE MINISTER'S WIFE: Yes, what difference does it make? If you find it easier—if you're more comfortable thinking of God that way, why shouldn't you?

THE MINISTER: It puts you out on a limb. The scientists will look up into the sky with their telescopes and report back that your "Person" isn't there. They'll tell you that if anyone were up there, he'd fall through space and be burned up by friction.

THE BIOCHEMIST'S WIFE: Then where *is* God?

THE MINISTER: *Everywhere.*

THE BIOCHEMIST: Just as I said—the force and the power behind everything. The *supreme intelligence.*

THE MINISTER: Exactly. The *infinite spirit.*

The man of science and the man of religion agreed, in the end, that they were looking at the very same thing, even though they stood at different windows.

There are lots of windows to look through. In my reportorial rounds I came upon many definitions of God, perhaps all different, perhaps all the same. A schoolteacher said, "God is wisdom." A businessman said, "God is nature." Many people said, "God is love." Others said, "God is truth," "God is mercy," "God is the creator," "God is the supreme being," "God is the father."

Reverend Albert D. Betts, a Methodist minister from the little hamlet of Travellers Rest, South Carolina, gave me a rich, inclusive definition. Said he, "God is the creator and governor of the universe, the all-knowing, the all-just, almighty, supreme intelligence. God is spirit. God is light. God is love."

"One could give a hundred and one definitions, and all of them might be truthful approximations," remarked Rabbi Abba Hillel Silver, of The Temple in Cleveland. He tilted back thoughtfully in the chair of his book-lined study and offered this one—"God is the thinking and creating mind of the universe. He is the source of all its laws, physical and spiritual. The universe is a manifestation of God."

Having given the definition, the Rabbi sat forward and said, as if humbly to withdraw it, "Perhaps Maimonides was right——" (Moses ben Maimon, or Maimonides, Spanish Jewish philosopher, 1135–1204) "Maimonides said that it is impossible to describe God, that one can only say, 'God exists.' "

A week later I was at the Catholic Centre of the University of Ottawa, in Canada. William E. O'Meara, a staff member, said to me, "There is a big difference between knowing *about* God —and *knowing* God."

That started me off on the next phase of the search. Definable or indefinable, God exists. But how can we *reach* Him?

There is something called "religion." That's supposed to be the way, at least the official way, to contact God. How have we regarded religion in the past twenty-five years? How often has it been something a man kept in his closet like an old tuxedo, out of style, not a good fit any more, rather uncomfortable, but absolutely vital to drag out and don on certain occasions?

People in some cases have even been ashamed of religion. It has been smart to be cynical. What rough-and-ready man of the world wanted to be caught *believing?* Can you imagine "J.B." saying to his secretary, "No phones for the next few minutes, Miss Jones. I'm going to pray"?

Lin Yutang, in one of his incisive observations on our culture of the West, said that Americans often feel about religion the way they feel about their sex lives—"a strictly private matter," not to be owned up to freely.

What about religion in church and temple? Reverend Cayley said in a radio broadcast, "Too often our worship services are packed with meaningless rigmarole. . . . Our prayers may be eloquent and frequently verbose, but on a bright Easter morning they don't seem to turn many of the worshippers' wandering eyes from hats to heaven."

Venerable Dean William Ralph Inge, firebrand of St. Paul's in London, complained at Britain's Modern Churchmen's Conference, "Do we really expect the workingman to come to church to sing, 'I will think upon Rahab and Babylon' . . . or such gibberish as the verse of the 68th Psalm beginning, 'Rebuke the company of the spearmen'? I am told that the correct translation of these words is, 'Rebuke the hippopotamus.' " (Literal translation: "the wild beast of the reeds.")

Simplicity is, and always has been, the brightest garb of truth. For clergymen, the truths of religion may be perfectly clear despite the archaic language and obscure allusions. But the average man and woman hasn't attended the seminary, hasn't studied theology, isn't much more familiar with the special language of religion than he is with the lingo of lawyers or the shoptalk of nuclear physicists.

Why should religion hide its light under a bushel?

At Reverend Cayley's house, at supper with his wife and four children gathered around him at the table, everyone held hands in a circle when it was time to say Grace. This is the Grace which they said:

"Thank you, God, the food is fine. Make us grateful all the time."

It was that clear, that direct, that simple. The children knew what they were saying. They understood.

Don't adults, in their religious observances, also want to know and understand? Otherwise, on Easter morning how are you going to turn their eyes "from hats to heaven"?

Religion has sparked some of the most surging, irresistible movements in human history. It also has slumped into doldrums. Rabbi Barnett R. Brickner, as I talked with him at Cleveland's Euclid Avenue Temple, regretted that religion in the last few decades hasn't had a moving force, a "dynamic."

"When religion has a dynamic it sweeps all before it. But it hasn't had a dynamic. It has grown too static. It has become concerned with housekeeping," he declared. "Too many of our clergy have been peddling the trappings of religion, not the essence. The trappings will not help people. Only the *essence* will."

The fragmentation of religion into multiple faiths and denominations, often with hot rivalries, certainly has not helped to bring people the *essence*. Rabbi Brickner pointed out, "When a man sees four different kinds of houses of God on four corners his natural reaction is, 'Where is the truth? They can't even agree among themselves.' "

He suggested a "Parliament of Religions," a kind of spiritual United Nations in which all faiths and denominations could proclaim the Fatherhood of God and the Brotherhood of Man.

It would be one way of stressing that which is common to all major, enduring religions: mankind's bond of love to God. This, most theologians agree, is the *essence* of religion. When one feels the warmth and strength and everlasting security of that bond he is having a religious experience. No matter whether he feels that bond in a church or temple, at his desk in an office, at home with his wife and children, or out in the country looking at a tree; the important thing is to feel it.

Albert Einstein, who has poised human intellect athwart the universe like cosmic calipers, describes the religious feeling thus: "The most beautiful thing we can experience is the mysterious. It is the source of all true art and science. He to whom this emotion is a stranger, who can no longer pause to wonder and stand rapt in awe, is as good as dead: his eyes are closed. This insight into the mystery of life, coupled though it be with fear, has also given rise to religion. To know that what is impenetrable to us really exists, manifesting itself as the highest wisdom and the most radiant beauty which our dull faculties can comprehend only in their most primitive forms—this knowledge, this feeling, is at the center of true religiousness."

The key is religious experience; not simply to be religious, but to *feel* religious. I was discussing human happiness with a priest in Canada, Father Andrew Guay, when he said, quoting one of the Roman Catholic philosophers, *"Joy is the echo of God's life in you."* That seemed to sum it up. If one can feel God living within himself, then indeed he knows true religion. He knows the comfort, the *joy*—as the philosopher put it—of the inner presence of God.

That is how we reach God. That is the God factor in human beings. Without the God factor, the playing of a violin is just horsehair scraping on catgut. With the God factor, it is music. The British physicist, Sir James Jeans, once said that the universe resembles not so much a mathematical formula or a mechanical law as a "great idea." Take the word "universe" itself. Etymologically it means "turned into one"—one physical system, one cosmos. Add the God factor and it means "one verse" —*one poem.*

But in my reportorial rounds I found that people who were searching for God weren't satisfied simply to try to define God, or even to reach God. They wanted to *understand* God.

At Heidelberg College, in Tiffin, Ohio, while the Korean war was raging, some of the students were hard pressed to understand God in connection with the bloodshed. During a week of nasty fighting, a group of students got together on Sunday night for one of their fireside conferences at the home of a faculty member. This time they fired their questions at the president of the college, Terry Wickham.

"Why does God let people kill one another?" they wanted to know. "If God *is* God, why does He let such awful things happen? Why does He let human beings get into such messes?"

Wickham leaned back in his chair and slowly replied, "God is not going to solve our problems for us." Then he went on to explain. . . .

When God created man, he did not simply design a robot. Probably the most wondrous thing about the creation of man is that God *withheld his hand*. He made man a self-directing being. He gave us humans a certain freedom of choice. We are free to work *with* God or *against* Him. We can accept the leadership of God, or reject it.

We have, then, our own human responsibility.

Responsibility . . . We have no right to blame God every time we get ourselves into a mess. *We* got into it!

But there is an even broader perspective. What is life all about? Do we really know, or do we just catch the most shadowy glimpses? "The essence of faith is the belief that God *has* a purpose in human life," remarked Reverend Arthur E. Wilson, of the Beneficent Congregational Church, of Providence, Rhode Island. He continued:

"Our lives, as individuals, can be used to live out that purpose. But we mustn't become preoccupied with life itself, as if our sole objective were to save our physical lives. It is easy to fall into that trap in these days of atomic fear."

Once Reverend Wilson was discussing "atomic fear" with a group of students in Providence. The question came up: "What if an atom bomb hit where you were? What if you were buried under heaps of debris? What if you were virtually mummified, like the people of ancient Pompeii?"

"Well, if that were the case," Reverend Wilson answered, "and if some archaeologists dug me up a few hundred years later, I can only hope they'd find me making my rounds in the parish, doing God's work as best I could, and not feverishly digging a bomb shelter!"

Many an individual has difficulty in accepting the idea of life's ultimate purpose. He isn't willing to throw in with the rest of humanity. He insists that God pay attention to him *personally,* that God sit on his shoulder, as it were, and guide his every step and ward off all misfortune and deliver to him every kind of earthly sugarplum.

"That's turning God into a divine bellhop," says Reverend Cayley. "Certainly God is interested in each one of us, the same as I am interested in every corpuscle in my body. I am definitely interested in corpuscle No. 7,792,678—even though I may not constantly be in personal attendance upon it!"

Man would be a pretty insignificant creature if God were, indeed, sitting on his shoulder guiding every move. Even man himself can make such creatures—marionettes, robots, automatons. But God made something special, a creature in his own image; since man, like God, has powers of creation, decision, inspiration, and love.

Perhaps these powers are what man is reaching out for in these troubled times. Perhaps he wants to team up with God again, to live and act as God's image, to realize the God within him.

On a bus in New York I sat behind a middle-aged woman who was reading the Bible. I leaned forward and asked, "Do you read it often?"

"Every day," she replied.

Her husband was seriously ill, she said, and the two of them read the Bible together.

"Do you think if you read the Bible, God will help you?" I inquired.

"No, not especially," she said softly. "But we will be more able to *help God.*"

2

WHAT SCIENCE HAS LEARNED ABOUT GOD

Is it scientific to believe?

A reporter starting out on any big assignment wants to take in the overall view first. If he is covering a flood area, he flies over it first by plane for the big picture, then moves in on the ground for the details. If he's covering a war, he checks in at the briefing room to examine maps of the entire front, then picks the sector where he thinks the news is hottest.

In the search for God I first took my big swing around America. From it I got the "feel" of the story, the overall view, a sizing-up of the heart hunger of our time. Then, like any other reporter, I wanted to move in where the news was hottest. That's why I chose science as the sector to cover first.

We're in a scientific age. All of us are saturated with science, from the moment we plug in our electric razor in the morning until we snap off the television set at night. We live in a world of incomprehensible gadgets which, fantastically beyond us as they are, we take more or less for granted. The symphony conductor Andre Kostelanetz remarked in the dawn of the television era, "There are a host of things about the universe which I do not clearly understand, any more than I can understand, for example, the technicalities of the process by which we can be heard and seen in this new dimension, the miraculous television screen. Such finite things as these inventions were inconceivable mysteries a few years ago."

If science is so wise, perhaps it can tell me about God, I thought. It knows about so many other things I only vaguely understand—including the miraculous television. Perhaps it has secrets all its own: secrets of belief, or even secrets of disbelief. I wanted to move in close and investigate. So I went into the laboratories and took scientists away from their Bunsen burners, and their retorts and their cyclotrons and even their nuclear reactors. And we talked about God.

One I remember best is Dr. Paul Francis Kerr, a noted mineralogist. From him came the first big reorientation. And you do have to reorient when you wade into science. Earth isn't earth any more, at least not quite as you always had figured it. And man isn't quite man any more as you always had known him. And space and the universe and *all there is* must be thrown into new focus.

I met Dr. Kerr in his laboratory at Columbia University. As we talked he strode across to a table on the other side of the lab and picked up a chunk of rough iron.

"It's a visitor," he said. "It dropped on this earth from somewhere in outer space. Where did it come from? What's the universe like outside—*up there?*"

Don't we wish we knew!

A few moments later Dr. Kerr took from a cotton-stuffed box a small black chunk of what looked like coal. "Uranium oxide," he announced. "It is continuously giving off radioactive particles. A residue of lead is left behind. By measuring the amount of lead we can find how old this chunk of material is."

"How old is it?" I asked.

"Somewhere between 643,000,000 and 950,000,000 years," he replied.

Whew!

But that's nothing. Hobnob with the scientists very long and you'll be living on a diet of exclamation points. The astronomers told me that the sun which warms our earth is just one of 100,000,000,000 suns in our galaxy alone—and there are at least 1,000,000,000,000 galaxies! These (within the limits of the so-called "observable universe") are somewhere in a band of space which extends outward from the earth 12,000,000,000,000,000,000,000 miles.

But that's just the *big* universe. The nuclear physicists took me on an opposite journey into the *little* universe.

How big is a hydrogen atom? Well, think of an inch on the ruler. Divide it mentally into hundredths. Now divide the hundredths into hundredths. Take one of those "hundred hundredths" and divide that into hundredths! Don't get dizzy, just divide by a hundred once more—and then divide by two. You've got it, the diameter of a hydrogen atom!

That's still large as nuclear physics goes. Suppose the nucleus of that tiny hydrogen atom were the size of a baseball. Then, in proportion, the electron, which whirls around it, would be a speck eight city blocks away!

Where is a place for God in all this? I went to the scientists to learn what they have *found out* about God, what they *think* about God, how they *feel* about God. Have they proven, in their scarcely comprehensible excursions into the macrocosm of the heavens and the microcosm of the atom, that there *is* a God? Or have they proven there is no God? Is there a place in the billions of miles or in the billionths of an inch for a factor known as faith?

Or has science made God old-fashioned?

Dr. Kerr, as he put the meteorite and the uranium back into their laboratory niches, said, "I cannot believe that the facts of science are mere accidents. The more we study the earth, the more sense it makes. Our findings give us more of a background for faith. I do not believe, as some do, that our faith is becoming vague. No, we are just stripping away some of the superstition and mythology. We are getting closer to the essence."

"Just what do you mean—'closer to the essence'?" I inquired.

"Well," said the scientist, "what I have learned about the earth has made me no less a believer in a Supreme Power, but actually more so. You see, some of the early philosophers simply *guessed* there was a God. All they could say was, 'God *is*.' But we have so much more evidence to go on. We have seen so much more of His handiwork. We can say, 'God *must be*.'"

Primitive man, then, on a purely logical basis, could have settled for a fourth-class god. But modern man—with his excursions into the tiny atom and the mammoth cosmos—knows what a terrific creator God must be. Dr. Kerr felt we were lucky to live in an age when so many wondrous evidences of the greatness of creation had been brought out in the open.

Far from debunking God, the scientist—as Dr. Kerr saw it—was merely chalking up another one of God's glories with each fresh discovery. He was piling up the "evidence for faith."

Dr. Kerr, as a mineralogist, had garnered his evidence from the earth itself. As we left his laboratory and stood outside Columbia's Schermerhorn Hall I noted an Old Testament quotation chiseled in the stone above the entrance: *"Speak to the earth and it shall teach thee."*

In Cleveland, Dr. Jason John Nassau didn't speak to the earth; he spoke to the sky. He spoke to it through a giant Schmidt-type telescope (a 36-incher) in the Warner and Swasey Observatory of the Case Institute of Technology. What had it taught him?

"It makes me marvel," the astronomer said, "not so much at the bigness of the universe, but at the ability of man's mind to comprehend it. The mystery is that this little creature wandering around on the face of the earth has a machine in him—a *mind*—which can reach out to the universe.

"I think the essence of our faith is in the relationship of this human mind to the universe. Simply studying the universe alone does not bring you to a belief in God. The universe is physical. God is spiritual. But if you *do* believe in God, then the study of the universe, its bigness and its complexities, is sure to make your belief richer and strengthen it. It has for me."

Dr. Nassau and other astronomers have found out a good deal about *how it is* up there, but not much about *why it is.* So you have your billions of suns and galaxies. Who put them there? Why are they there?

I turned to Dr. Jan Schilt, head of the astronomy department at Columbia, an expert on the star systems, the scheme and pattern of the cosmos. Photographs of the heavens, taken in Johannesburg, Union of South Africa, were analyzed and "diagnosed" in his New York laboratory. I put the question to him: *Why* is it so?

"The hope and faith of astronomers is that eventually we will find that it is so because it couldn't be otherwise," Dr. Schilt replied. "The greatest shock would be to find that it all just happened by chance."

Where does *man* come in? A much earlier astronomer, Galileo, ran afoul of contemporary beliefs because, in discovering that the earth wasn't the center of the universe, he seemed to cast aspersions on man's importance. How could man be such a hot shot if he were just a little mite on a planet whirling around the sun?

How about it, Dr. Schilt? What have you and other modern astronomers done to man if—now—he is just a mite on a planet whirling around one of 100,000,000,000 suns in 1,000,000,000,000 galaxies! Is man less significant than a flea on an ant's back?

"No," the astronomer replied. "Finding all these star systems, these patterns, is just a game—an artificial game. The thing we really have to account for is the *observer:* man. Without the observer one can make a universe on paper.

"Now, if the earth is the only place where there is an observer, then it certainly is the center of the universe.

"It is conceivable that there are other planetary systems revolving about other suns. But it is also conceivable that there is no other planetary system outside our own. Likewise it is conceivable that there may be life on other planets—and equally conceivable that no life exists except on our own earth (with the possible exception of lichens on Mars which some scientists believe exist, but without certainty, and which, if they do exist, may result from the earth's influence).

"It makes more sense to me that man *is* the center of the universe, that he is the sole observer. I don't see any sense in all this being duplicated. I don't think other astronomers are looking at *us*."

If Dr. Schilt was correct, then man is a much hotter shot than ever he was in Galileo's day. All those billions of suns up there —are really no more than the lights on man's Christmas tree!

At the Lederle Laboratories in Pearl River, N.Y., I talked with Dr. Benjamin Minge Duggar, the discoverer of aureomycin. As a biologist, Dr. Duggar had wrestled with the toughest problem in all science: What *is* life anyway? In fact, Dr. Duggar tried to create life. At the University of Wisconsin, during the 1930's, he spent five years trying to make living matter out of nonliving.

He took a combination of salts such as is known to exist in living organisms; he took material to furnish carbon; he took several materials to furnish nitrogen. By heat and filtration he rendered all his ingredients sterile. He put them in flasks, put some of the flasks in incubators and some in a room subject to normal conditions. At intervals he "harvested" the flasks to see if he had produced any life. Over the five-year period he varied the experiment in dozens of ways, correcting errors, trying new methods, new conditions, new variations. "But in the end," he said, "we were not able to establish any change even to give us the hope of living material."

"In other words," I said, "you put all the necessary ingredients of living matter together——"

"Exactly."

"But it wouldn't live."

"Correct!"

This has been the cul-de-sac of the scientists for a long time. But for Dr. Duggar the failure to create life was not a negative experience. It was a building block in a scientist's philosophy. In seventy-eight years Dr. Duggar (he was seventy-six when he discovered aureomycin) had seen a good deal of the wonders of science. He said to me:

"I feel it doesn't matter much whether there is a creator of 'all this' or whether God *is* 'all this.' "

"But—scientifically—why allow for God at all?" I questioned.

He replied, "I *can't* conceive of nothing. I *can* conceive of something. Something can't come out of nothing."

At Wayne University, in Detroit, anthropologist George Lechler spoke of two widely held theories of how life began on this earth: (1) Heterogenesis—inorganic matter, at some point in time, turned into organic matter. (2) The Theory of Inoculation —organic matter came to the earth in splinters from other planets, via meteors.

But after a bit Dr. Lechler wheeled in his chair and blurted, "All this begs the question. The real question is how to explain the spiritual and the material. What is behind the origin of life? What is life? So many fall back on the explanation—'the law of chance.' But even this presupposes a 'law.' Whose law? For me, I prefer the belief in a creator, divine, supernatural. I cannot accept chaos."

Not all the scientists I met believed in God. A few were atheists. Many were confirmed agnostics.

One young physicist said frankly, "You either feel it or you don't feel it. I just don't feel it. I suppose it's like being in love.

"The supposition of God is a fine thing," he continued, "because it can't be disproved. But it can't be proved either. That's why I won't take a position one way or the other. As for science, the physical tinkering I do is like a kid playing with an alarm clock. I see no reason why I should believe in a Supreme Being."

A physiologist declared, "When I ask, 'What is life?' I'm up against a blind alley. I acknowledge that blind alley. But I am not going to use faith as a way out.

"I wouldn't call myself an atheist, because that in itself implies a belief. As a scientist, I have no more evidence that God *doesn't* exist than I have that He does exist. I would label myself an agnostic. That's the only position my scientific training would support. It means 'I don't know.' I'll go further and say, 'I don't think I'll ever know.' "

A chemist insisted, "I'm not an agnostic. I'm an atheist."

"On what grounds?" I asked.

"We are told that God is love," he replied. "Yet the world has gone through strife and horrors of ever-growing ferocity. If there were a God, it would have been perfectly possible for Him to have made the uranium-235 nucleus unfissionable. Then there could not have been an atomic bomb.

"In the laboratory where I work I see things governed by statistical law. There is no need for spirit, no need for divine power. I do not believe life has any purpose. Man has not been on this planet very long, and he won't be here much longer."

At Brookhaven National Laboratory, the atomic research center on Long Island, I heard two nuclear physicists debate the issue.

1ST PHYSICIST: I've always worried about death. I wanted to do something about putting off death. That's why I went into science. I feel death is the end of everything.

2ND PHYSICIST: Why?

1ST PHYSICIST: Because death is the total end of the organism. All of its functions have stopped. It couldn't possibly live again.

2ND PHYSICIST: But you're seeking a natural explanation of a supernatural thing. You're forgetting all about God.

1ST PHYSICIST: Is there a God?

2ND PHYSICIST: There *must be* a God.

1ST PHYSICIST: You can't prove it.

2ND PHYSICIST: Well, how did the world come into being?

1ST PHYSICIST: I don't know.

2ND PHYSICIST: Do you know that it did *not* come into being by supernatural power?

1ST PHYSICIST: I have an open mind on the subject.

2ND PHYSICIST: Then why don't you accept the belief in supernatural power?

1ST PHYSICIST: I'm right in the middle.

2ND PHYSICIST: No you're not. You've taken the opposite position. You say death is final. Why is it final?

1ST PHYSICIST: I go by the proof of my own senses.

2ND PHYSICIST: But you cannot prove by the senses that which is *beyond the senses.*

I heard many such discussions among the scores of scientists who had descended upon old Camp Upton, the scene of Brookhaven, after it donned its atomic dress. Even the young lab workers were intent on finding meaning as well as microbes beneath the microscopes. Twenty-four-year-old Rosalind DuBow, a junior cytologist, remarked, "I went into science on account of my desire to explain life. I want to believe in God because of the order in nature and the greatness of the whole universe. But I can't quite accept the idea of God that was taught to me in my childhood."

Perhaps, on that remote Long Island site where science was being pushed to its furthest limits, a few clashes with faith were inevitable.

The most fantastic machine I saw at Brookhaven was the cosmotron. I lost balance for a moment when I stepped out on a balcony and peered down upon this awesome gadget looking like the inside of an electric motor swollen beyond all belief. It gave me the dizzy feeling of suddenly stepping out of reality.

After a second or two I became aware of men working around the huge machine, so small they looked like lead soldiers.

I talked with one of the physicists involved with this fantastic device. What were they trying to do with it? Well, they didn't want merely to split atoms. They were after the infinitesimal particles inside the nuclei of atoms!

And how did they propose to get at them? The physicist explained that they'd get about ten billion protons whirling around the huge magnetic circle of the cosmotron. They'd whirl them around 3,000,000 times, which would take all of one second. That would speed them up to a velocity of 176,700 miles per second (nearly the speed of light). Then they'd bang the protons into a target of atomic nuclei.

In this way, the physicist said, a good deal more would be learned about the protons, neutrons, and mesons within the nucleus of the atom.

"All very well," I commented. "But tell me—do you feel there is any ultimate purpose in what you are doing?"

"Purpose?" he questioned. "What is purpose?"

"Why are you doing all this?"

"I'm a physicist. I like physics because it is fun."

"I mean, is there any ultimate good—any spiritual side—to all of this?" I inquired.

The physicist replied quite solemnly, "As a scientist I have to distinguish between questions which have meaning and those which do not. Vague terms like 'spiritual' and 'good' roll off the tongue very nicely—but that's all."

I asked, "Do you think there is any ultimate purpose in life itself?"

He replied, "That's meaningless because there is no way of checking. Anybody's answer is as good as anybody else's."

There was a long, uncomfortable pause. And then the physicist added, "I was always told as a child that I should have faith, and all that. But I examined those things and found they didn't hold water. So I threw them out. I feel better now."

I met a few other scientists who had done likewise. They didn't want any truck with "faith" unless it could be laid out upon a laboratory table, analyzed, proven or disproven.

But more typical was Seymour Block, a young Brookhaven physicist. He was very much the pure scientist when he developed the "Block model" ionization chamber, a gas sampler, in June, 1950. But while he was waiting publication of his invention in the scientific journals he became uneasy. What if someone else beat him to the punch?

"I began to get worried," he said. "I was really conscious of the God factor then. I sure hoped God would let me publish first!"

The scientist had come to the end of his controls.

I wondered what the men at Brookhaven's atomic pile thought about God, these scientists who sat all day at the esoteric controls of the huge reactor while the formidable process of nuclear fission went on. Did they see any place for God in these mighty machinations?

John J. Floyd, the reactor research co-ordinator, stepped out of the highly secret precincts of the pile into an anteroom and the two of us sat down on a wooden bench.

"Sure, as I work at the atomic pile I feel God is there," he said. "I have faith that in the long run atomic energy will be beneficial."

"Then you think God is personally masterminding this atomic pile?" I asked.

"No," he replied. "God simply set up the principles. We use them."

An engineer at the pile added, "If man developed a bomb capable of destroying the world, I don't think God would suddenly appear and stop it. No more than God stops forest fires." Atomic energy, the engineer implied, is man's baby. Man is responsible for what he does with it.

I asked him if he regarded it as "scientific" to speak of God. Did a scientist feel he could account for God "scientifically"?

"Certainly—by the physical laws of mass and energy," he replied. "Up in the pile we see mass disappearing and becoming energy, but nowhere can we add or subtract to the total of mass and energy. Where did mass and energy come from? We know we can't make it. We have found laws to prove we can't make it. Yet it must come from somewhere. There must be a higher power who *can* make it."

I noted when I went to a party on the Brookhaven site one evening that all the scientists—agnostics, doubters, and true believers—sang with equal gusto when the accordion and the guitar played, "Atomic power, Atomic power, *It was given by the mighty hand of God.*"

In many of the scientists I met in my travels I sensed a new mood of humility. Ten or fifteen years ago science thought it had the world by the tail. It was going to solve everything. As one elderly chemist remarked, "We thought science was magic." But today the best scientists know *how little* they know. They have pulled aside the veil of mysteries—only to find deeper mysteries.

I sat in on a bull session of scientists at the Carnegie Institute of Technology, in Pittsburgh, and heard even the champions of mathematics—the "absolute" science, the "exact" science—admit that science is neither absolute nor exact. "We even could make different types of mathematics if we accepted different axioms to start with," remarked Dr. George H. Handelman, assistant professor of mathematics.

Dr. Dennistoun W. Ver Planck, professor of mechanical engineering added, "Science—if you pursue it far enough—either takes you to a dead end or back to the beginning. Finally you have to fall back on faith."

In her lab filled with beakers, burners, bottles, and bell jars, a woman biochemist at Columbia University quietly observed, "Scientists used to place a lot more stock in 'facts' than they do today. They have found that many of their 'facts' aren't facts at all. And no matter how many 'facts' they've accumulated, there are still so many unknown facts out ahead."

She turned to her enormous shelf of glassware and gadgets. As her eye swept over it she added, "A scientist's faith begins where facts end."

The old conundrum, "When is a fact not a fact?" has dogged science for centuries. For while science, flourishing its lorgnettes of "fact" and "proof," often has looked down its nose at other fields of knowledge, it also has had to swallow, on occasion, such "facts" as that the world is flat and the sun travels around it.

If science has had its comeuppance, it may be because a number of "facts" have backfired in recent years. What science called a "solid" turns out not to be a solid, but a collection of empty spaces. Matter, which science regarded as "indestructible," turns out to be not indestructible—but convertible into energy. John Dalton, English chemist, gave science the "fact" that the atom was "indivisible, eternal, and indestructible." Actually it has none of those three qualities. Euclid gave science the "fact" that the whole is always equal to the sum of its parts. But the whole of an atom weighs less than the sum of its parts (explained by a new principle called "mass defect"). Physics has had as its very backbone the principle of *certainty* (physical laws would guarantee a given result from a given cause *every time*). But today physicists have a new toy: the *uncertainty principle.*

In northern Iran in April, 1951, a University of Pennsylvania anthropologist dug up human bones dating back to the Ice Age —evidence that modern man, Homo sapiens, apparently lived at the *same time* as such subhuman species as the Neanderthal Man. This rocks the whole theory of evolution. At the University of Arizona, Dr. Edwin F. Carpenter in December, 1950, even upset science's idea of an evolving universe. He had found, he said, new evidence that the entire universe was condensed out of a primeval gas in *one, single act.*

No wonder Dr. Schilt quizzically remarked, "We knew more about the universe ten years ago than we know now."

When the nation's top nuclear physicists met at the University of Rochester late in 1950—mid-point in the Twentieth Century—they were more baffled than enlightened by their newest experiments. They had found out just enough to put crimps in most of their theories. In a world which had regarded science as "magic" and scientists as "knowing everything," it was refreshing to receive from this meeting the honest report: "Nobody knows what holds the atom together, nor why there are so many particles, nor why they have electrical charges, nor why the atoms don't disintegrate, nor why the universe itself holds together."

In his laboratory at Wayne University, Dr. Charles W. Creaser, professor of zoology, sat beside a table on which reposed in rather unprepossessing circumstances (floating upside down in a jar of formaldehyde) a frog of the variety known as "Burnsi." He was, in the language of science, a Mendelian mutant, inasmuch as he was a spotted frog without spots. As such, this unfortunate fellow was ideal for teaching students Mendel's law of genetics.

But Dr. Creaser quickly dispelled any notion that the "Burnsi," or any other of the trappings of science, provides an open-sesame to truth. We call it Mendel's law. Mendel discovered it. Who wrote it? Who decided that frogs should have spots in the first place?

"We speak of the 'scientific method,'" commented Dr. Creaser. "People think the scientist comes into his laboratory and starts in methodically to make his discoveries. Actually, he finds out a lot of things by indirection. He backs into them. He follows clues and tip-offs. He has a few facts to start with—then he draws on insight, even revelation, to leap beyond the facts."

The things which science calls "facts" Dr. Creaser referred to as "almost true." He said, "They are very useful and very interesting—but they are not like the philosopher's truth."

One of his colleagues, Dr. Katherine M. Chamberlain, professor of physics at Wayne, recalled that Newton had likened himself to a child playing on the seashore while the ocean of truth lay undiscovered. "We are still on the seashore," she said. "What we *know* is just the tiniest fragment. For the whole, we depend upon faith."

The new mood of humility becomes science, even in the view of scientists, far more than the erstwhile attitude of Mr. Know-all. Dr. Nassau, the Cleveland astronomer, commented, "It is too bad the public has regarded scientists as makers of gadgets, as magicians. The best scientists are philosophers. Science is an art, like poetry, and it too seeks to reach the higher truth. It is interested in ethical matters and moral matters and the eternal aim of life to bring about more human happiness."

This was impressed upon me dozens of times. In many scientists I found a passion for the ethical life, for human values, for a better world. When I asked, "What do you basically believe in?" a typical answer was—"My faith is in humanity. I believe that as man now harnesses physical forces, so he may one day be able to harness the mind and emotions. In the ultimate purpose of creating a better world—that's the nearest I can come to God." This came from William A. Higinbotham, chairman of the Federation of American Scientists.

In a biological laboratory I met a young technician who was busily making a new index. He was hunched over a half-dozen file drawers spread out at odd angles. "Terms, thousands of terms!" he exclaimed. "This is biology, the science of life. But in the whole darned index you can't find the words 'kindness,' 'gentleness,' 'joy,' 'love'—the things which affect life most!"

Perhaps as scientists show more that they are poets and philosophers those words will find a place in the index.

I met a few scientists who were too bashful to admit they were reaching for idealistic goals.

Take Dr. Redginal Hewitt, parasitologist. His entire life, virtually, had been devoted to the war against three tiny worms, *wuchereria bancrofti, onchocerca volvulus,* and *loa loa.* These worms cause a tropical disease known as *filariasis,* the symptoms of which may be the grotesque swelling up of parts of the body (elephantiasis) or blindness.

Dr. Hewitt had sweated through the tropics on the trail of these parasitic worms, worked doggedly with natives in Central and South America to rid them of the disease, performed innumerable experiments with animals, tracked the worms to their breeding places in tropics all over the world. On the back of his desk at the Lederle Laboratories was tacked a scientist's "war map"—colored pins sticking in it wherever he had found his enemy, the worms, in action.

Finally, during 1945–7, Dr. Hewitt developed a drug which destroys the worms and cures the disease. Four hundred million people in the tropics, one fifth of the world's population, need no longer fear this scourge of deformity and blindness.

"What egged you on to do it?" I asked him.

"Well, I certainly wasn't spurred on by any burning desire to be of benefit to humanity," Dr. Hewitt replied. "I don't regard myself as any kind of do-gooder or humanitarian. I just did it because I was interested in it. It was a challenge."

"What about Ehrlich and Pasteur, don't you think they were humanitarians?" I countered.

"No," he replied. "I think they were just scientists. I think they just had a problem and were interested in licking it."

But a few moments later Dr. Hewitt told of the surge of joy he felt when he first used his drug among the natives and saw an eighteen-year-old girl's enormously enlarged leg return to normal and a blind boy's sight restored.

"Is it just a coincidence," I asked, "that you discovered a way to help those people? Why not devote your energies to spreading the disease, to making it worse?"

He laughed. "Hell, I'd never do that."

"Why not, you said you weren't a humanitarian."

"Well, I just can't explain it."

A few days later I repeated the story to Dr. Nassau, raising the question, "Just why do scientists want to do good anyway?"

"Maybe that's the God in us," Dr. Nassau responded.

Robert A. Millikan, distinguished elder statesman of American science, once said, "Just how we fit into the plans of the Great Architect and how much He has assigned us to do, we do not know. . . . But fit in we certainly do somehow, else we would not have a sense of our own responsibility."

The elder scientists, I found, had the deepest spiritual awareness. Most of them had gone through the phase of agnosticism. They had moved on. As one elderly geneticist remarked, "When we think we know a lot, we're agnostic. When we learn how insignificant our knowledge is—we return to God."

While the young man, cocksure in his laboratory, says, "How wonderful I am! Look what I've found in the atom!" the old man says, "Isn't God wonderful—look what He's put in the atom!"

3

IS THERE AN AFTERLIFE?

What happens to you when you die?

A healthy new respect for scientists came over me after my explorations among the telescopes and test tubes; not for the cocky whippersnappers of science who think they know everything, but for the wise men of science who know they know nothing, or next to nothing.

I had talked to some of the scientists about life, even their futile attempts to create life. Now a new question obtruded itself. What about death?

Death has been a fascinating subject always—and probably always will be. As a reporter I wanted to plunge right to the core of it, and I knew the core of it was one simple question, "Is death the end?"

That's why I wrote the name "Fred Sanders" in my notebook and why I knew I'd have to talk to him. Fred Sanders, who lived in Belvidere, New Jersey, was an average, everyday American in every respect except one: he had been "dead" once.

He was on the operating table at Warren Hospital, Phillipsburg, New Jersey, on July 7, 1951, undergoing a routine operation when all of a sudden his heart stopped beating. This is what the surgeons call a "cardiac arrest," but in layman's terms it means the man is dead. The basic engine of life, the heart, has stopped. The primary distinction between life and death, the heartbeat, has disappeared.

Fred Sanders was "dead," but he wasn't "pronounced dead." That's the technical difference. He was "dead" for five minutes. During that interval—a brief moment or an eternity (call it what you like)—Dr. Homer Bloom cut open Sanders' chest, carefully exposed the lifeless heart, and massaged it with his hands. The heart started beating again. Sanders, after five minutes of "death," came back to life.

What about his brief sojourn to what Shakespeare called "the undiscover'd country from whose bourn no traveller returns"? Had Sanders contradicted the poet? Had he actually "crossed over" and returned? Had he glimpsed the future life, the land beyond, the mysterious other side of the veil?

"I can tell you this," said Fred Sanders. "Life has been different ever since." He hesitated, groped for words. "I can't explain it. I must have gone through something. Life is happier. My job doesn't bother me. It just seems to be a different world."

As to the experience itself—"Everything was just like a dream." Sanders didn't know what had happened to him until it was all over. The operation was at 9 A.M. Saturday; he didn't regain consciousness until 4 A.M. Monday. "During that time," he said, "I ate ice cream and didn't even know it. The nurses told me later. I even asked for more and didn't know it." He added jokingly, "It must have tasted good."

Sanders recalled how, after it was all over, he expressed his thanks, literally *heartfelt* thanks, to Dr. Bloom. "Don't thank me," the doctor said. "Thank Someone much greater than I. I couldn't have done it alone."

Sanders, deacon and elder of the First Presbyterian Church in Belvidere, fully believes in the "Someone much greater" who enabled him to return to life. While in terms of finite sensation and worldly experience he has no memory of his five minutes of "death," he freely admits that he has come back a changed and different man, almost as though he had unconscious memories or perhaps even a glimpse of the great beyond, which, though submerged in the amnesia of worldly consciousness, has left a mark upon him.

"I don't worry about anything any more," Sanders told me. "I used to be a regular fuss-budget. I'd get all upset if the car was dirty or if the grass wasn't cut. Now those little things just don't bother me. I enjoy myself more. Why, I just came home from Florida and I had a wonderful time!"

Life seemed to have taken on a new bouquet for Fred Sanders. There was a sweetness in it and a tranquility he hadn't known before. I pointed out to him that many persons, in their last moments before passing on to death, show in their faces a quiet serenity, a relaxation, even a trace of a smile, as though they had caught a glimpse of what lay ahead and found it pleasing.

"Is it possible you caught a glimpse?" I asked him.

"Maybe so," he said. "All I know is—life is different!"

From the beginning of time and perhaps to the end of it human beings have wondered and will wonder what *happens to us when we die*. Is there an afterlife? Many have felt that if there *isn't* then life is hardly worth living. "If this puny planet is life's only locale, then 'the sooner it's over, the sooner to sleep,' " said New York's Reverend George A. Buttrick at the Washington Conference on Children in 1950. He made it clear, of course, that he felt this "puny planet" was not life's whole story. Nearly every profound belief, every religion, from the primitive redman's belief in a happy hunting ground to Christianity's heaven, has pivoted upon the mystery of life after death. Deep down, we all are concerned with it. Children display their first conscious fascination with death, and anxiety about it, usually at ages six to eight. From then on, throughout life, all of us carry in the deep wells of our minds a pervasive, if latent, concern.

Why not?

What journey is more important? What riddle more challenging?

In my explorations of faith in modern America, in seeking answers in the crowded cities and most isolated villages, in the roaring factories and the quiet farms, in the laboratories of science and the sanctum of philosophy, I found that death to many is not an *end* but an *adventure*.

"To me, death is the greatest adventure in living," said Stephen B. Bromley, at the Lederle Laboratories, Pearl River, New York, where "miracle drugs" are fashioned. He added, "I actually look forward to death. The only thing I fear is a *manner of death,* something which may be painful or ugly—but not death itself."

Dr. Robert Foster Kennedy, the famed neurosurgeon, remarked with a curl of the lip, "I don't think death is all it's cracked up to be." He debunked the fear, grief, heavy emotion we associate with death and scorned its special vocabulary of "loss," "sorrow," and "bereavement." Though a medical man, he seemed to be saying with St. Paul, "Thou fool, that which thou sowest is not quickened, except it die." Dr. Kennedy himself passed quietly into death early in 1952.

In Stevensville, Pennsylvania, Mrs. Ruth Sumner, a farm wife and onetime Bible student, told of her experience at the deathbed of her father:

"I asked him, 'Are you afraid? Do you have doubts?' And he replied, 'No, I'm just as anxious as I can be to see what's ahead.' I knew he had a deep belief that life somehow goes on. I asked him, 'Suppose you're wrong?' He looked out of calm and peaceful eyes just before he passed away and answered me, 'Well, I can't do anything about it now. I've believed and had pleasure believing.' "

A young woman scientist at the Brookhaven National Laboratory, the atomic energy center, took the opposite tack. She didn't believe. "I don't *want* to disbelieve," she said. "I'd be a lot more comfortable if I believed in God and the afterlife. The thought of death scares me."

Indeed, the thought of death scares millions and always has. Louis XIV of France had a new palace built just so he would not have to gaze out his chamber window upon the Church of St. Denis, where his ancestors were interred. He couldn't stand looking at the place where he someday would lie dead. In our own time, William Randolph Hearst had so marked an aversion to death, or even the thought of it, that intimates dared not mention the word in his presence. The subject, during Hearst's lifetime, had to be handled with kid gloves in his newspapers. The dismay of one of his editors was boundless when, owing to a typographical error, the phrase "heart attack" appeared in the newspaper as "hearst attack."

By contrast, I met on his return from Mulungwishi, Belgian Congo, Bishop John M. Springer, a missionary to Africa for forty-nine years. He not only didn't fear death; he was ready to receive it with open arms.

At his home in Mulungwishi, near the old stamping ground of Livingston, Springer kept a wooden crate, a coffin, stored away and ready for use when he had need for it. He didn't mention it to the natives, who were up to their necks in superstition and probably would have fled the mission in fright. But one day the natives got wind of it. A delegation of three came climbing up the rocky bluff to Springer's house and asked in astonishment, "Is it true—you have a box—all prepared—to die in?"

The good bishop sat down and explained to them his thoughts about death. Then he showed them the crate he had prepared and gave his reasons for having it ready: the climate was hot and gummy, there were no undertaking facilities, burial would have to be the same day. Hence the bishop, not a young man any more, was ready. Here was the box, and there was a grave already dug in the rocky hillside.

I asked him, "What are the thoughts about death of a man who can approach it so unafraid?"

He shot a question back at me, "Aren't you thinking of death as the worst thing that could happen? Look at Romans, 8:28."

I did, later—"And we know that all things work together for good to them that love God, to them who are the called according to *his* purpose."

Springer continued, "I have no more fear of death than fear of going out the door of this room. I know there is something nice out there. . . . Why should we be afraid to go home?"

In my belief that in the innate wisdom of everyday people lie embedded the nuggets of truth, I went to Detroit to talk to workers in factories. I vividly remember the fiery foundry of the Cadillac plant, where molten iron flowed from the cupolas into the great bull ladles. I talked with several men who had been working all day around licking, lapping flames. One of them remarked, "It looks like hell around here"—and he meant it literally.

"What about it?" I asked John Matthews, a crane operator working under the fiery maw of a cupola. "Is this the sort of hell-fire that awaits us if we're bad?"

"No," Matthews said thoughtfully. "I don't believe the good Lord would stand for anything like that. I think he's *for* us, not against us."

I put the same question to John Young, whom I found working on the "shake out" (shaking out the iron engine castings from the sand molds). Yes, Young believed in hell, all right. But he didn't believe it was a place of fires. It was a place of torment. "Like a jungle, with thorns," he said. As for heaven, he had a simple, satisfying belief about that: "just a place where there's nothing to worry about."

Willie Collins, who was testing the hot iron as it came out of the cupolas for engine blocks and cylinder heads, had a personal experience which helped shape his view of the afterlife. It was in 1934, after he'd undergone an operation. On the third day of recovery, the bad day, he was hemorrhaging seriously. He lay, not unconscious, but as he put it, "half awake, half asleep.

"I had a vision then. I saw myself flying around buildings up in the air. I heard someone say, 'Doctor, is there any chance for him?' Then I felt myself going away. I had golden wings on my shoulders. I don't know how I got them. But I flew around until I came to a large white building. I flew around it—and then I woke up. Y'know, I could see myself in heaven flying around with those gold wings just as clearly as I can see you now!"

A more earthy view of immortality was voiced by Lester Walden, who was grinding cam shafts on the night shift. "Is death the end?" he asked rhetorically. "Not exactly. After all, the elements are there. You may fertilize a rose!" He smiled wryly. "I just can't think of a great soul coming to an end. Take Abraham Lincoln. I can't imagine a spirit like that ceasing to exist."

An assembly-line worker, Albert Youngblood, summed up the view most workers held of life after death: a Biblical, religious belief in spiritual survival. "Our souls will never die," he said. "The soul was made unto the image and likeness of God. God is a spirit. Our souls are spirits. Once we die this life on earth won't matter at all. The only thing that is important is when we stand before God."

What about it? Do we collect rewards if we've been "good"? Are we punished if we've been "bad"?

Frank Licari, an automatic screw-machine job-setter, cautiously ventured, "If we do something here on earth that's worthwhile, we might have something upstairs that's worthwhile, too." He looked around the room, then added, "People say 'rest in peace' . . . but the evil ones won't rest."

Twenty-one-year-old Clara Wiktorowski, who drove a hundred Cadillacs a day, ferrying finished cars from the end of the assembly line to the loading dock, had little doubt that we humans are punished for our sins. "I think one of the worst punishments is not to have a happy death," she said.

"A happy death?" I queried.

"Yes, like passing away quietly in sleep," she explained. "Compare that to long suffering and a lingering illness."

Billie Brewer, a young fellow who put on the left-rear spring as the cars went by, saw it still another way. He didn't see why *everyone* shouldn't get a crack at the "better place." He felt everyone should be graded alike. "After all," he said, "if people have a bad time here, maybe it was caused by something outside them. Take a bad guy—he may be pushed by something. Maybe he doesn't *want* to be bad, but at the same time he's just got to be bad." Merciful Brewer would make a spot in heaven for him, too.

While the idea of immortality—in some form—seems ingrained in human consciousness, the *precise form* remains a tantalizing mystery. Lester Walden, in the factory, had said, "You may fertilize a rose." I heard that idea again, weeks later, from one of New York's outstanding psychiatrists, Dr. Carl Binger, of Cornell Medical School. A lover of nature and a believer in the endlessness of the process of life, Dr. Binger speculated, "Wouldn't it be satisfying to have one's remains dug in at the base of a rosebush, to live again, as it were, as a beautiful flower?"

Benjamin Franklin, at the age of twenty-two, already was concerned with the *form* of immortality, though he did not dispute the *fact* of it. He wrote his own epitaph, as follows:

The Body of
B Franklin Printer,
(Like the Cover of an Old Book
Its Contents torn out
And stript of its Lettering & Gilding)
Lies here, Food for Worms.
But the Work shall not be lost;
For it will, (as he believ'd) appear once more,
In a new and elegant Edition
Revised and Corrected,
By the Author.

Mrs. Franklin D. Roosevelt, late in 1951, was taken to task by a Catholic prelate for saying on a radio program, "I don't know whether I believe in a future life . . . I think I am pretty much of a fatalist." The great lady didn't mean any harm, of course. She was being honest, as always. But to clarify the record, she announced a few days later:

"I do believe in immortality, but I haven't been able to decide exactly what form it might take. There are so many possibilities. For example, there is a question in my mind whether we will appear physically as we appear now. [Whatever the form] we won't be able to change it, and we must accept it. And we must meet it with courage and do our best."

This simple, courageous acceptance of life as God made it was what Mrs. Roosevelt meant by being "pretty much of a fatalist." Her inability to know (as no one can) whether immortality means actual physical reliving was her basis for not knowing whether she believed in a future life. But in God and *some form* of immortality she most certainly did believe.

Such beliefs are personal. Often we go through most of our lives only vaguely aware of just what our beliefs are. No one has called, as it were, for a vote, a show of hands, a statement of position. Then, one day, life itself calls for such a declaration. The poet Kahlil Gibran, deeply moved by the death of his sister, Sultana, reached into the inner recesses of his heart and said to a friend who was with him in the time of grief:

"Everything dies that it may be born again in another form. The rock dies to become stones and pillars in the temple; the candle dies to be transformed into light; a piece of wood dies to give birth to the fire within it; a fruit dies to give birth to the seed, which dies in turn to give birth to the tree. Everything goes back to its origin. Life is a going forth; Death is a coming back. Life is an investment; Death is a dividend. Life is a thought embodied; Death is a bodiless thought. While God is both—Life and Death."

In my reportorial search for God, I explored beliefs in many and varied forms of immortality. There was, for example, the belief of Reverend Albert D. Betts, of Travellers Rest, South Carolina.

Betts held to that fond hope of many a frail human in life's hours of grief: to be united in a blissful hereafter with loved ones who have passed on. "I believe in personal immortality," he told me. "I do believe in reunion with our loved ones, not in bodily form as flesh and blood but in some form as individuals." He added that in this reunited state all of us would have "freedom of the universe." We would be able to participate in "God's greater enterprises."

In Providence, Rhode Island, Reverend Arthur E. Wilson insisted that the afterlife is not for the dust-made, earth-bound protoplasmic mechanisms we know as our physical selves. The afterlife is for the *real person,* which Wilson described as "personality, mind, essence."

"In death this spirit, this *soul,* continues without the limitations of the body in an existence similar to ours on earth but with much greater opportunity," he said.

"Just where? In what place?" I asked.

"No 'place' is needed because there is no physical body," Wilson replied. He smiled, "When we on earth keep insisting on a 'place' for the life hereafter, we are like the goldfish looking out of his bowl and wondering how people can possibly live outside without water."

The great humanist wave which swelled in the latter nineteenth century and broke over into the twentieth brought rational, down-to-earth notions of immortality. Never mind things we cannot comprehend, said these thinkers. Let's explain life after death in terms we *can* comprehend; let's be logical. I found strong traces of humanism in modern America, particularly among the businessmen, the men of affairs, the impassioned exponents of the theory that two plus two equals four.

"The only immortality is through our children," said an industrialist in Pittsburgh. "We give them life, and they carry on. But when *we* die, we're six feet under. Brother, that's all."

"Oh, I suppose there is a form of life after death," mused a politician in Los Angeles. "Our deeds live after us. People either mark us good or mark us lousy. And in my business that's something to think about!"

A clubwoman in Boston remarked, "The ones who miss us and keep on loving us—that's the only immortality I believe in. The worst thing is to die unloved and forgotten."

Finally, I came upon the immortality-of-the-ghost cult. These were the patrons of the séances, who thought of life after death as a flitting about in ectoplasmic abandon with nothing better to do than haunt houses, carry messages, and amuse oneself passing from room to room without benefit of doorways.

I visited a woman medium on upper Broadway, in New York, and heard from her not only all about the ghost world of those who had "crossed over" but also got a personal message from a purely fictitious relative of mine. I invented the relative, "George," just to see what would happen. The medium, enthroned in the inner sanctum of her expensively furnished apartment, proceeded forthwith to bring "George" back from the "astral plane." She sat with a trance-like stare and solemnly conversed with his ectoplasmic spirit, which, she insisted, was hovering over my left shoulder.

"Oh, George is fully materialized now," she clucked. "He's smiling at you. My, what nice broad shoulders he has! Make yourself at home, George. That's the way. . . . Ho, ho, you know what he's doing now? Why, he's sitting on top of the lamp shade. What a pity you can't see him, as I can!"

Hokum artists, from the days of totem worship in darkest Africa, have preyed upon man's anxiety over death. They have combined fear and grief with the innate wish to believe, spiced these ingredients with magic, and taken many an emotionally upset human along the road of bunko and deceit.

Religion, philosophy, and science all have fought against such high jinks. And many a calm thinker has been glad, after all, that we do not live in a world of disembodied departed ones who are here and not here at the same time. Mrs. Roosevelt once mused, "I think all of us wonder at times whether those we love who have died are somewhere near, and whether only our own lack of sensitivity keeps us from having contact with them. If they are, and they have to watch helplessly while the earth people make mistakes, it must be a desperately difficult situation."

The three main religions of America—Protestantism, Catholicism, Judaism—tell us about the afterlife largely in Biblical terms. They give us, quietly and with love, anchors of faith based upon what the devout believe to be the revealed word of God.

Reverend David Roberts, of the Union Theological Seminary, in New York, succinctly set forth the prevalent Protestant belief: "The soul continues to live and at the end of time is reunited with the body, which is resurrected in spiritual form."

This "end of time" and the resurrection of the dead is thus foretold in the New Testament: "For the Lord himself shall descend from heaven with a shout, with the voice of the archangel, and with the trump of God: and the dead in Christ shall rise first: Then we which are alive and remain shall be caught up together with them in the clouds, to meet the Lord in the air: and so shall we ever be with the Lord. Wherefore comfort one another with these words."

As to damnation (hell) and salvation (heaven), Protestant beliefs range widely from Calvinist predestination, which holds that at the beginning of time God elected some souls to be saved and others to be damned, to Universalism, which holds that everybody is going to be saved because God is all-loving.

The individual Protestant finds his belief somewhere between these extremes. Many believe with Reverend Chasteen T. Murray, of the Vermont Avenue Baptist Church, Washington, D.C., that "there certainly will be a separation of souls . . . Dillinger and I won't be in the same category."

What is salvation? "One achieves fellowship with God," Roberts explained. What is damnation? "The soul undergoes continued torment, or even is annihilated."

Christian ideas of heaven, hell, and judgment are rooted deeply in the final book of the New Testament, The Revelation of St. John the Divine. Of judgment we find, "And I saw the dead, small and great, stand before God; and the books were opened: and another book was opened, which is the book of life: and the dead were judged out of those things which were written in the books, according to their works."

As for hell: "But the fearful, and unbelieving, and the abominable, and murderers, and whoremongers, and sorcerers, and idolaters, and all liars, shall have their part in the lake which burneth with fire and brimstone . . ."

And heaven: "The twelve gates were twelve pearls; every several gate was of one pearl: and the street of the city was pure gold, as it were transparent glass. . . . And there shall be no night there; and they need no candle, neither light of the sun; for the Lord God giveth them light: and they shall reign for ever and ever."

Between the extremes of heaven and hell, the Catholics add a third or "middle" state called purgatory. This is a place of temporary suffering and penitence where the souls of those who have sinned, but not sinned sufficiently to be damned to hell, are cleansed so that they may qualify for heaven.

The logic of this belief is explained in a Catholic instruction book as follows: "Scripture tells us that nothing defiled can enter into heaven. Likewise, passage after passage tells us that hell is eternal. It would indeed be cruel that anyone be condemned forever for just a slight fault. In purgatory slight offenses and punishment due to forgiven sins are cleansed 'so as by fire.' Besides we are asked to pray for the dead. . . . But those in heaven need not our prayers and for the damned they are of no avail. There must then be a middle state."

Judaism never has stressed the afterlife with the same vigor as has Christianity. Prior to the dispersion of the Jews from the Holy Land in 70 A.D. there was little religious emphasis on life after death. But with the subsequent persecutions in Europe and the seeming pointlessness of life on earth Jewish thinkers turned for solace to the contemplation of a hereafter.

Today the Reform wing of Judaism believes in the finality of physical death but in the immortality of the soul. Rabbi Hirsch E. L. Freund, executive director of the Synagogue Council of America, explained, "The body dies and is laid in the dust, but the spirit lives on in the shelter of God's love and mercy." The Orthodox wing believes in bodily resurrection. As explained by Rabbi Freund, "The bodies of the dead will be resurrected when the Messiah arrives on earth." This millennium, says Orthodox Judaism, will come either when the world becomes all good and is saved or becomes all bad and must be remade.

As to heaven and hell, Orthodox Judaism clings to notions of reward and punishment. Live a good life and you will earn happiness in the world to come; succumb to evil and you will be punished. But Reform Jews place more emphasis on making a heaven or hell right here on earth. As explained by Rabbi Freund, "If we make a better world right here, the next world may be better too."

One naturally wishes he could prove immortality in finitely understandable terms. The three main religions throw us back on faith. Why can't we prove this thing scientifically? Why can't we put it in a test tube, spread it out on a laboratory table, express it in a foolproof formula?

I never expected, in my explorations, to find scientists who would touch the matter of life after death with a ten-foot pole. I was mightily surprised when I did.

At Duke University, in Durham, North Carolina, Dr. J. B. Rhine told me he was satisfied that he and his experimental research staff had proven that man has a soul. "The question of the human soul," he declared, "boils down to this: Is there anything extra-physical or spiritual in human personality? We have proven in our laboratory that there is. We now have experimental evidence that such an extra-physical factor exists in man."

For two decades Rhine, pioneering in the field of extra-sensory perception, had been conducting experiments in the nonphysical properties of the human mind. He had been investigating such phenomena as precognition (the ability to know things in advance), clairvoyance (the ability to know that which is not present to the senses), telepathy (the ability to communicate from mind to mind), and psychokinesis (the ability of mind to influence matter).

I reviewed the many experiments of Duke's Parapsychology Laboratory, even participated in some demonstrations. I knew then what Rhine meant by an "extra-physical factor" in man. He meant the strange ability of the human mind to reach out beyond the senses, without regard to time and space. Even in the most elementary experiments—predicting the symbols on cards drawn out of a pack—Rhine had shown that the human mind goes far beyond the laws of chance. Such research is still in its infancy. Yet Rhine feels it has established a basic premise:

"In the sense that we have found evidence of nonphysical properties of the mind, we have sustained the soul theory of man by experimental research," he declared.

As to life after death, Rhine reported:

"When extra-sensory perception was found to function without limitation from time and space, this discovery was taken to mean that the mind is capable of action independent to some degree of the space-time system of nature. Now, all that immortality means is freedom from the effects of space and time; death seems to be purely a matter of coming to a halt in the space-time universe. Therefore the conclusion that there is at least some sort of technical survival would seem to follow as a logical derivation from the extra-sensory perception research."

There are, of course, some who dispute Rhine's findings and

many who would take his spiritual conclusions charily. Yet I found many top-flight men of science who thoroughly believed in an afterlife though they have found no way of proving it in the laboratory, just as they thoroughly believe in life itself though they have found no way of creating it in the laboratory. Typical was Dr. James H. Williams, director of research at the Lederle Laboratories.

"I certainly do not believe that death is the end," he asserted. "I believe there is a great deal more to the system than our mere existence here. I have a feeling there is a purpose that goes far beyond life as we know it. I cannot think of anything more unsatisfying than approaching death with the feeling that death has no purpose or that life had no purpose."

This I accepted as one scientist's credo, one scientist's faith. But in all my probings, the proposition which best stuck to my ribs was a simple, elementary exercise in logic by the straight-talking Reverend Murray A. Cayley, of Rochester, New York.

"Let's compare the universe and all creation to a school system," said he. "Here we are on this tiny thingumbob called earth. We are first-graders, and like all first-graders we don't know much about where we came from or much about where we're going. Now wouldn't it be a poor superintendent of schools who got us through the first grade and then thumbed his nose and said, 'Ha, ha, that's all there is!' Why I could run a school system better than that!"

As Cayley pointed out, all of us—or nearly all of us—believe in some Creator, some Supreme Power, some Ultimate Intelligence behind the marvel of the universe. Isn't it reasonable to suppose that this Superintendent of Schools has more than the first grade to offer us?

4

GOD AND PSYCHIATRY

Is psychiatry Godless?

Early in the search for God—if I may compare myself to a voyager upon a vast sea—I came upon a continent which demanded exploration. I could not sail around it. There it loomed, rising from the sea with a great challenge. It was the new, still only vaguely charted, continent of psychiatry.

I had to explore it.

Perhaps I would find there new trails to the God I was seeking. Or—one could not tell—perhaps I would find there a substitute for God, an ersatz god, or even the unnecessity of God.

Psychiatry in its modern form is a twentieth-century phenomenon younger than a good many of the doctors who practice it. It has cut as wide a swath as any movement of our time, influencing not only the treatment of the mentally ill but also art and literature, science and government, philosophy and religion. It has been called a fad, a cult, a gimmick of screwballs. It also has been called a road to truth, the greatest advance in man's knowledge of man, and the hope of the world.

But at the heart of the debate there seemed for me a central question: Does psychiatry have a place for God?

In my search for the answer I turned first to Dr. Leo H. Bartemeier, of Detroit. Being an outstanding Catholic layman and a psychiatrist also (once president of the American Psychiatric Association), Dr. Bartemeier seemed a pivotal witness. I put the question to him point-blank, "Is psychiatry in conflict with your religion, or in any way a threat to your concept of God?"

"Certainly not," Dr. Bartemeier replied. "I am an active Catholic and a devout one. Psychiatry does not impinge on my religion in any way. It is a medical specialty, no more against God than surgery or any other branch of medicine."

I entered the statement in my notebook. Over the ensuing weeks and months more statements of a like tenor found their places across the pages. From the expensive specialists' offices of Park Avenue, New York, to the public clinics of San Francisco, I found psychiatrists of many religious persuasions who saw no conflict between psychiatry and their concept of God.

To them, psychiatry was simply new knowledge. And, expectedly, it made a good many timid folk tremble lest, in accepting it, they would have to throw all old knowledge out the window. But, these psychiatrists pointed out, every scientific leap forward —in physics, biology, astronomy—has met the same sort of resistance. Galileo was condemned to a dungeon for insisting that the earth revolves around the sun. This, some believed, would undermine all religion. Yet certainly no Catholic, Protestant, or Jew feels today that his religion has been wrecked because Galileo put the earth where it belongs.

This was one side of the story.

I also found the other side.

One psychiatrist I interviewed in New York said to me in the quiet of his private office, "I'm afraid I cannot help you in your search for God. You see, I don't believe in God."

"Are you an atheist?"

"The label isn't important," he said. "I just have no need for what you call 'God,' nor do I believe any such being exists."

Another psychiatrist observed, "The necessity for God and religion is a hang-over from childhood. God becomes the grown-up's substitute for father, a 'father figure' as we say." Another said, "If I were forced to declare myself in one camp or the other, the best I could do would be to call myself an agnostic. I just don't know—and I'm not going to pretend I know. I am a doctor, not a preacher."

As a reporter, I was up a tree. It was clear that psychiatry could be described as "God loving" or "Godless," depending upon which particular psychiatrists you were talking about. But, as a reporter, I often have discovered that when you are up a tree you get a better view. The better view in this case was the view of psychiatry as a branch of science in which individuals of many, and contradictory, personal philosophies could be found.

Dr. Bartemeier had compared it to surgery. Is surgery *for* or *against* God? I'm sure there are surgeons who are devout Catholics, Protestants, and Jews—as well as some who are agnostics and atheists.

I shifted my approach. Instead of questioning individual psychiatrists (each entitled to his individual belief), I would examine this new branch of knowledge itself. Was there anything about psychiatry *per se* which was at odds with God? Or could this new science be of service to religion? If it was atheistic or anti-God, let's say so. Or, if it had something valuable to add to, and not detract from, man's religious nature, let's say that too.

The new trail led to Boston. . . .

I went to Boston for a two-day meeting called the "National Conference on Clinical Pastoral Training." It was held at the Boston University School of Theology. When you stripped away the verbiage and looked beneath the labels, what this meeting really amounted to was a co-operative conclave—a kind of trade conference—between preachers and psychiatrists. Dozens of speeches were given, some by state hospital superintendents, some by professors of psychiatry, some by practicing psychiatrists and pychoanalysts; and some by ministers, chaplains, and rabbis. The first thing which struck me was that unless you listened carefully to the introductions or consulted your program, you frequently couldn't be sure—just by the content of the speech—whether the speaker was a psychiatrist or a clergyman.

The theme of all the speeches was, basically, "How can we help people?" As far as this theme was concerned, both the psychiatrists and the clergymen were in the same line of business.

During a recess I slipped into an anteroom for a talk with Reverend Charles C. Howse, of Boston's First Baptist Church. Howse was a minister who had taken a psychiatric orientation course—and he had taken it at the same time he was doing graduate work in the New Testament.

"How about it?" I asked him. "Here we have modern psychology, the basis of the psychiatric branch of medicine. Is it in conflict with religion?"

Reverend Howse replied, "I haven't found a bit of the New Testament which is at odds with psychology. Quite the reverse, I have found that modern psychology really is *based on* the New Testament."

That seemed to state the case for synthesis pretty strongly, but later in the conference I met a preacher who stated it more strongly still. "Christ," he said, "was the first psychiatrist."

Just before the conference adjourned I met an old friend, Reverend Otis Rice, religious director at St. Luke's Hospital in New York. I set down in my notebook a remark he made: *"All truth is God's truth, so the more of it we discover the closer we should be to Him."*

I couldn't forget that simple statement.

Perhaps here was the nugget in a mountain of controversy. Perhaps the so-called conflict between psychiatry and religion was no conflict at all, any more than there is a conflict between engineering and religion, or arithmetic and religion. Perhaps it was a trumped up conflict, a phony war.

Back in 1947 Bishop (then Monsignor) Fulton Sheen had fired a powerful salvo at psychoanalysis, charging it was based upon "materialism, hedonism, infantilism, and eroticism." There was a thunderous reverberation in the press and the battle was joined. Ever since, an occasional new barrage has been laid down.

Trying at least to clear the smoke (even if he couldn't spike the cannon), Dr. William C. Menninger, psychiatry's leading spokesman, lamented, "Unfortunately a few religious leaders have made a great effort to set up a straw man of conflict between psychiatry and religion."

It became my job to investigate the "straw man." Boston was a good start. I went on from there.

In New York I found that a neighborhood psychiatric clinic had been established—in the parish house of a church. "Without the co-operation of the church we could never have launched this venture," Psychiatrist Fredric Wertham, the founder, told me. Reverend Shelton Hale Bishop, of St. Philip's Episcopal Church, had welcomed psychiatry with open arms. Would he have done so if it were Godless?

At the Sinai Temple in Mt. Vernon, New York, I met a rare combination—a rabbi-psychologist. Rabbi Henry E. Kagan had earned a doctor's degree in psychology and was proving himself a doubly effective spiritual leader to his flock, bringing them the everlasting truths of religion enriched with psychiatric knowledge. "Psychiatry," he told me, "is a willing servant of religion." His days were filled with counseling appointments—"helping my people toward a healthy life with God."

Then one day I came upon psychiatry in a Catholic setting. It was down in the busy core of New York City, on a traffic-choked side street, in old St. Francis' Church. I had heard of the old church before as one which all but lost its parish as the skyscrapers trampled down the last few dwellings in the area. Now the church had a new function. It was a counseling center. On their lunch hours, after work, between shifts, troubled people elbowed their way down West Thirty-first Street and came with their problems to this church of St. Francis.

I sat in one of the counseling rooms with Father Alfred Martin. Here was a priest who for five years studied psychology and psychiatry at the Catholic University of America. It was, of course, psychology and psychiatry distilled through the retort of Catholic doctrine. Its basic truths were there.

"I find the combination of modern psychology and the Catholic religion wonderfully effective for today's problems," Father Martin told me.

Later, his mentor at the Catholic University of America, Reverend James VanderVeldt, under whom the priest had taken his training, spoke to me enthusiastically of the fine work being done at St. Francis'. "We find in modern psychology and psychiatry many implements for good which are not at all in conflict with Catholic principles," he said.

The "straw man" of conflict between psychiatry and religion was rapidly falling apart. A few mere months of searching and digging and there was hardly enough left to make a scarecrow.

Look at some of the evidence:

Detroit's Dr. Bartemeier, I found, had frequently been called upon to give lectures on psychoanalytic therapy to Catholic nuns. Can you imagine this occurring if psychoanalysis were atheistic or pagan? And one of New York's prominent psychoanalysts lectured for two years as an associate in psychiatry at the Catholic University of America. Could this have happened if the new science were anti-God?

Judaism, I learned, was diligently schooling its rabbis in psychiatric background. At the Hebrew Union College-Jewish Institute of Religion, all rabbinical students were given courses in pastoral psychiatry. The dean of the New York school, Dr. Abraham Franzblau, was a psychiatrist. The New York Board of Rabbis even was conducting a training program in pastoral psychiatry—"Not to make our rabbis over into psychiatrists, but to make them more effective rabbis," a spokesman told me.

Where was the "conflict" now?

And in Protestantism, the great synthesis was even closer to full flower. Two organizations, the Council for Clinical Training, headquartered in New York, and the Institute of Pastoral Care, headquartered in Boston, were doing a mass production job of "psychiatric orientation" for theological students and practicing pastors. At centers all over the country—in mental hospitals, general hospitals, and correctional institutions—they were giving men of God a new knowledge of God's man. These clergymen were going back to their flocks, after training ranging from six weeks to a year, better equipped to serve God because they were better equipped to serve men.

"We have taken psychiatry under our wing," one trainee said to me.

To put it another way—I found that psychiatry was not taking over God; God was taking over psychiatry.

I have used the word "psychiatry."

Perhaps that's just a dodge, you may think. Perhaps "psychoanalysis" is the real villain.

I wondered myself. I found that opponents of psychoanalysis often tried to split it from the rest of psychiatry. Psychiatry is all right, they would say, but psychoanalysis is the devil's own hash.

The only thing wrong with this argument is that it doesn't jibe with the facts. I found that virtually all of modern psychiatry is "analytically oriented." This means that while many psychiatrists do not use the classical couch-and-free-association method of analysis, they nonetheless lean heavily upon the three Freudian pillars: (1) Man has an *unconscious* as well as a conscious mind. (2) Much mental illness stems from emotional conflicts which are *repressed* in the unconscious mind. (3) Mental health is restored when these repressed conflicts are brought to the surface, recognized, and resolved.

There are, even in the ranks of psychoanalysis itself, dozens of variations on the Freudian theme. Go to any psychiatrists' meeting and somebody with a learned paper to read is bound to be "rejecting Freud" for something or other. By the same token we may reject Columbus because the American Continent is not the East Indies—but we cannot reject the American Continent.

I went to Dr. George E. Daniels, clinical professor of psychiatry at Columbia University and one of the best-informed men on the countless schools, schisms, and factions in modern psychiatry. Was it possible, I asked him, to split off psychoanalysis from the rest of modern psychiatry. He replied that fully sixty per cent of the psychiatrists in the United States were "analytically oriented." Five per cent, he estimated, were hostile to analysis and still believed in the old custodial methods of treating mental illness: put the patient away, give him wet sheet packs or tepid baths, and keep him quiet (the refined snake pit). The remaining thirty-five per cent were neutral, but, according to Dr. Daniels, were constantly using psychoanalytic techniques. The minute a doctor becomes concerned with his patient's childhood relationships, his dreams, his inner conflicts, his unconscious, he is going straight back to Freud.

It was analytically-oriented psychiatry which the Army used in World War II. Dr. William C. Menninger, as a brigadier general, headed the Army psychiatric services—and he was a psychoanalyst. It was this kind of psychiatry which healed combat mental casualties so effectively that sixty per cent of the "emotionally wounded" were able to return to duty. It was this kind of psychiatry of which Reverend David E. Roberts, of the Union Theological Seminary, declared, "Only analytically-oriented psychiatrists give us any hope for conquering mental illness. The others, for the most part, are mere custodians."

I asked myself, "Whence come the charges that psychoanalysis is dark and sinister and godless and all the rest?" The answer, I found, was in the mires of ignorance which surround this new science, the misinterpretations, the nonsense which has sprouted up around it.

Take the matter of sex. Because Freud faced sex for the tremendous force it truly is in human life he has been attacked as an advocate of promiscuity, a destroyer of the sanctity of marriage. This is quite a charge—but the evidence is all to the contrary.

Freud actually regarded promiscuity as a neurotic trait, a symptom of mental maladjustment. To him mental health meant the wholesome fusion of full, free, sex expression with adult love. To him the Don Juan males were infantile, and the promiscuous females were as surely in need of emotional therapy as females suffering from frigidity.

If you haven't time to read Freud (and he was quite a dull, long-winded writer) you might take the word of a witness who could hardly be accused of being pro-Freud. The learned Catholic professor, Thomas Verner Moore, of the Catholic University of America, affirmed that Freud "regards it as a serious mistake to advise the indiscriminate satisfaction of sexual cravings as a cure for unhappiness."

Freud, actually, was mighty close to Catholicism's own moral code in his basic attitude toward sex. He defined mental health as a state in which both man and wife, in sex relations, are motivated by *deep inner desires to have children.* That's how the Catholics want it, isn't it?

But isn't psychoanalysis at war with religious morals? We hear frequent charges that it advocates a libertine, go-out-and-do-what-you-please policy.

"This is irresponsible nonsense," Dr. Lawrence S. Kubie, of the New York Psychoanalytic Institute, has insisted. "Not only was Freud himself an ascetic in his personal life, but repeatedly in his writings he has emphasized the importance of curbing unbridled pleasure-seeking. He speaks of this as the restriction of the 'pleasure principle' by the 'reality principle' in life. Psychoanalysis points out that whereas conscious mastery and restraint lead to health and strength, unconscious repression all too frequently leads to neurotic illness. Irresponsible critics often misrepresent this as meaning that psychoanalysis lifts the lid on license. Nothing could be further from the truth."

The charge that psychoanalysis is against morals must have sounded like a cruel joke to the many analysts I found working with drug addicts, prostitutes, nymphomaniacs, homosexuals, and criminals—trying to reclaim them for wholesome, productive roles in society. Many a doctor and sociologist told me that psychoanalysis, or some modified form of psychotherapy, is the one hope we have for saving such unfortunates.

In my reportorial rounds, I saw analytically-oriented psychiatry used for the treatment of drug addicts at Lexington, Kentucky, for promiscuous girls in San Francisco, for homosexuals in New York, for criminals in New Jersey, and for alcoholics and other unhappy neurotics in Topeka, Kansas. Talk about morals. Who could be a greater guardian of public morals than the psychiatrist who works to bring such people back to wholesome living?

What about the problems of daily life? In the less lurid circles of existence is psychoanalysis a breaker or a bastion of morals?

I went to see Dr. Bertram Lewin, then President of the American Psychoanalytic Association. What he said, in sum, was this: "The goal of psychoanalysis, when confronted with marital or sexual difficulties, is to work toward sexual adjustment and happy marriage. We are constantly striving toward the cure of promiscuity and other abuses of the sexual drive. Personality adjustment on an adult level has saved many a home from divorce, and brought many a married couple to the true moral blending of sexual expression with mature love."

What is the first thing that often is said to someone who is morally on the skids? "Why don't you see a psychiatrist?"

Dr. Bartemeier recalled, "Just recently a clergyman and I worked together on a case in which an emotionally ill woman wanted to plunge headlong into divorce. Both the clergyman and I agreed that divorce was not the answer. We set out, working co-operatively, to restore her to mental health—both of us knowing that the difficulty was not in her marriage, but in herself."

Certainly there was nothing libertine, immoral, or licentious about that.

There was yet another charge to explore, another shred of the "straw man." Does psychoanalysis deny free will, a basic tenet of religion?

Here is the answer I found:

Psychoanalysis does not deny free will. It rather seeks to help those who are themselves *denied of free will* by twisted character formations. The goal of analytic therapy is to free the individual from those emotional bonds which make him a victim of circumstance and environment. Once freed, he is able to tap more and more those treasures of free will which religion talks about. The premise here is a religious one indeed: "And ye shall know the truth, and the truth shall make you free." (John 8:32.)

Far from chucking all sense of responsibility for one's actions into the wastebasket, psychoanalysis helps the patient see the truth about himself, face his unconscious drives, understand his motives, cut the puppet strings of neurotic compulsion, and emerge a freed individual—able at last to exercise free will.

From the clergyman's viewpoint, as Reverend Roberts put it, "Patients begin treatment expecting to have all of the inconvenient consequences of their neuroses removed, without having to relinquish the neuroses themselves. They end with the humbling discovery that their most important gain has been in the power to take responsibility for their own difficulties instead of blaming them on other people or upon fate."

Such a revitalization of personal resources would seem to be the very soil in which free will thrives.

Indeed, in many areas psychoanalysis—once the "straw man" of conflict was brushed aside—seemed to be religion's helper.

One of the nation's leading theological seminaries, I learned, had sent forty of its own students to be psychoanalyzed. It felt they would be better men of God if they improved their state of mental health. A spokesman for the seminary told me, "Not one of them has left the ministry. They completed their analyses and went on with new vigor to lives dedicated to religion and God." He added, "I've known many fellow clergymen who have been analyzed—but I am yet to find one of them leaving the church."

To top it all, I learned from one of the leading Protestant ministers in New York (what we call in the language of reporting "an unimpeachable source") that ten psychoanalysts had presented themselves to him for confirmation in the church. They kept right on being psychoanalysts—but they needed religion, too. Their study of man had led them to the inevitable goal: faith. They had found that beyond the first glare of the new science of dynamic psychiatry there was a mellower light. In it psychiatry and religion could be seen not as angry gladiators but as allies.

Allies . . . I spent the next few weeks of my search for God watching psychiatry and religion work together as allies, not in the conceptual realms of 25,000 feet up but right down to earth in the grassy, gardened, family-studded communities of our country.

I remember Spring City, Pennsylvania, a little textile town. It was a Sunday morning when I reached it, after driving through a dismal rain for hours and over seemingly interminable detours. I went to Spring City to see Reverend Joseph L. Schantz, pastor of the Spring City Evangelical Lutheran Church. In the office of the Council for Clinical Training, at New York's Academy of Medicine, I had picked his name from the alumni list; he was one of the ministers whom the Council had given its psychiatric-orientation course. Pastor Schantz took the training, under guidance of a minister-supervisor, at the New Jersey State Hospital, Greystone Park.

He was at the door of the church when I drove up. The rain had stopped, a few random sunrays were peeking through, and the young minister stood framed in the doorway shaking hands with his people.

"What additional good can he do for them now that he has taken on psychiatry?" I wondered.

Pastor Schantz answered the question later as we sat in the parish house. "People's problems are a big part of a minister's work," he said. "That's as it should be. We are here not only to preach, but to *help*—and that means helping in the problems which disturb people, which throw them off the track.

"Clinical training gives us a background in human behavior and emotions. When people come to us, we are able to catch maladjustments early. We can spot the direction in which they are moving and help people when they are approaching the edge of a cliff instead of waiting until they have plunged over it."

People in Spring City, even many outside of Reverend Schantz' congregation, had come to him with parent-child problems, marital problems, problems of getting along with bosses and neighbors. "Without clinical training, I don't think I could have helped them much," he said. "I suppose I just would have given them the old exhortation—you know, told them to pick themselves up by their bootstraps—and sent them on their way."

"Well, what do you do now?" I asked.

"I don't play psychiatrist—don't worry about that," he laughed. "In fact, that is the first thing we learn in clinical training. We learn to spot cases where people actually need a psychiatrist, and we refer them for proper treatment. We learn to differentiate between the situations we can handle and the ones we cannot.

"But where we can help on a counseling level, we try to give skilled counseling. We employ the insights of psychiatry and the skills of psychological counseling. We listen more than we talk. We don't pour out advice; we try to help people work through their own problems and come upon their own solutions."

"It takes more time that way, doesn't it?" I asked.

"And a good deal more patience. But the individual is growing and improving all the time," the pastor replied.

"What happens to his religion?"

"It grows in strength and maturity, just as the person himself does. Instead of paying lip service to God the person who has worked through his own problems is able to feel and know the presence of God in himself and in the world around him." Pastor Schantz walked to the door of the parish house. The sun was streaming down brightly now.

"I'll sum it all up for you," he said. "The tools of psychiatry have enabled me to do God's work much better than I ever could before."

From Spring City, I barnstormed from town to town, exploring this business of doing God's work. Pastor Schantz had spoken of "well-meaning mistakes" that many a minister may make simply because he lacks up-to-date know-how in human behavior. I collected a notebook full of such "mistakes."

In one small town a young man who was sliding swiftly into the abyss of homosexuality went to his pastor in a desperate hope to be helped back to normality. The pastor was well meaning, of course. He wanted to help the young man. But he just didn't have any knowledge of sex deviation. Psychiatry to him was still a dark and forbidding continent which he had never dared to explore. After hearing the youth's story, he advised him to "marry one of our nice young girls and settle down."

What about the young man gaining a little insight into himself? What about unraveling the tangled skein of his personality and helping him back to emotional health?

The youth did marry a "nice young girl" and—as any clinically trained minister could have predicted—proceeded to wreck her life as well as his own.

In a Midwestern city, an untrained minister was baffled by an alcoholic in his parish. Nothing he did seemed to help him. Finally the minister persuaded him to sign a "contract with

God." It was drawn up legalistically—"On pain of death and everlasting Hell I do hereby contract, pledge and promise to God Almighty that I will never touch a drop of liquor again."

The poor alcoholic went out and drank again (as a compulsive drinker must, so long as the compulsion is there). With the crushing realization that he had violated a "contract with God," he staggered into the cellar of his house and hanged himself.

What would a clinically trained pastor have done? He would have recognized alcoholism as an emotional illness. (The man is sick and he drinks. The man has a cold and he sneezes. You can't stop the sneezing without treating the cold; you can't stop the drinking without treating the sickness.) The trained pastor would have directed his counseling toward finding the *causes* of the compulsion to drink, helping the sick man to understand his own sickness. He might also have sought the help of Alcoholics Anonymous or, if necessary, urged psychiatric treatment.

In a city in the South, an untrained pastor was visited by a parish woman who complained of unhappiness in her home. Her husband seemed to be losing interest in her. She feared he was straying. They had no children because, as the woman put it, "My husband just doesn't want children."

In the course of counseling the pastor learned that the woman had been using a diaphragm to avoid pregnancy. He advised her to leave off the diaphragm secretly for a few weeks—"Become pregnant, have a child—that will hold your husband for you."

Another of those "well-meaning mistakes" Reverend Schantz had talked about. . . . Instead of ministering to the maladjustments of the husband and wife, the well-meaning but untrained pastor had appointed a child to be the brunt and target of the parents' ills.

I was glad when the trail led to a parish in upstate New York which was lucky enough to have a minister with psychological know-how. He had served in the ministry for twelve years before enrolling with the Council for Clinical Training. He had taken his year off and gone through the paces of psychiatric orientation, then returned to the parish. I was interested in the *before* and *after* contrast.

"I did my share of bungling *before,*" he related. "I'm afraid I manhandled and mishandled a good many people who came to me for counsel.

"There was a young woman who had committed adultery. I was terribly shocked when she came to me. Yet I had no knowledge of *how she got that way,* what pushed her over the edge of the precipice. I didn't realize it at the time, but I was a carpenter without tools—not even knowing how to begin to help her. All I did was preach to her about the evil she had done. I had her in tears. When I got her to agree to baptism in the church, I thought her problem was over."

The minister drew a yellowed newspaper clipping from his old parish records. "You see," he said, "her home broke up anyway. This tells of her divorce. I hadn't helped her after all."

He continued, "Once I caught a boy stealing money from the offering box. I wasn't yet trained to inquire into the *why* of it. The best I could do was make him write out his definition of Christianity a hundred times. Can you see where I failed? Actually I was practicing an unchristian doctrine of blame and punishment, instead of understanding and help. I didn't help him at all.

"Then there was the alcoholic. I made him keep a record in red ink of every saloon he went into, and a list of drinks. Then I'd look into it with raised eyebrows and say, 'Aha, seven ryes, three beers, and one port! You've slipped again!' I didn't realize what a failure I'd been until he left my counseling with a farewell note saying, 'I see you have no intention of listening to the things I really want to tell you.' "

That was the *before.*

What is the *after?*

The minister looked pensively upward through the gothic window of his study. "Since I took clinical training," he said, "I don't ask people to swallow prescribed and premasticated nostrums. I merely help them analyse their own problems and seek their own solutions." He spoke of "substituting humanness for shame and taboo" and "helping people grow up."

When I asked for an example the minister told me of his "lost week end"—how he had recently handled an alcoholic, in contrast to the red-ink inventory he had used before. It began with a call from the man's wife:

"Pastor, I'm afraid Arthur's pretty bad. I'm worried."

"Perhaps I'd better stop by."

The minister drove to Arthur's house, finding him glazed and sodden, suffering from the big jitters.

"Oh, parson! Please get me a drink!" Arthur begged.

"Let's go for a drive instead," said the minister. He helped the flaccid fellow out to the car and they started driving. They drove for hours, into the gorgeous country of the Finger Lakes. They stopped for dinner, the first solid food Arthur had eaten for days.

They drove some more, drove and talked, drove and talked. Soon the minister wasn't talking any more. Arthur was. He was pouring out a monologue, a great gush of fears and feelings of inadequacy. They came home by darkness and the minister went into Arthur's house, stayed with him, finally put him to bed, and stayed up late talking to Arthur's distraught wife.

"Please don't go," she pleaded. "He'll be in a terrible way tomorrow."

The minister stayed for two days, as faithfully as he would have stayed at the bedside of a man dying. He talked a little, listened a lot. Finally they reached the point short of which no alcoholic can get well: the man admitted he was helpless. "I'm licked," Arthur said. "I can't beat this myself—I need help."

The minister continued to work with him for months.

"Was it worth the trouble?" I asked.

"Worth the trouble!" the minister exclaimed. "If you save a man from drowning, is it worth the trouble? Arthur has thanked me a million times over—not in words, but by becoming whole again. Today he is a happy, productive human being. And not only that—he is helping others get well!"

I met several other clergymen who felt that psychiatric know-how had enabled them to do God's work better than they ever had done it before.

One of them told me, "A man in my congregation was dropping ten- and twenty-dollar bills into the collection plate. In the old days I would have been delighted. I would have called him a God-fearing man, even though he was forcing privation on his family to make these large offerings.

"But clinical training had made this pattern all too clear. I knew the tens and twenties were his defense against strong, underlying feelings of guilt. I didn't abruptly demand, 'What are you trying to do, bribe God?' But in long sessions of counseling, he got around to seeing that for himself. He uncapped a terrific pressure of guilt feelings.

"He got along with his family, his fellow man, his church—and God—much better after that."

Another minister related, "A woman came to me full of fears that her six-year-old son was going to be killed by an automobile. She was 'absolutely sure' it would happen. She was constantly on edge with worry."

An untrained pastor might have tried to "talk her out of it," laugh off the idea, or even prove with statistics how exaggerated her fear was. But this minister—thanks to psychiatric orientation—quickly recognized *neurotic* fear. He knew this woman's feeling, detached as it was from reality, stemmed from her own tangled emotions.

His counseling had little to do with automobile accidents or statistics. Instead, he guided the woman on a quest for self-understanding. Slowly she unearthed bits and pieces of unconscious hostility toward the child. Slowly she gained the insight to see that guilt over this smoldering feeling had thrown up its own smoke screen—in the form of hyper-solicitude for the child's safety. As she resolved the hidden hostile feelings her relationship with the child changed subtly on the surface, but profoundly beneath. By the last few counseling sessions she actually could laugh over what previously had been grueling and debilitating fears.

The minister concluded, "I felt the woman had been made whole again—not so much through what I did, but what I helped her do herself. Isn't that a minister's job? Didn't Jesus ask, 'Would ye be made whole?' "

I said at the outset of this chapter that I *had to* explore the continent of psychiatry. I could not sail around it.

In my explorations I expected possibly to find that psychiatry was against God. Instead I found it was a path to God. The ministers who used psychiatry to do God's work were daily proof of that. But there was even more dramatic proof.

People treated by psychiatrists were coming home to God. With their inner conflicts quieted and their hearts and minds opened to the love that is in the world, they were able to say with Job of the Old Testament, "Now mine eye seeth Thee."

Many a psychiatrist has found himself with a patient who was utterly atheistic and emerged, after psychotherapy, a firm believer. Dr. Philip R. Lehrman, former president of the New York Psychoanalytic Society, told me of a patient who came to him steeped in hatred of God and religion. He was a severe neurotic, unable to look after his business, unable to care for his family—utterly consumed by his blasphemous bent.

"Psychoanalysis brought out that the root of this God hatred was repressed hostility toward a brutal grandfather," Dr. Lehrman related. "This he had carried up from childhood, when the grandfather image became confused in his unconscious mind with the image of God. His militant atheism vanished during the course of the analysis."

Another patient, Dr. Lehrman recounted, was a Catholic girl so violently anti-religious that, in her mental illness, she raved and ranted against the church and even performed sordid acts of desecration.

"What did treatment do for her?" I asked.

"The neurotic origins of her attitude were unearthed and resolved," the doctor replied. "She began to see how unreal and how *sick* her emotional attitude toward religion was. She also found that this 'God hatred' was actually a disguise for unconscious feelings which she had been unable to face. It took a long time to unravel. But early in the analysis, the young girl's hatred of the church completely disappeared."

Dr. Lehrman certainly didn't consider himself a missionary, but I'm sure he had regained for the church one who could hardly have been brought back to the fold by conventional methods.

Still, some ministers themselves, aware that the healthy human mind reaches out toward spirituality, have not been averse to using a touch of psychiatry to good missionary purpose. At the Fifth Avenue Presbyterian Church in New York, Reverend John Sutherland Bonnell told me of a young woman who came to him complaining that she was "unwanted of God." She believed that God had no interest in her and was "neglecting" her.

Being a minister who, as he put it, "employs practically every form of analytic insight in my work," Reverend Bonnell easily spotted the neurotic nature of such an attitude. He worked with the young woman along analytic lines until finally she saw the root of her trouble. She had felt, in her formative years of childhood, that her parents didn't love her or want her. As she grew up she had transferred this feeling to God.

She was, of course, won back to God's side.

When Columbia University conducted a scholarly inquiry into the matter of religion and health, I went to the chairman of the project, Professor of Philosophy Horace L. Friess, and asked, "What about the impact of psychiatry upon the religious nature of the patient?"

He replied, "I can easily conceive of the patient emerging

better attuned to his religion, with a truer concept of God, with stronger faith—in short, a more deeply religious person."

So far as I know we have no sawdust path down which psychiatry's converts can rush to be counted. But we occasionally come across a witness who makes a public breast of it. Such a witness was Lucy Freeman, the New York *Times* writer who underwent psychoanalysis and wrote a book about it entitled *Fight Against Fears*. In it she stated, "Analysis gave me what feeling I possess for religion. 'Spiritual—it's a lovely word,' I said [to the analyst] one day. 'Funny, it never meant anything to me before I came here.' I had been too busy fighting inner devils to give much thought to the reality of spirituality. I began to read the Bible. I started to think about why I had ignored religion."

But there is, of course, religion and religion. There is what the psychiatrist might call "healthy religion," and there is also "unhealthy religion." Every mental hospital has experienced delusional patients who imagine they are saints or self-appointed saviors. I remember visiting St. Elizabeth's in Washington and seeing a patient strolling along the walks in a long blue, kimono-like gown with gold lace along the edges. "We call him 'The Saint,' " a doctor said. In daily life, too, there are religious fanatics and people who still think of God as a Santa Claus and people who use religion as a drug and a nostrum.

It is this neurotic fringe of religion, and not the true core of faith, which Freud attacked when he called religion an "illusion" and which modern psychiatrists regard clinically as "infantile dependency" or "escapism." All of us have seen, probably many times, the abuse of religion by people who use it as an escape from responsibility, as lip service, or as the childish magic which saves them from the obligation to face life maturely.

Haven't you known the pious hypocrite who thinks he is "religious" because he goes to church one day a week while he spends the other six days hating and exploiting his fellow man? Haven't you known people who, in daily life, are as far from the precepts of Jesus, Moses, or Mohammed as any human being could be—yet hide behind cloaks of piety and charity?

Haven't you known people who avoid every duty and responsibility in life in the childlike thought that blandishments to a magical diety will solve their problems? Or the reverse—people who are forever in a prison of infancy because they fear some vengeful, wrathful diety instead of growing up to a mature relationship with a loving God?

Against these "unhealthy religions" both the psychiatrist and clergyman fight shoulder to shoulder.

Likewise, they fight together for the triumph of true religiousness.

Psychiatry's stock in the powers of love and the potentiality for love in all human beings is like the very voice of the Bible: "Let us love one another, for love is of God; and every one that loveth is born of God, and knoweth God."

This Biblical line is just about the psychiatrist's credo. He struggles as a medical scientist to remove hatred from the human heart. He struggles to free his patient from the dark bonds of envy, jealousy, resentment. He struggles to release an inner potential for love—which is of God.

Freud himself wrote of "that way of life which makes love the center of all things and anticipates all happiness from loving and being loved." Every psychiatrist knows that love is his primary medicine. He gives love to the patient. He helps the patient give love to others. If psychiatric treatment could be summed up in a phrase, that phrase might be, "Helping love to triumph over hate."

Is that Godly?

One of psychiatry's foremost teachers, Dr. Karl A. Menninger, stated, "It is the essential spirit of the prevalent religions of the earth—Buddhism, Confucianism, Judaism, and Christianity—that one cannot live to oneself, but must love one's neighbor. And this is the same conclusion that we have arrived at in psychiatry."

Well, then, is psychiatry itself a religion?

No, it is a science. But it opens up a man's heart and frees his mind for the upward thrust of faith. It can prepare a man for mature belief.

William Ernest Hocking, professor emeritus of philosophy at Harvard University, put it this way: "It is, in the end, a man's religion which must finish what psychoanalysis begins."

One day a parishioner who had been psychoanalyzed came up to Reverend Bonnell and said, "My illness is over. I feel that I understand myself perfectly and I should be able to go ahead now on my own steam." He paused. "The trouble is I haven't any steam left."

The steam this man needed was continuing faith, some sense of relationship between himself and the infinite universe around him.

"This I was able to give him through religion," Reverend Bonnell told me. He explained it with a parable from the Gospels in which man's life is compared to a house possessed by a demon. "Man expels the demon, cleans out his house, and leaves it, as Jesus said, 'swept and garnished'—but empty. As long as the house is untenanted the demon may return.

"Thus," Reverend Bonnell concluded, "while the science of psychiatry can expel the demon, it is necessary that the faith of religion move into the house—lest the demon return and find it untenanted."

This is the great synthesis.

When I had explored the new continent of psychiatry in my search for God I knew that it was no hostile or isolated land. It was a fertile new part of the world of faith, friendly, asking only for more colonization and a swifter trade of ideas.

It too was God's country.

5

"THANK GOD I'M AN ATHEIST"

The nonbeliever

Walter Damrosch, the symphony conductor, composer, and critic, who lived to be almost ninety, said on his eighty-second birthday, "An atheist is a man who has no *invisible means of support*."

In my reportorial search for God, I found occasional men and women who called themselves atheists.

A coast guardsman in San Diego, California, told me, "The very use of the word 'God' can denote only a cerebral disturbance."

An aged sugar-beet grower in Colorado said he had been "searching for God" for eight decades and "the results have been nil." If there is a God, he complained, "Let Him search for me for a change."

Were they really *atheists?* Were they totally self-sufficient, without, as Damrosch quipped, any invisible means of support?

I wondered if it were psychologically possible to believe in *no God*. John Donne told us, "No man is an island" in this world of ours. Could any man be an island in the universe? The psychologist, Erich Fromm, recently wrote, "There is no one without a religious need, a need to have a frame of orientation and an object of devotion."

To lash out at the atheist, to "debunk" him, would be easy enough. But this is not the reporter's way. Instead, I sought to ferret out the atheist—to meet him on his own ground, hold him up to the fluoroscope of a reporter's questions, see what makes him tick.

The prime spokesman for atheism in America was Woolsey Teller, general secretary of the American Association for the Advancement of Atheism, Inc., an organization headquartered on Park Row, in New York, chartered in 1925, and known to its adherents as the "4A's."

I found Teller a pleasant, scholarly gentleman with white hair and dominant, deep-set eyes. His face was lined, yet he had a youthful look for a man of sixty-two who had been fighting a mighty adversary for forty-seven years.

Woolsey Teller and I faced each other across a table. We started in to examine atheism at the very bottom. Teller didn't duck a single question. In fact, he fired a few sharp ones back at me. A tape recorder took down everything we said.

Here is the story:

WHITMAN: Do you, Mr. Teller, really call yourself an atheist —I mean, no dodges, no punches pulled?

TELLER: I call myself an atheist and I have been an atheist since I was fifteen years of age.

WHITMAN: And atheism with you is not a dodge or a pose?

TELLER: I believe there is no God—the same as I believe there is no devil. I reject God as I reject demons, angels, and other supernatural beings. I take the position that there is no God. I say distinctly that I deny the existence of God.

WHITMAN: Well, Mr. Teller, when you deny the existence of God, do you deny the existence of any *particular* God. For example, if I were in a primitive tribal setting in Africa and someone held up a totem pole and said, "This is God," I could say that vis-à-vis the totem pole I am an atheist because I do not regard it as God and I do not believe in it. Do you deny any *particular* God, say, do you deny the God of Christianity and Judaism?

TELLER: In my denial of God I take the definition of God as found in the dictionary: God as an "intelligent being." Whether He has long whiskers or short, whether or not He is the Old Testament Jehovah, God is supposed to be an intelligent being who comprehends what He is doing.

Spinoza said—and this was pantheism on his part—that the universe was God. I am certainly not disputing the existence of the universe, but I think it is very unreasonable to say that God is the universe or that the universe is God. It is just as preposterous as saying that the Brooklyn Bridge is God or a cucumber is God.

No, I think the clear definition of the God believers is that God is an intelligent being behind and operating the universe.

WHITMAN: And this you totally deny.

TELLER: I do.

WHITMAN: Do you have any doubt about it, or——

TELLER: I'm just as sure that there is no God as I am sure there is no Jack Frost. We know how the God idea arose. We can trace it through primitive life up to the present time. When a savage's hut blew down and he couldn't see the cause of it he naturally felt that some invisible being, some enemy, was trying to punish him for evil he had done. Or when his crops were ruined he naturally looked to an unseen being. This primitive man had a whole collection of gods. But many gods have been reduced to three—the Trinity in Christianity—and much modern belief is centered more or less on one. We atheists go just a little further by claiming that even one God is one too many.

WHITMAN: That God is one too many?

TELLER: Yes, one too many.

WHITMAN: What do you think of the Bible?

TELLER: The Bible? Just look at it. As the story goes, God

made the world and it went along for a time until He was so dissatisfied with his own handiwork that He decided to drown nearly everybody in it. According to the story there was a universal flood, or at least a flood that wiped out everybody except those who entered the ark.

Now the story of the ark is so preposterous. Noah, who was supposed to have built the ark, was a tender of vineyards, an agriculturalist in a small way. What did he know about boatbuilding? But he built this boat into which pairs of animals were put in order to save them. After the flood, presumably, the polar bear went to the north polar region and the kangaroo jumped to Australia. The whole thing belongs to the world of fantasy, and the tragedy is that many people believe it.

WHITMAN: All right, Mr. Teller. You express not only doubt but downright disbelief in the Bible as one might read it literally. In my search for God I have found many, many religious people—God believers as you'd call them—who do not take the Bible literally. I have discussed the point with scores of clergymen and found many who are not bound to the Bible in a literal sense.

Oh yes, I also have encountered plenty of Fundamentalists, who do feel totally bound by the Bible, word for word—but they are only one group of people who believe in God. Vast, vast numbers of religious people and God-fearing people can view the Bible as, to some extent, folklore, to some extent mythology, to some extent symbolism—but, by and large, a vehicle for the conveyance of eternal truth to mankind. And they do feel that there is within the Bible stories—even if you do not take them literally—an ultimate source of truth.

Compare it, if you wish, Mr. Teller, to one of Aesop's fables. The story of the fox and the grapes—it is sheer make-believe, the fox and the grapes never existed; but there is a gem of truth in that fable.

Many believers in God are willing to accept the Bible as a receptacle of the *great truths* about man and the mystery of life on earth, even though these truths may be conveyed in simple stories which are not to be taken word for word as literal facts. The important thing is that *the truth is there.*

TELLER: But these things in the Bible *must* be taken literally, or else the whole idea of religion falls to pieces. If Eve didn't sin by eating the fruit in the Garden of Eden then there was no fall of man. Now it's either a true story or it isn't. If it's not true then the whole scheme of redemption is blown sky high, because it was Jesus who came to redeem the world from original sin.

If we're not to accept the stories of the Bible as historically true, then the whole plan of redemption and the very meaning of Christianity fails. Jesus said he came to redeem the world from sin. It wasn't the sin of his time; it was the sin brought about by Eve's transgression in the Garden of Eden.

WHITMAN: Suppose that the Garden of Eden story were simply a symbol for the sin in all of us? Suppose that "original sin" is the sin original in human nature? Suppose that the idea of redemption refers to the struggle of good versus evil that goes on inside of every man?

I mean the struggle of you and I as we go about our daily lives in society; I mean, too, the struggle of the human race onward and upward, its determination—even though it constantly stumbles and fumbles—to overcome sin and to embrace that which is good. Must we accept the Biblical truth of sin and redemption as stemming literally from the eating of the forbidden fruit in the Garden of Eden, or can we not accept this Bible story as symbolic of mankind's rejection of God?

TELLER: Well, this is merely an attempt, Mr. Whitman, to hold onto that which has no historical significance. There is no need to fool around as the ancients did, or as even some of our moderns do, with the idea of symbolization.

Everything we do in our life in society must be anchored to intellectual integrity. The only way we know whether an act is good or bad is by its consequences. In our relationships with one another we must base our conduct on something more substantial than Bible mythology.

WHITMAN: What do we base it on?

TELLER: On personal well-being—and by looking at the consequences. It may be very tempting to some people to rob a bank. But bank officials are going to resent it, depositors are going to resent it, and society itself is going to resent it. And so, however tempting it may be, very few people rob banks.

WHITMAN: Is that what determines behavior?

TELLER: The consequences—of course.

WHITMAN: You mean, Mr. Teller, that if I had a thousand dollars in my pocket and you absolutely knew you could get away with it and never be blamed or punished, you simply would pick up a club and hit me over the head?

TELLER: Oh, you're talking about morality. Morality is constantly changing. There are certain basic crimes such as murder. Since nobody wants to be killed, laws are enacted against killing. Yet we do kill. We kill the murderer in the electric chair. In times of danger, when our country is threatened, we thrust a gun into a man's hands and say, "Go out and kill or be killed."

I'm pointing out that everything is conditioned by the determining factors around us.

WHITMAN: Well, on basic morality . . . Do you believe in the Ten Commandments?

TELLER: I certainly do not. Take one of them, "Thou shalt have no other gods before me." Now that's just a tribal god speaking; he didn't want any competition. It has no meaning for us, no meaning whatsoever.

WHITMAN: We were talking before about killing——

TELLER: You mean—"Thou shalt not kill."

WHITMAN: Yes.

TELLER: Now, what does it mean? As I say, we make it legitimate to kill at times—war, capital punishment. Not only that, but it is regarded as perfectly legal and moral to kill in self-defense. Your commandment, "Thou shalt not kill," has no meaning.

WHITMAN: Aren't you begging the question? Along the Merritt Parkway in Connecticut the signs tell you the speed limit is fifty-five miles an hour. That's the law, the commandment. But it certainly is understood by everyone that if a fire truck or an ambulance comes along on an emergency mission it can go faster than fifty-five miles an hour. We all understand that the signs mean fifty-five miles an hour is the speed limit under ordinary circumstances.

TELLER: That's right.

WHITMAN: And so with the commandment. In the interest of terseness the commandment states, "Thou shalt not kill."

TELLER: Yes.

WHITMAN: But it doesn't say "Thou shalt not kill a steer in order to have meat to eat," or it doesn't say "Thou shalt not kill a murderer," or in wars that "Thou shalt not kill an invader," or it does not say "Thou shalt not kill a burglar who enters your house and threatens to kill you——"

TELLER: That's the fault of the commandment, Mr. Whitman. It should be specific.

WHITMAN: —But by and large, the proposition is that I shall not kill you, that it is wrong to kill, that in ordinary circumstances of life to kill a man because you hate him, or because you want his money or want some advantage over him—is wrong. Don't you accept that?

TELLER: No, I don't accept it. There's a lack of qualification in this commandment. In our jurisprudence we are very careful of the wording of regulations and statutes. Just a blanket order "Thou shalt not kill," is not enough. This commandment means nothing in a world where we want precision.

WHITMAN: Do you actually reject the Ten Commandments?

TELLER: As divine teachings—yes.

WHITMAN: Yes, I presume you would reject the idea that these commandments were delivered by God through Moses at Mt. Sinai. But what about revelation through the human mind? Suppose the God force of the universe revealed these Ten Commandments to man when man was in a primitive stage of civilization and hence not capable of accepting the Annotated Code of the State of New York or the United States Constitution? But at such an early stage man could accept the first, fundamental body of law. Do you accept or reject the proposition that the underlying concepts of law and morality embodied in the Ten Commandments could have been given to man by a higher power?

TELLER: As I deny the existence of a higher power, I deny that such a power could have given mankind anything.

WHITMAN: Mr. Teller, do you ever pray?

TELLER: What would I pray to?

WHITMAN: Have you ever found yourself in a position where you wanted to reach out to some power in the universe greater than yourself?

TELLER: Yes, I've been in swimming and found it very comforting to reach out to a life raft. That was greater than myself at the moment.

WHITMAN: But you've never felt in your mind that you would like to reach out and address yourself to something which we who believe call "God"?

TELLER: It would be ridiculous for one who doesn't believe in the existence of that Being to reach out for Him. You might as well expect me to reach out for the numerous gods of ancient times. Reaching out for numerous gods is just as fantastic as reaching out for one.

WHITMAN: Have you never prayed in your life that you can remember?

TELLER: No. I was not religiously reared. I did go to Sunday School as a boy, but merely to be with my schoolmates or chums on Sunday. I attended the Baptist Temple in Brooklyn and two other churches. This was at about the age of ten. I was never impressed; in fact, I never understood what it was all about.

WHITMAN: Did you believe in God at any time in your life?

TELLER: I never did.

WHITMAN: You've been an atheist since you were——

TELLER: About fifteen, when I first took an interest in the subject of religion.

WHITMAN: Mr. Teller, when you were a young boy didn't you write a story for a Brooklyn newspaper in connection with Thanksgiving?

TELLER: That's right. I was a schoolboy and the Brooklyn *Eagle* was holding a contest for Thanksgiving essays. I contributed one which happened to win one of the prizes.

WHITMAN: Would you describe the story you wrote?

TELLER: I wrote it according to what I felt was the atmosphere required and expected. It was something which would please the religious people. The story was of an Indian who was about to scalp some settlers. He approached their cabin and looked through the window. He saw a very happy gathering of father and mother and some small children. They were reading the Bible. He was so impressed (as if a savage would be impressed by seeing anyone reading a book!) that he put his tomahawk aside and went away. The whole thing, of course, was childish fiction. Stupid as it was, it won a prize.

WHITMAN: You didn't believe it?

TELLER: No, I knew I was writing fiction. Just as anybody would write a story, I created characters and these characters fit in with what I thought would be acceptable.

WHITMAN: I see. You wrote this story because you thought it would make a hit?

TELLER: Yes, that's right.

WHITMAN: Now, Mr. Teller, a person who believes in God must seem somewhat ridiculous to you because he cannot *prove* there is a God. Is that correct?

TELLER: The one who makes a statement is expected to prove it. It is up to the believer to give evidence, either direct or indirect, that will have some bearing on this supposed God he believes in.

WHITMAN: And you say the believers in God can't prove there is a God.

TELLER: Exactly so.

WHITMAN: And therefore you refuse to accept their position?

TELLER: That's right.

WHITMAN: If they could prove to you that there was a God, would you believe in God?

TELLER: Well, I certainly would have to answer yes if the evidence warranted it. If it were proven to me, that would be the answer itself.

WHITMAN: That would be the end of your atheism, wouldn't it?

TELLER: Naturally.

WHITMAN: So you contend that since the believers in God cannot prove that there is a God therefore they must be wrong.

TELLER: That's correct.

WHITMAN: Now, you are an atheist. That means you have a belief.

TELLER: That's true.

WHITMAN: And your belief is what?

TELLER: That the universe has no need of a God. It operates entirely by itself.

WHITMAN: You believe there is no God.

TELLER: There is no God.

WHITMAN: That is a belief of yours?

TELLER: It is.

WHITMAN: Now, Mr. Teller, can you *prove* it to me?

TELLER: Positive evidence and negative evidence are somewhat different. Suppose I come to you and say, "Mr. Whitman, in the adjoining room there is a whicker-whacker." You ask me what I mean—"What is this whicker-whacker?" "Well," I tell you, "it's an unseen being." And when you ask to take a look at him, I reply, "Oh, I can't let you do that. He's *unseen.*" So you naturally ask, "How do you know there is a whicker-whacker?" And I reply, "Oh, I *know* there is!"

Now the shoe is on the other foot. Just try to prove there isn't a whicker-whacker in the next room, Mr. Whitman. That's what you're telling me to do. On that basis—on the basis of negation—it is impossible to disprove anything. Anybody can make a statement and if you can't disprove it, he thinks he has proven his case.

WHITMAN: But suppose I want you, by *entering the room,* to prove there isn't a whicker-whacker in the room? You have taken the position, without going into the room, that there isn't a whicker-whacker in there.

Now many a scientist who had never gone inside the atom could have taken the position that electrons do not exist. He couldn't see them. He could have called himself an "electronic atheist." But now we finally have gained admission to the atom through our scientific methods and we find that there are electrons there. Where is your "electronic atheist" now?

TELLER: Mr. Whitman, the parallels do not hold. When we get down into the atom, where there are electrons and protons, we are dealing with matter in every sense of the word. We are dealing with material particles. This is a far cry from the existence or non-existence of a whicker-whacker in the adjoining room.

WHITMAN: But I contend that——

TELLER: You are dealing with material things. I am dealing with immaterial things when I talk about God and the whicker-whacker.

WHITMAN: All right, Mr. Teller. Back to the main line—I am challenging the positive position of the atheist, who says in so many words that there is no God. If you say to me that the believer in God cannot go into the next room and show me the whicker-whacker, I say to you that you can't go into that room and show me that the whicker-whacker *isn't* there either.

TELLER: That's very true.

WHITMAN: Then aren't you really an agnostic, rather than an atheist, Mr. Teller? The agnostic simply takes the position, "I don't know," because he recognizes that he cannot prove the existence of God—or the non-existence of God.

TELLER: I'm not an agnostic. I'm an atheist. The agnostic just isn't consistent. Look—why is the agnostic's attitude focused only on God? Why are there no agnostics in regard to the existence of witches? Do you ever hear an agnostic say, "I don't know whether or not there are witches"? Or, "I don't know whether or not there are demons"? Or, "I don't know whether or not there's a devil"? No. Yet God is in the same category of invisible, mythological beings.

WHITMAN: No, I think here we have to take into account man's progress. The God concept has evolved a great deal in the course of human history. We know that at one time people worshiped thunder, or the sun and the moon. When they learned more about the universe around them their religious concept changed. In modern religion the God concept goes beyond material things.

It is as Jesus said—"God is a spirit." So we must look for something beyond material things, and that is why I cannot walk into the next room and show you God, nor can you walk into that room and show me that God isn't there.

Take something else which goes beyond the material. Take beauty, for example. I, who may have a great appreciation of beauty, try to tell you that beauty exists in the world. And you say, "Prove it!" And I say, "Look at that sunset, isn't it beautiful!" And if you cannot appreciate beauty you say, "No, it is not beautiful"—you see, you are a kind of atheist in regard to beauty. You don't believe in it. But I say this to you: *Maybe it's that you don't see it.*

TELLER: In regard to that, Mr. Whitman, you have raised a nice point. When you deal with beauty you are dealing with an abstract term. You can only have beauty in connection with that which is material. It may be a sunset, it may be a gorgeous panorama, it may be a beautiful woman—it is an abstract term. No atheist questions that there is beauty in the world any more than he questions that there is ugliness also.

Or, you might bring in goodness. The only way we can recognize goodness is by observing types of behavior. We see both good and bad.

These are merely abstract terms, having nothing to do with the existence or non-existence of God.

WHITMAN: Yet in my rounds as a reporter in search of God, I asked people to define God and scores of times I heard, "God is goodness," "God is beauty," "God is truth"—and we know the apostle John told us "God is love."

Now suppose we take love, Mr. Teller. In Charles Dickens' story, "A Christmas Carol," a man like Scrooge could say there is no love. He could call himself an atheist as far as love was concerned. For him there was no love in the world—because he could not see love. But does that deny that love exists in the hearts and feelings of those who are capable of responding to it?

TELLER: Of course not. Even in ancient times men had reactions and feelings. Each man has his responses.

WHITMAN: Well then, does love exist, Mr. Teller?

TELLER: Yes, as an abstraction, a term that covers certain feelings known as love.

WHITMAN: But does *love* exist?

TELLER: You mean love as a word or as a thing in itself?

WHITMAN: I mean love as a concept. Does it exist? Is there love in the world?

TELLER: There are people who love.

WHITMAN: Well then, is there love in the world?

TELLER: If you wish to use it as an abstraction, yes.

WHITMAN: Can you show me a handful of it?

TELLER: No.

WHITMAN: Can you put it on the table?

TELLER: No.

WHITMAN: Can you go into the next room and—call it a whicker-whacker or anything else—can you say, "There is love"?

TELLER: Love is an emotion.

WHITMAN: Yet you know it exists, don't you?

TELLER: It doesn't exist as something tangible. It exists only as an abstraction. It has no physical existence.

WHITMAN: But it has manifestations. If, out of the love in a man's heart he is able to do something good for his neighbor, then love has manifested itself in something which we actually can see. We can see the good which was done because we see that a man went over and plowed out his neighbor's driveway when the neighbor was ill and couldn't do it himself.

TELLER: Love and hate manifest themselves through the agencies of physical organisms known as human beings and animals. There you have tangible expressions of love, hate, and other feelings. But your abstractions are mere concepts. This is a fault into which all believers in God fall: they talk about abstractions, spiritual values. They talk about spiritual beings.

WHITMAN: I have no trouble following such concepts.

TELLER: But what has this to do with a supreme being up in the sky?

WHITMAN: Suppose I said, "But we're not speaking, necessarily, of a being in the sky?"

TELLER: Then what are we speaking about?

WHITMAN: We're speaking of a concept of God. There are a great many firm believers in God who would reject—as much as you would—the idea of God as a "being in the sky" who sits on the edge of a cloud with a long, white beard.

TELLER: Then they are virtually atheists.

WHITMAN: Are they? They believe in the spirituality of God. They believe in God as a force, a concept, a spirit.

TELLER: Which doesn't exist.

WHITMAN: You mean which doesn't exist in *material* form.

TELLER: There is no other kind of existence.

WHITMAN: Wait, Mr. Teller. Let's examine that. Take poetry for example. Here is a poem. I read it. It is beautiful to me. It is full of meaning. Do you mean to tell me that that beauty and that meaning do not exist? Or isn't it a fact that poems and writings and songs have stirred people to action and shaped the course of history?

TELLER: Very true.

WHITMAN: And ideas! What about the reality of ideas? Take the ideas set down in the Declaration of Independence. They are intangible. They are not a bit *material.* They are ideas—floating around like your man in the sky—but what power those ideas have put forth in the world!

TELLER: But remember that there actually is a Declaration of Independence. It is a physical document.

WHITMAN: So is the Bible. So are the Ten Commandments.

TELLER: But the idea of the Declaration of Independence is right and good.

WHITMAN: Can't you say the same for the idea of God?

TELLER: I certainly cannot!

WHITMAN: Why not?

TELLER: Just examine this "God idea" of yours. We are told generally that God is benevolent. He's represented as an all-loving Father who cares for His children.

Now does he? Let's look around. What do we see? We see a world in which there is terrible misery, stark poverty, plenty of pain, plenty of suffering, disease after disease. In the last war we were fearful that some of our enemies were going to use disease germs. But look at this God of yours! He is using disease germs against us every day in the year! The world is alive with these germs. Where is God's benevolence? That's where belief in God breaks down—when it pictures a benevolent being responsible for everything.

WHITMAN: Yet mankind still exists. You and I, Mr. Teller, are not being eaten up by disease germs. We are sitting here, we are pursuing knowledge, we are trying to enlarge human understanding by whatever iota we can contribute here.

Mankind does continue to go forward. I mean—I am not trying to tell you that all that ever has happened in the world has been good, but I am saying that there is a kind of forward motion. Mankind falls on his face, he suffers plagues and he learns how to conquer plagues, and then he gets into terrible wars and right now we're trying to learn how to eliminate war. Some people think we someday may do it. Some say we never will. But by and large mankind continues.

I think that anyone would have to agree that whatever the God force is, its purpose—obviously—is not to make everything on earth plum cake and sugar candy.

TELLER: All right. But let us compare this supposed father in heaven with an ordinary, decent father on earth. Now what father on earth, barring some degenerate, would bring into his home innumerable disease germs, those of tuberculosis, infantile paralysis, and the rest. I don't have to give you the list. The hospitals are full of misery. A human father who intentionally brought disease germs into his home would be regarded as a criminal.

WHITMAN: Yes, there you're judging God by our own earthly standards.

TELLER: What else have we?

WHITMAN: We have the knowledge of how little we know.

TELLER: We have the knowledge of what we do know, too. We know that we can distinguish a good father from a bad father. Anyone who did the things that this bad father in heaven does would be punished for his crimes.

WHITMAN: I had reference to Socrates, and how he has inspired all intellectuals since his day with the crowning statement of his wisdom, "The one thing I know is that I know nothing." And I know, Mr. Teller, that you are a great admirer of the scientific approach. It was Isaac Newton who said the scientist was like a small boy playing on the sands of the seashore while the whole ocean of truth stretched out unknown before him. That's what I meant by saying *we know how little we know*. How then can we judge God? How can we say, as you do, Mr. Teller, "Well, if God were such a good God—by my standards—he wouldn't have any plagues, any floods, earthquakes, or tornadoes"?

TELLER: Why should God be any more immune from criticism on the basis of our earthly understanding than anyone else? All we have to go on is our earthly understanding.

WHITMAN: But we don't know what God's purpose is, do we? You want to condemn God because He allows tragedies to occur. But let's remember who is doing the condemning. We human beings are doing it—we humans, we are so wise, so all-knowing, that the greatest intellect we could produce, Socrates, said, "The one thing I know is that I know nothing." Do we humans presume to know what is in the mind of God, or what the ultimate purpose of reality may be? Take these tragedies—these "criminal acts of God," as you would call them—do we know where they fit into the entire, infinite picture?

TELLER: There you go assuming again that God exists. You ask me how I know what the purpose of God may be. I reply to you that there is no need of trying to find out the purpose of that which does not exist.

WHITMAN: Basing this on an assumption which you cannot prove either—that God doesn't exist.

TELLER: To me the non-existence of God is proven. It is proven by the fact that we can observe in the universe factors which show definitely that no such being as God is required to account for the phenomena we observe.

WHITMAN: For example?

TELLER: Consider the long, drawn-out history of the evolution of this planet and the life on it. What do we find in the early geologic strata? We find, first of all, only the lowest forms of life. You have to bear this in mind if you want to imagine your God behind evolution. He wastes time with a lot of microscopic animals. Geologic ages go by, animals evolve slowly, slowly. This God is supposed to have as his objective the coming of man, yet he blunders through the reptilean age. In this long period of time, was he more interested in reptiles than in man? Why all this needless beating around the bush, all this waste motion, before reaching man? No, evolution does not suggest intelligent guidance at all.

WHITMAN: Aren't you saying, Mr. Teller, that if you were God you would have done a better job?

TELLER: Unquestionably. God should have consulted me when the earth was being formed. There isn't an individual who couldn't plan a better world. The fact that man is trying so hard to improve things here on earth shows how many things are wrong. And who made them wrong? Well, according to the God believers, God made the world. He must be responsible.

WHITMAN: Who made the world according to you?

TELLER: The world was not made. It has always existed. Matter in its totality has always existed. It merely changes its form.

WHITMAN: Where did it come from?

TELLER: It didn't come from anywhere. It was always here.

WHITMAN: Can something come out of nothing?

TELLER: No, it cannot.

WHITMAN: Again—and I call upon your reverence for science—one of the first principles of physics is that there is only a change in the form of matter——

TELLER: That's right.

WHITMAN: —that it cannot come out of nothing.

TELLER: I didn't say it came from nothing. I said it didn't come from anywhere, it was always here. The universe as a totality has always existed.

WHITMAN: Who created it?

TELLER: It wasn't created. It is self-existent.

WHITMAN: Now isn't that a little bit like this whicker-whacker in the next room?

TELLER: No, on the contrary, it is the God believer who starts with a ghost. God is his whicker-whacker. Take yourself, Mr. Whitman. May I ask what your definition of God is? What is He, or what is it, or what isn't it, that you call God?

WHITMAN: I feel that——

TELLER: You're in a jam, Mr. Whitman.

WHITMAN: No, I don't think I'm in a jam because I can define God to you in a number of ways. For example, I accept the fact that God is love, that God is goodness, that God is beauty, that God is wisdom. I also accept the fact——

TELLER: Is beauty God?

WHITMAN: Beauty is an aspect of God, a manifestation of God to my mind. What man is able to create in a painting, or what nature creates in a sunset, or in the magnificent unfolding of a flower, or in the apple blossoms that cover the trees in my orchard at home—there to me are manifestations of the beauty of God.

TELLER: All of these are manifestations of matter. Your rainbow, your aurora borealis, your beautiful landscape, can thrill the atheist just as much as they can thrill the God believer. They are all basic physical phenomena. There is no God involved.

WHITMAN: But that which responds to it is *the God in you,* Mr. Teller. I believe there is God in you, despite the fact you call yourself an atheist.

TELLER: When I enjoy a beautiful statue or a beautiful painting, what am I responding to? Why, that which is pleasing to my sense of form or color. It has nothing to do with a God, either inside or outside of me.

WHITMAN: Yes, but your sense of values—where does it come from? Why don't you value ugliness instead of beauty? Why don't you value hatred instead of love? Why don't you value killing instead of the saving of a life? Why don't you value a wicked deed instead of a good one?

TELLER: There are certain standards that come into one's life.

WHITMAN: Exactly. From something beyond ourselves, from a force greater than ourselves—in short, from what we call God.

TELLER: You don't expect me to accept that, do you?

WHITMAN: As a practicing atheist, no. But as an intelligent human being, perhaps. Look, Mr. Teller, you are a man, an individual, and you are alive and you are following a course of life. Don't you think there is some ultimate purpose behind it? Isn't there some fundamental purpose in life itself?

TELLER: Each individual must find his or her own purpose in life. There is no ultimate purpose in the universe.

WHITMAN: What is your purpose in life?

TELLER: My purpose in life is to pass time pleasantly, to kill time pleasantly. Now what I mean by that is—I'm here, and I know that the time will come when I'll cease to exist. And when I'm dead I'm going to stay dead.

So time is a valuable factor. I have tried to formulate a life which will give me enjoyment. I find stimulation in literary work, I enjoy the great masters, I enjoy my research in science, I like writing, and I like some people—*some* people. Other people, I suppose, find me as difficult to get along with as I find them. As for the general run of the human race, they could, as far as I am concerned—the way they think, the way they behave—they could all jump in the lake.

WHITMAN: That's how you feel about humanity?

TELLER: They could probably tell me to do the same thing. The great work of the world has been done by the few. It's like hauling a donkey up a mountainside, trying to get the great masses free of superstition, free of their idiotic notions. It's like dragging a donkey up a mountainside and then getting kicked in the bargain.

WHITMAN: Do you think life is worth living?

TELLER: It has been for me. I've found it tremendously enjoyable—a real adventure. It has plenty of possibilities for one who is alert and alive. I can take a long walk by myself and not feel alone. I am never in bad company with myself. With my own thoughts I can live in a world of ideas. I am never bored with life.

WHITMAN: You feel that life has no purpose beyond death?

TELLER: Absolutely none.

WHITMAN: What do you think happens to us when we die?

TELLER: There is a complete disintegration of the body. The

average crematory remains are, so to speak, only a handful of dust; and the rest goes up in gas. Man's body, you know, is mostly liquid and there's very little residue after you are put into the flames.

WHITMAN: What about man's mind?

TELLER: Man's mind? Here too is an abstraction. There is no such thing as an entity called the mind. The word is used to designate cerebral activities—vibrations of the nerve cells in the brain. When the brain ceases to function, that is the end of what you call "mind." The average individual, Mr. Whitman, is unconscious one third of his life.

WHITMAN: In sleep, you mean?

TELLER: In sleep.

WHITMAN: Well, you think death is like sleep? We sleep, we're unaware?

TELLER: I do.

WHITMAN: You mean it's like sleep without ever waking up.

TELLER: My "life" hereafter will be the same as it was before I was born. It's *nothing*.

WHITMAN: It's nothing?

TELLER: That's right. And it won't be painful. I'm already used to non-existence. I wasn't around when the pyramids were built and I won't be around when other events stir up the world.

WHITMAN: You don't believe there is any essence in man beyond the material? He ends up as just liquid and a handful of dust?

TELLER: That's right. The parts of the body are just parts of a machine.

WHITMAN: But where is the beauty created by the poet, or where is the love of man for man, or mother for child, in this mechanism which—according to you—is just so many parts of machinery strung together?

TELLER: A mother's love for a child is based on material factors. The infant sucking at her breast gives her a pleasant sensation.

WHITMAN: Yes, we know that. In sex education we tell young mothers not to be alarmed by this fact.

TELLER: All these things have a biological basis for the mother. This love for her child gratifies her sense of private possession—something she can pour her emotions out on.

WHITMAN: Yes, you're speaking now of some of the, shall we say, corruptions of love——

TELLER: No, I wouldn't call them corruptions.

WHITMAN: —the *possession* of a person, and what has been called "smother love." But I would like to think now of a healthy form of love where there is a real affirmation of one person by another, a respect for the integrity and innate worth of another life, another human being—the kind of love, say, that Lincoln was capable of having for all humanity. Now where do you think that comes from in this little package that becomes so much moisture, so much dust?

TELLER: It comes from the same little package that everything else comes from—the same as hate, the same as cruelty, the same as brutality. These are all products of the same machine.

WHITMAN: And you do not perceive—in the universe, in the course of history, or in your own heart—a force which strives toward the triumph of the good over the evil, a force which we call God, Mr. Teller?

TELLER: Mr. Whitman, I am not going to take this God concept any more seriously than I take Jack Frost. When you point to the window on which beautiful frost designs appear and you say that Jack Frost made them, there's no doubt in my mind that they were not made by Jack Frost—they were no more made by him than the universe was made by God.

WHITMAN: Let's take Jack Frost for a moment. I have a son five years old. If I tell him that Jack Frost painted the windows with those beautiful designs, I am telling him something intended for the five-year-old level of comprehension. It is like telling him a fairy tale, like folklore.

But as the boy grows up he will not retain the idea of Jack

Frost as a huffing-puffing fellow dressed in snow and icicles. He will begin to evolve Jack Frost into the concept of a force of nature.

TELLER: He'll change Jack Frost into God?

WHITMAN: No. But in a way, now, you may have something there. Because he will change Jack Frost into a force of nature as he learns about the condensation of moisture against the window pane——

TELLER: Ah!

WHITMAN: And then as he grows older still he will wonder, "What is behind this? Who is the author of the force of nature? Who is the creator of all this?"

Right now, you see, my five-year-old son knows only that we are living in a world and that up the road is another town and that we take a long trip in the car and there are more towns. But someday soon he will get an idea of the whole world, and then of the universe outside our world. He will learn that there are billions of stars and billions of galaxies, and in his own mind he will begin to wonder, "What is the meaning of all this?"

At that time he will be far beyond the Jack Frost idea and ready to cope with a mature God concept. He will wonder about such things as a first principle, a creator, a supreme intelligence, an ultimate purpose in living, a source of beauty, wisdom, and truth.

Do you throw that out, too, Mr. Teller?

TELLER: I throw the whole business out because it is just a trick to perpetuate the idea of God.

WHITMAN: What would you tell the child, Mr. Teller?

TELLER: I would focus the child's mind on the idea that everything is natural, that there are no supernatural beings.

WHITMAN: What, then, would you say to the hundreds of people I met in my reportorial journey who asserted, "God is nature?" Would you simply agree with them—and come back to the ranks of the believers?

TELLER: They are quite wrong. They want to label as "God"

that which has no right to the label. Spinoza did it and he did it for a good reason. There was a time, you know, when it was unsafe to be known as an atheist. Spinoza was virtually an atheist. He said that God and the universe are one. That's pantheism, a poetic form of atheism.

WHITMAN: In a talk I had with Rabbi Abba Hillel Silver in Cleveland, this outstanding religious leader made the statement, "The universe is a manifestation of God." Now do you approve of that?

TELLER: How can I approve? How can it be a manifestation of that in which I do not believe?

WHITMAN: All right. But you are trying to take Spinoza into your camp because he said the universe was God. I'm asking if you would take Rabbi Silver into your camp and call him an atheist because he said the universe was a manifestation of God.

TELLER: No, there's a difference.

WHITMAN: One of the scientists I met in my journeying said that to him it didn't matter much whether God *created* "all this" or God *is* "all this." Either premise was bedrock for his faith. There you have a believer, a person of faith who somehow believes in a God principle which involves a dynamic in life.

He cannot look out into space and say "all this" is one colossal accident, that it came from nowhere, that it never began, it never was created, it has no regulator, has no wisdom.

Look at the clockwork mechanisms of the universe, Mr. Teller. The astronomers can tell us that in 1999 at such and such an hour, such and such a celestial body will move to such and such a point.

TELLER: It isn't because the universe is "on time"; it's because we set our time to moving bodies. A revolving or rotating body is registered by means of observation. It isn't that it keeps time with the clock—our time is set to the revolutions and rotations of celestial bodies.

WHITMAN: And how rhythmic they are that we can set our watches to them!

TELLER: I am inclined to believe that this solar system of ours is something of a freak. We have millions upon millions of stars and they're mere points of light—that's all we see, points of light. I hold with the theory that our solar system was an "accident." It came about when two stars came within a certain distance of each other, one pulling out a long film of gas from the sun. The cigar-shaped film then broke up into particles, forming our planets.

Now the point is: what are the results? You say we should look for a God behind this—and what do we find? We find a wasteful process in order to bring about one inhabited planet. I said the solar system is a freak. There are other freaks right on the earth, plenty of them. Why is it, for example, that Venus's flytrap, an unusual type of plant, exists only in the Carolinas? Why is it that the kangaroo is found only in Australia? You would think that in a universe where "God rules" and all His forces are at work you'd get more satisfactory results.

WHITMAN: Again you are saying, in effect, that you could design a better universe.

TELLER: Yes.

WHITMAN: You really believe that?

TELLER: I do. As Ingersoll said, "I'd make good health catching instead of disease."

WHITMAN: Yes, if that were consistent with your ultimate purpose——

TELLER: If I were designing a universe, I would have a purpose in mind. I would have suffering reduced to the minimum and happiness raised to the maximum.

WHITMAN: That brings us to your former statement that you exist for—was it, *enjoyment?*

TELLER: Planning a happy world would be part of my enjoyment.

WHITMAN: Yes, I want to return to that for a moment. Is enjoyment your sole purpose in life?

TELLER: I would say yes. But the word "enjoyment" covers a

large field. It isn't narrowed down to being frivolous or wasteful of time.

WHITMAN: No.

TELLER: It can have its serious aspects, it can have its lighter vein.

WHITMAN: Yes, you might get enjoyment out of reading philosophy or studying ancient Greek.

TELLER: Another might get it from dancing, another from bowling or billiards.

WHITMAN: And that is your sole purpose?

TELLER: I find it a worth-while purpose. What other purpose do you have in life, Mr. Whitman.

WHITMAN: Oh, I have other purpose.

TELLER: I'm not here to question you, Mr. Whitman——

WHITMAN: Why not? I'll gladly answer. My deepest purpose in life is growth as a person, growth toward self-realization and fulfillment. I am fully cognizant of how badly I do, how woefully I fail—but the goal is there. It gives purpose and direction to life—and meaning. It is man's eternal struggle to grow toward unity with God.

TELLER: For myself, I'll take hedonism.

WHITMAN: Why are you spending these days of hard work in your office promoting atheism in the world? Does that give you pleasure?

TELLER: It certainly does. I enjoy fighting organizations that are befuddling the human mind. I think the Catholic Church and the Jewish Church are swindling the people by giving them all this superstitious nonsense and ritual.

WHITMAN: You left out the Protestants.

TELLER: Well, I should have included them. I'm glad you mentioned them.

WHITMAN: I mentioned them because the Protestants have been called "the people of the Book." They have to a large extent raised the Bible to its high estate in the world today. Remember what you said about the Bible?

TELLER: It was my mistake leaving out the Protestants. I could include all religions, but I focus on those which do the most damage. The Christian Scientists and the Mormons also teach superstition.

WHITMAN: But again now, I ask you—is your hard work at the American Association for the Advancement of Atheism simply part of your pursuit of hedonism? Do you do it for enjoyment?

TELLER: Well, the enjoyment comes not only from the work itself but also from the responses we get. It is a satisfaction to have people express their approval. We find there is a breakaway from all kinds of religious orthodoxy.

WHITMAN: A breakaway from religious orthodoxy is one thing; atheism is quite another.

TELLER: That's true. But once they are rid of their orthodoxy, they are ready for atheism. That's our speciality.

WHITMAN: The Reform Jews have broken away from religious orthodoxy. Protestantism in its entirety was a breaking away from the religious orthodoxy of the early church. There are within Protestantism today 222 denominations. Each one of them is a breakaway from something which was found unacceptable—but *none of these are breaks away from God.*

TELLER: "God"—that's one word they try to retain. But when you ask them, "What is this 'God'?" their troubles begin. Their thinking gets fuzzy. It gets nebulous. You can see in the expressions on their faces how embarrassed they are.

WHITMAN: Mr. Teller, if I ask you, "What is a table?" can you tell me? Can you define it?

TELLER: Well, my definition might not satisfy you, but I think I can define a table.

WHITMAN: Would you please?

TELLER: I would consider it an object with a flat surface on which you may put things. It can have one or more legs. It is used to serve food on or hold various articles.

WHITMAN: I accept that as a definition of a table——

TELLER: It can be made of wood, it can be made of metal, it can be made of various materials.

WHITMAN: Yes, you have no trouble getting up that definition at all.

TELLER: That's right.

WHITMAN: Now I want to ask you if you will define a building.

TELLER: A building is a structure made out of wood or metal or some other material which is used as a dwelling or for business purposes or for storing things. It is any type of structure that serves as a shelter from the elements.

WHITMAN: Now would you define a person?

TELLER: Yes, I would say a person is a man or a woman or a child, either male or female.

WHITMAN: Now would you define justice?

TELLER: There you are dealing with an abstraction. We have formerly dealt with concrete, material things; now we're dealing with a concept. Justice is the application of the law to give proper treatment to people. Justice will be defined variously according to geography and the time element. It was "just" at one time to have slaves in this country. You want justice? The South thought it was perfectly just to keep slaves. No question about it. The slaveholders even quoted the Old Testament in favor of the justice of keeping slaves. Then there was an alteration, there was a change in the attitude. Justice is subject to a great deal of change. It was "just" to put witches to death right in this country, only yesterday—relatively speaking—in New England. It is no longer "just." You think justice is static, that it can't move, that it has no changeability. History shows otherwise.

WHITMAN: Now, Mr. Teller, I asked you first to define three tangible, relatively simple things: a table, a building, a person. You gave concise, clear definitions. I had no quarrel with them. You had no need to qualify or to show that a table wasn't always a table, that sometimes it was something else; or to show that a building wasn't always a building, that it depended on which age you lived in whether it was called a building or whether it was called a bird or something different.

But when you came to justice, your attempt to give a definition was not the same. You took a different approach. You brought many more words and many more ideas to bear upon your attempt to speak to me of justice. In fact, part of your definition was almost to deny that there is justice in showing how——

TELLER: No, not to deny that there is justice, but to show that our concepts of justice change.

WHITMAN: Correct.

TELLER: In other words, what might be just one day might be unjust at some other time. So really, there's no tangibility behind the term "justice." People merely regard a certain form of behavior toward others as signifying their understanding of justice.

WHITMAN: So justice is something which exists in the concept of the person——

TELLER: That's right, it has no——

WHITMAN: —seeking justice, or dispensing justice or thinking of justice.

TELLER: That's right. It will be determined by the time and the group.

WHITMAN: Now would you say, therefore, it doesn't exist?

TELLER: I would say that these various concepts of justice exist.

WHITMAN: Would you say, then, that concepts of justice exist but justice itself does not exist?

TELLER: A concept is not a tangibility—like a table or a chair.

WHITMAN: No, you cannot see it in this room as we see this table, nor can you define it as you defined a table.

TELLER: That's right.

WHITMAN: Then are you going to be an atheist with regard to justice, Mr. Teller? Are you going to say it doesn't exist?

TELLER: I would say that my ideas of justice might differ from yours.

WHITMAN: And your ideas of God might differ from mine.

Among the hundreds of people I talked to in my reportorial rounds, there were scores of varying ideas of God. But does that say that God does not exist? Do varying ideas of justice say to you that justice does not exist?

No, Mr. Teller, we cannot take justice and put it under a bell jar on the laboratory table. Yet we do not deny justice exists. We accept it, we strive for it. We seek to grow toward it.

TELLER: Where does your "God" come in?

WHITMAN: The concept of God is certainly as hard for the human being to approach as is the concept of justice, perhaps a good deal harder. I was going up the scale when I asked you first to define table, building, person, and then justice. I could have asked you further to define beauty and love and finally goodness, purpose—and God. You, or anyone, would have had tremendous difficulty. It is doubtful if the highest realm of ideas even is amenable to verbalization. So often we all are blind men trying to figure out what the elephant is, and it seems different to all of us.

In art, Mr. Teller, the greater the painter the fewer people are going to be able fully to appreciate all that he has put into his canvas and the more time it is going to take before mankind has caught up with him and his achievement of beauty becomes recognized.

TELLER: But you go to the Metropolitan Museum of Art here in New York City, and what do you see in the galleries? You see a person lingering for some time in front of a particular painting. You may pass by and glance at it and not be overly impressed. You may go to another painting and be absorbed by it. A third person may come in and join you or the other party, or prefer a third painting. Beauty is a matter of taste.

WHITMAN: What if someone came into the museum and saw all these people, each looking at the painting which appealed to him, and this person stood in the gallery and said, "There is nothing in any of those paintings which appeals to anybody?"

TELLER: Well, what am I supposed to answer? It would merely mean that in his case there was no art appreciation. That has nothing to do with God or no God.

WHITMAN: What I am getting at, Mr. Teller, is—is it possible that you have no God appreciation? The world is full of people who believe in God in one way or another. Some look at the landscape and some look at the seascape and some look at the still life (to carry out your figure of people in a gallery). Some think of God in the Catholic concept, some think of God in the Judaic tradition, some think of God in the Protestant light, or some think of God in terms of the Mohammedan Allah. Still others think of God as transcendent over all these formalized religions, but as somehow a Supreme Power in the world or perhaps as a Supreme Intelligence or perhaps as an Ultimate Purpose or perhaps as simply the Vastness of Creation—Spinoza's "universe as God" or Rabbi Silver's "universe as a manifestation of God."

Are you going to say to these people that none of that exists because you, Woolsey Teller, do not see God in any of that? Wouldn't you then be like the person without art appreciation—except that in this case it's without God appreciation?

TELLER: It isn't a question of appreciation but a question of evidence. No one is denying that those paintings exist.

WHITMAN: No. No more than you deny that a human being exists. Yet you, as an atheist, look at the human being and say, "There is nothing immortal about him, there is no God in him, God is not interested in him, he should not be interested in God because there is no God. When you add this human being up, he is just a handful of dust out of an urn in a crematory or so much liquid squeezed and condensed out of cell tissue."

Now, by the same token, would you walk into the museum and say, "I don't deny that the picture is there. Why, I see two board feet of chestnut wood, which is the frame, and I see one square yard of canvas, which is so many fibers woven together, and then there are certain pigments on it which are called colors, and if you scraped them off you'd have a dust of some kind which you could sprinkle on the floor."

Is that a painting?

TELLER: How are you going to disprove atheism by talking about beauty? You've seen pictures which are not beautiful.

WHITMAN: The ugly pictures might be compared to the floods and the hurricanes and the plagues and the diseases, which are sheer ugliness, sheer evil, if you wish, on the face of the earth. Do the ugly pictures deny the existence of beauty—or do the ununderstandable occurrences which seem (to us) to be filled with evil and wickedness deny the existence of God?

I might even say that we cannot have God without the anti-God. This has been in religion constantly—the Christ and the anti-Christ, God and the devil, good versus evil.

TELLER: Religion itself has been an evil influence. Look at all the squabbling, all the fighting, all the misery, all the wars of religion and all the antagonisms—where is the love and beauty in that? If the followers of God are set apart in different armies and are fighting one another, where is the good of religion? Get a Jewish rabbi and a Protestant preacher and a Catholic priest together on a platform and they'll express in public the most lovable feelings. But listen to what they say behind each other's backs!

WHITMAN: But hasn't much of the trouble with religion—the wars of religion and all the evil that has been done along with the good in the name of religion—hasn't it been due to the failure of man to perfect his concept of God? But isn't he moving onward and upward?

In the Old Testament story, Abraham was about to sacrifice his son to God on a burning altar. It was a step forward when, through revelation or inspiration, if you will, the idea came to him, "Look, that's not necessary in the name of God." At other times the concept of God has required rituals of pain and suffering, as in the ordeals of African tribes, and at other times the

God concept has required a denial of pleasure and the enthronement of pain. In our times religion is liberating; it is trying to move people toward love and understanding. Who knows what religion may have for mankind in a hundred years?

TELLER: You say religion is doing this, Mr. Whitman. You've spoken about a number of different religions, and they all are fighting one another. They can't get together on anything except that there is a God.

WHITMAN: That, indeed Mr. Teller, is the essential truth in all of them.

TELLER: The whole business is superstition.

WHITMAN: Mr. Teller, I have wondered as we have been talking whether you really are an atheist. I have wondered if, like so many in history who have called themselves atheists or been labeled atheists, you really are just an anti-church person who is intent on religious reform.

TELLER: No, not reform. You can't reform that which is not true.

WHITMAN: I've wondered whether you simply want to take that which is primitive and superstitious out of religion——

TELLER: I throw out the whole business.

WHITMAN: —if, in your zeal to remove that which is superstitious and primitive about religion, you haven't thrown the baby out with the bath water.

Should we throw out the concept of democracy because political parties squabble, or because some of the things done in the name of politics give us the horrors?

You speak of the abuses and the wrongs done in the name of religion and I say to you, "Why do you throw out God because the approach to God has been strewn with blunders?"

Should the physician abandon all attempts to conquer disease simply because there is sickness in the world—or should the fact that there is sickness in the world strengthen and speed his efforts to find the cures for sickness?

I have found, Mr. Teller, in my treks across the country many,

many people who believe in God, yet do not hold with any formal religion. Some even are anti-church, as you are. Yet they say, "I have a personal belief in God and I also abhor the evil which has been done in the name of religion. But I do not throw out God. I rather seek constantly to improve religion by growth and reform."

I also have found many people who are ardent in their espousal of a particular formal religion, a particular church—yet hope the day will soon come when there will be a parliament of religions or, better still, one religion for all.

We're on the way, Mr. Teller. We haven't got there yet. But because the religions cannot all get together here and now, must we throw out that which is the essence of them all—a God concept?

Woolsey Teller's final words were, "Why must we throw out God? The answer, Mr. Whitman, is very simple. Because no such Being exists. There is no God."

Such was the atheist's parting shot.

As I left Woolsey Teller I could not feel, somehow, that I was leaving a man who believed in *no God*. I felt, rather, that I was leaving an intellectual rebel. He was fed up with superstition in the world, with childish beliefs. He could not accept the anthropomorphic God, the God with a long, white beard, sitting on the edge of a cloud.

But there are many firm believers in God who likewise have gone beyond this primitive concept. They see God as a force, an ultimate purpose, a fount of meaning in the world. They throw out superstition, and fear, and other neurotic aspects of primitive belief and substitute a mature relationship with the ultimate power of the universe.

They do not renounce God. They learn to know God.

I thought, as I left Woolsey Teller, that perhaps he too knew God—in his own way. His denials were so vigorous, his protestations so acrid; yet I couldn't help feeling that the gentleman, as

Shakespeare put it, "doth protest too much." Perhaps inwardly he had a God concept of his own.

One militant non-believer summed it all up with the phrase, "Thank God I'm an atheist!"

Another, an old man who had been an atheist all his life, broke down and became a believer on his deathbed. It wasn't that he was afraid of death. It was just a line his daughter uttered, "You may not believe in God, Dad. But He believes in you."

When I was a boy my father told me of a rock-ribbed atheist who was dared by his cronies to go out into a cemetery at midnight, hammer a wooden cross into the ground, and shout three times, "There is no God!"

He took the dare. He went to the cemetery. He knelt down and hammered the cross into the ground. He shouted, "There is no God!" three times and then started to get up to go away. But he could not move. Something held him fast. The shock of it so frightened the man that he dropped dead.

What held him fast was a very simple thing. He had hammered the wooden cross through the hem of his overcoat.

As Woolsey Teller would say, "The thing that held him fast was a natural physical phenomenon."

But it didn't stack up that way in the man's heart of hearts.

6

FATALISM—IS EVERYTHING WORKED OUT IN ADVANCE?

Luck, chance, God, and you

While I was journeying through the back country of Iowa, away from the towns and highways, dusk overtook me in Grundy County and I put up for the night in a farmhouse. I slept in an old brass bed in a garret room. But before I went to bed I sat up with my host, a rugged, weather-tanned corn farmer, and the two of us, bobbing back and forth on a pair of old wooden rocking chairs, talked about the quest for God.

The old farmer kept referring to "God's will." I finally asked him just what God's will was and how he knew God had a will.

"How do I know?" he blustered. "Because I'm alive today, that's how I know."

I asked for the details.

"Well," he said, "I near drowned twice, all but shot myself once, stabbed myself, and was pronounced dead in the hospital. The near drownings was when I was a boy. I was picking up flood trash down by the riverbanks near home. I waded in too far, I guess. The river was a-comin' and a-boomin' and I was just swall'ed up.

"I remember me bein' under the water and seein' how the air bubbles went up. They looked like silver balloons going clear up to heaven. All I could think of was, 'What'll Ma say!'

"Twice I near drowned like that.

"Then the near shootin'—I was rabbit huntin', y'know the way we did it in the old days, with a ferret? Well I had my gun and I went to set it up against a tree. Now y'know how an accident can happen. Blamed thing went off and I don't think the bullet missed me by two inches.

"Well sir, I did go ahead and stab myself. That was another time, when I was skinnin' a gray squirrel. What I was doin' was takin' off the tail for my daughter. Knife just slipped I guess.

"Yes, and I was sick in the hospital once and the docs gave me up and pronounced me dead. In fact, the word got out and my friends was already fixin' to take in the funeral. But I just wasn't dead at all, as you can see for yourself, sir."

The farmer fixed his eyes on me and concluded, "Now, *is* that or *isn't* that the will o' God?"

He had pinpointed a question that rapidly was rising to number one position in my search for God. More and more people I met were raising it in one form or other: "Does God actually control our lives?" "Are we personally responsible for what happens to us, or is it just God's will, whatever happens?" "Is it right to be fatalistic?" "Is everything worked out in advance?"

Certain events seemed also to thrust the question forward. As I went from place to place I recorded them, inquired into them. They were tantalizing events. Events such as:

In Norfolk, Virginia, a naval lieutenant in command of a transport was leaving his ship on a landing ladder when suddenly he fell, struck his head against the pier, plummeted into the water —and drowned.

Tragic, but why so unusual, you may ask. It happens that the man, Lieutenant Philip G. Nolan, whose life was snuffed out in this freak accident, was on a merchant ship which was torpedoed during World War II. But on that occasion he survived. He survived one of the most grueling ordeals in maritime history. He survived adrift in a lifeboat for thirty-nine days!—until the craft reached a South American port, having been tossed about the sea for 2,000 miles.

This, one of the longest open-boat experiences in naval annals, Lieutenant Nolan survived—only to be rubbed out in one of those silly things, a fall on a ladder, which happen day in and day out. It's like the acrobat who survives every death-defying antic on the high trapeze, then slips on a banana peel and breaks his neck.

Then, in Chicago, a minister delivered a sermon entitled, "The Touch of God." No sooner had he concluded it (he was still in the pulpit) than he collapsed with a heart attack. He died a few minutes later.

Was this, indeed, a "Touch of God"—or was it just happenstance? Not only was the minister, Reverend Howard C. Fulton, suddenly snuffed out, but the church treasurer, Henry F. Weiler, who rushed to the minister's aid, also collapsed and died. Both men had served the Belden Avenue Baptist Church for many years.

Was it God's will to call them to Him together? Was He gathering them to life eternal as a reward for long and faithful service? Was it all planned that way? Or was it just the capricious arm of coincidence reaching into human affairs?—one man simply being struck down by a cardiac phenomenon (at an odd moment) and another man dying from the shock of it.

Then there was the little town near Birmingham, Alabama. A minister told me the story. He had gone on a condolence visit to a small farm in the hinterland where a little girl had fallen down a well and been drowned.

"I was surprised, almost shocked, at the mother's attitude," the minister related. "She wasn't a bit grief-stricken. She seemed to be taking the whole thing in stride—too much in stride, if you ask me."

"What do you mean?" I inquired.

"Well," the minister went on, "she just sat there shelling a bowl of peas and saying, 'It had to be. That's all there is to it, it had to be.' "

"And you object to that?"

"Now, I don't know," said the minister. "I agree that we must accept God's will and all of that. But when you just accept everything that comes along by saying, 'It had to be,' I think that's carrying it a bit too far. I felt like telling her so. I felt like saying, 'Maybe it didn't have to be at all! Maybe you should have got that husband of yours to put a fence around the well! Maybe you should have watched your child!"

The question was thus sharply posed.

I wondered where best to search for the answer.

What individuals are most concerned with the question of fatalism? And then I remembered my experiences as a war correspondent during World War II. Of course. Soldiers are the most concerned. They are the most concerned because, for them, life is the most uncertain, the most shadowed by unpredictable circumstance. I remembered that phrase I heard so often in bull sessions behind the hedgerows of Normandy—"if a bullet's got your name on it . . ."

And so I headed for Fort Sam Houston, Texas, to talk to soldiers. There were a good many action veterans of World War II there, and also, at the time, the Army was evacuating freshly wounded soldiers from Korea and flying them in hospital planes to the big Texas base.

I would see what soldiers knew, or believed, or just felt in their bones about this challenging question of fate. . . .

On his hospital bed at Fort Sam Houston, Corporal Ray Mooney told me what happened to him in Korea. He was leading a squad south of Hamhung hoping to entrap some Reds, but instead his own squad was trapped. Red fire poured in on it for six hours, during which Corporal Mooney, a bright-eyed lad of twenty-two from Rodeo, New Mexico, was hit four times—in the chest, the right calf, the left leg and left foot.

The only wound which might have killed him was the chest wound. And it probably would have, but for one of those mysterious, tantalizing things which happen in war. No, the bullet didn't hit a Bible in Mooney's pocket, or a locket with a picture of his mother. It hit another bullet!

Mooney, just before he was hit, had been firing his machine gun and it jammed on a long round. He pulled out the round, a .30 caliber cartridge just a trifle longer than it should have been, and slipped it into the right chest pocket of his jacket. That's what the Red bullet hit. It crashed into the cartridge, was slowed way down, deflected sideways, and slid for an easy wound into Mooney's chest.

Mooney propped himself up on his bed in Brooke Army Medical Center. "I believe God had something to do with it. I swear I do," he said. "I'll never know till the day I die why I slipped that cartridge in my right pocket. I had two hand grenades in my left pocket. What if they'd been hit!"

I asked the young corporal if he ever prayed when he was at the front. "No, I didn't turn to God. I just turned to my machine gun," he answered. "I never was much on church. The only time I prayed to God was afterward—after that cartridge saved me—y'know, just a little thanks. But I sure did go to church when I got home to Rodeo—to pay my respects. From now on, any time I pass one I don't think there's a bit of harm in stopping by."

As with so many of the other wounded at Brooke, hot lead had stirred a whole new birth of wonder in Corporal Mooney. The very air of war does that. Life suddenly seems to dangle from invisible strings. The day and night seem alive with an unseen power, and puzzled people reach out to feel it and to plumb its mysteries.

Not only the wounded. At "Fort Sam," as the big San Antonio army base is called, I found this groping out among the green young lads just checking in at the reception center as well as among seasoned generals, among Wacs and nurses, among battle-scarred veterans of World War II, and, at nearby Randolph Air Force Base, among B-29 pilots and starry-eyed cadets who soon would fly jets and B-36's.

Fort Sam itself was a symbol of this search for meaning. When I arranged with the Pentagon to go there, someone joshed, "I guess you know God is a Texan." At any rate, from the old field-stone watchtower in Fort Sam's quadrangle you could see a good deal of God's country. You could see planes with wounded on their way in, and buses with selectees on their way out. And at your feet in the quadrangle, while these earnest affairs of men were in progress, young deer grazed peacefully and Fort Sam's famous peacocks strutted and preened as though nothing really mattered.

Fort Sam is the successor to the Alamo. That famous old mission stands just a gunshot away. From within its besieged walls, Lieutenant Colonel William Barret Travis, the commandant, wrote on February 24, 1836, *"The Lord is on our side."* But was the Lord on his side? Ten days later the Alamo had fallen. Travis, Davey Crockett, and their gallant band were killed to the last man and their bodies burned into dust by Santa Anna.

Where was God at the Alamo? I thought perhaps in my stay at Fort Sam I could find out—and I think I finally did, but not until I had found out a good many other things about God and soldiers. . . .

Private First Class Cletis Barlow got hit forty miles north of Pyongyang. He was driving an ammo truck when a bullet smashed into his right hip. The truck somersaulted over a thirty-foot embankment and the next moment of consciousness Barlow knew, he was in a cast from his neck to his knees. I found him in the paraplegic ward at Brooke. How did he account for what happened?

Quite simply. "If your time comes it just comes, and there isn't a damn thing anyone can do about it," he said. "If you're gonna get hit, you're gonna get hit—and it doesn't matter how big a hole you're in. You can get hit even on your knees."

Many soldiers shared this fatalism. As a wily old master sergeant remarked, "When the old man swings that scythe, there's no use ducking."

But if it's all cut and dried, I inquired, what's the use of taking any precautions? If it's your time, you get it. If not, you don't. Same with people worrying about atom bombs, or even crossing the street. Why try to protect yourself? Why be careful?

"Fate is fate, but there's no use rushing it on," one soldier answered. "You can't avoid it when your time comes—but you can push it up closer by being a damn fool."

A flyer at Randolph put it this way: "If a bullet's got my name on it, I don't mind getting hit by it. But I sure don't want to get hit with one that's marked 'To whom it may concern'!"

The shoulder patch of the Fourth Army, which has its headquarters at Fort Sam, is a four-leaf clover. That stands, not for fate, not for inexorable kismet, but for a volatile, capricious thing called luck. A good many soldiers prefer to believe in just that. They prefer the wheel of luck to the scythe of destiny. Take Bill Vail, for example . . .

First Lieutenant William H. Vail, Company A, Fifth Cavalry, was caught in one of those early infiltrations in Korea, in the first year of the war. He went to the top of a hill and, strangely (he still can't understand it), he heard no shots but saw his buddies falling all around him. His company commander got hit. Bill found himself in command, but only for ten minutes. He knelt to give a soldier morphine, and a moment later (he still heard no shots) he was spinning around with a bullet in his right arm.

People say to Bill, "God was good to you. You got by with a wounded arm."

But Bill says, "Baloney. What about my buddies who were better than me—and yet they were killed. It wasn't God at all. Sure, I believe in God, but I don't think He's wasting his time looking out for me personally. If God was good to me to get me *out*—well, He got me *in* in the first place! No, sir. Don't put it on God. It was just luck."

Flyers traditionally are superstitious. They wear lucky boots. They carry charms up with them. They make magic signs at take-off.

"The hell you say. I'm not superstitious," a pilot at Randolph insisted. He held out his hand. "See this ring? Three times I've gone up without it, and each time I crashed. But that was just coincidence—I know that. The ring had nothing to do with it."

"Do you ever go up without the ring now?" I asked.

"Not if I can help it," he replied.

Your witness.

I met a flight surgeon at Randolph who, during World War II, was himself regarded as a lucky charm. He flew forty-six missions in Italy, not because he had to, but just because bomber crews got the idea he was good luck and begged him to come along. "If doc comes along, we're safe," they'd say.

"Anything to it?" I asked the flight surgeon.

"Just this—" he said. "I don't believe that anyone, or any supreme power, is looking out for my destiny. It's just pure blind luck whether a plane gets hit. I just happened to be running in a lucky streak."

Other soldiers reach out for deeper explanations of the cosmic mysteries. They can't accept either blind fate or dumb luck. They want to get into the act. So they come up with the *power of believing*. Believing makes it so.

Master Sergeant Warren Orr, a B-29 radio operator, served on a B-24 (Liberator) crew in World War II. Eight crews trained together and flew over to Europe in eight new B-24's. Only Orr's plane, the "Penelope," came back. All the others were shot down or crashed. Some of their crews wound up as casualties or PW's.

"But our crew—we got only scratches," Orr told me. "And I mean scratches. Our bombardier got hit by a burst from a

20 mm. and it just nicked his face, no worse than you'd get from shaving. Every one of us came back.

"Why did we come back? I'll tell you why—because we *believed* we'd come back. We believed it had to be that way. It couldn't be any other way."

"Did you believe in anything else?" I asked.

"You mean the Good Lord?" Orr replied. "Sure, everybody believes in the Good Lord. But you don't suppose God put His finger down and said, 'These men will come through.' Naw, He had more important things to do. We came back because we ourselves—in our hearts—*believed* we would."

Private First Class Clovis Bevill also had that strong, unshakable belief. When his outfit moved into Korea he knew he'd come back. Even on that August 15 when his platoon was pinned down trying to take a hill along the Naktong River, Bevill knew he'd come back.

"I just made one mistake," the twenty-four-year-old farm lad told me. "I believed I'd come home, yes. But I wish I'd believed I'd come home *good.*" "Good" was his way of putting it. For he spoke to me from a wheel chair in the paraplegic ward at Brooke. A Red machine-gun bullet had hit him in the back, torn up some of the spinal nerve tracks.

"It's all in what you *believe* will happen," Bevill went on. "We had a sergeant who believed the wrong way. He told each fellow in the squad what he could have in case he (the sergeant) got killed. He gave me his watch and said, 'You can have yours right now.' He was killed a day and a half later."

Bevill held out his arm, with the sergeant's watch on it, and silently watched it tick for a few seconds.

All of these soldiers, whether they believed in *fate, luck,* or the *power of believing,* also believed in God. But here were the question marks: Does God look after each one of us individually? Does He author our fate from moment to moment instead of having it all written out in advance? Does He control our luck? Does He respond to our believing?

"Yes, God's in the thick of it right with us," argued the colonel who was headquarters commandant at Fort Sam. He had gone all through World War II with nothing more than a nicked finger. "It *must* be God," he insisted. "Men were killed beside me, in front of me, all around me—and me with just this." He held up the finger.

"Once I heard a shell coming," he continued. "They say you don't hear the close ones, but you sure do. I dropped on the ground. I was still fully exposed. It hit so close you'd think there wasn't a chance, but I wasn't touched. I got up and saw that another man—in a foxhole, well protected—was killed by it. Now what do you make of that?"

The colonel looked up with cool, serious eyes and answered his own question: "God must decide these things."

God must decide . . .

That's how Private First Class James Seybold felt when he was hit near Inchon. A piece of shrapnel went clean through him. Another piece lodged in his spine. His thoughts as he passed into the shimmery gloom of unconsciousness were, "If the Good Lord wants me he'll take me."

The next he knew he was on a hospital ship and somebody said, "You'll live."

Seybold answered, "That's fine," and lapsed back into coma.

He underwent five operations in Japan but never once had the slightest doubt that he'd come through. In his heart was the feeling, "God had his chance if he wanted me. He didn't take it. I'll get through now."

Jim Seybold, a twenty-year-old from Waukesha, Wisconsin, still had that feeling when I saw him at Brooke, his legs paralyzed, his face and eyes yellow with jaundice, his name on the serious list. "God has his idea of what He wants to do with each one of us—that's all," he said to me.

I talked to an army nurse, a very experienced high-ranking one, Lieutenant Colonel Augusta Short, who had seen a good deal of the life and death of soldiers. For fifteen years she had given anesthetics and had seen patients flutter at the ends of those gossamer threads which separate now from eternity. She had seen the doctors dispensing their skills behind masks, the gleaming equipment of the operating room, the vessels full of science's newest medicaments.

"Yes, we do all we can," she said with a toss of the head. "But there is always a point where we say, 'Now it's up to you, God!' And when it is all over and the lad has pulled through we never know whether we did it or God did it."

Could it possibly be teamwork?

Captain Dexter Green, who was teaching cadets to fly at Randolph, believed there was plenty of teamwork in the wild blue yonder. He was convinced God was the co-pilot. He became convinced while flying a B-25 into Mobile, Alabama, and hearing that awful cough that means one engine is gone. His ship was losing altitude, floundering through an overcast that blotted out the ground. He had to pick one of two emergency fields that showed up on his map. If he picked wrong it would be curtains for one B-25 and one Dexter Green.

"I didn't pray, and I didn't guess. I just picked. It came to me out of nowhere. It was just plain inspiration," Captain Green recounted. "Once I made the decision I didn't hesitate a moment. Other times there'd be a question on a decision. This time there was no question, no review. I just did it. I let down through the overcast and there was the field just ahead. If I'd have shot for the other field I could never have made it."

"That," said Captain Green, "is the 'God factor' in flying. Where all the sciences—weather science, mechanics, aerodynamics—leave off, that's where God begins."

No. 54011333 also thought the secret was teamwork. No. 54011333 was Ernest (Buddy) Barefield, who said he was "just a number" because he was newly drafted, had just reported to the Fort Sam reception center, and was still in faded blue dungarees when I met him. Twenty-one-year-old Buddy learned about God in the oil fields of New Mexico where he worked as a "roughneck," a derrick hand.

One winter day he was ninety feet up on the derrick, on the "board," as they say, unlatching stands of the pipe as it was pulled up from the well. There was ice all over the board. Buddy fell. He sailed through space and was caught by his safety rope. As he caught his breath and dangled there, at this peculiar way station between life and death, Buddy thanked God with all his heart. He kept thanking God as he scrambled up the rope to safety.

"You think God saved you?" I asked.

"Sure He did."

"Did you ever fall again?"

"No. I brought a hatchet up after that," said Buddy. "I chopped the ice off and covered the board with soda ash and a 'toe' sack."

"Why those precautions—if God was looking after you?" I persisted.

"Listen," said Buddy, "I trust God all right. But I've got to do my part. *He's got to trust me, too!*"

Buddy, without even a uniform yet, was thinking along much the same lines as a four-star general I talked to later on, General Courtney H. Hodges, commander of the First Army in World War II. "There may be *several* bullets with your name on them. But with intelligence and care—in a soldier's case, with good training—you can avoid a good many of them," the general said. "That's just giving God a little co-operation."

I noticed an unusual thing at Fort Sam. While people I met everywhere were more or less glad to be alive, the wounded at Fort Sam—especially the grievously wounded—were *really* glad to be alive. Some had wounds so serious you'd wonder, "What's there to live for?" But they didn't see it that way.

Just how did they see it?

There was Private First Class Reinhart Stepan, a lad with green-blue eyes, flaxen hair, who had enlisted with his parents' permission at seventeen. Stepan was still seventeen when I saw him, but he had aged a lot. It happened during three days in Korea, near the Chosan Reservoir . . . Left leg blown off by a mortar shell . . . Right leg frozen (and later amputated) in two days and nights of crawling through snow to a village . . . Both hands frostbitten.

Stepan sat in his wheel chair, held up his bandaged hands, and said calmly, "They're going to take me down Monday and whack four fingers of this hand (right) and one off this one (left). One already fell off."

Then he drew up the stumps of his legs, wrapped his bandaged hands around them and said, "I feel damn lucky myself."

Lucky! I winced to hear him say it. But he wasn't putting on. Stepan had absorbed a lot about life in that two-day-and-night crawl through the snow. He summed it up with the crisp line, "People ask for too damn much!"

In a nearby bed lay Private First Class Roland Robins, who was hit near Taegu. His left femur was shattered and he was trussed up in a weird traction contraption. "After two or three weeks at the front I didn't care what happened," he said. "But after I got home I realized that I should have cared all along. I have more faith in God now than I ever did before." The traction was pulling his leg upward at a forty-five-degree angle and he was sweating from the grueling position.

But glad to be alive . . .

Private First Class Billy Williams had some shrapnel in his back and a shattered right hand, souvenirs of a hand grenade thrown at him near Wonju. He had a little different perspective. The war had made him very curious—*about war*. Here's what he said:

"I'd been living a clean life as a civilian, but left church out completely. Last Sunday I was well enough to visit home in Houston. I went to church for the first time and I intend to keep it up. I've never read the Bible, don't know what's on the first page. But I intend to find out. The whole thing over there seemed so senseless, full of things I don't understand. Maybe the Bible will throw some light on it. Why do there have to be wars? What about the guys who get killed? Does God want wars to go on?"

Williams hurled those questions like spiritual grenades.

Where is God in war?

Just a stone's throw from Fort Sam, in the office of an insurance company he then headed, I found "Skinny" Wainwright—General Jonathan M. Wainwright, the hero of Luzon and Corregidor, who spent three years, three months, and eighteen days in Japanese captivity. He had plenty of time, if nothing else, during that long "rot," as he called it. He played 8,632 games of solitaire. He also did plenty of thinking.

I decided to put the question to him. "General," I asked, "do you think God has a hand in war?"

Wainwright shot back an answer: "You know what Napoleon said—'God is on the side of the strongest battalion.' I believe that."

"But isn't there a time when a soldier turns to God in weakness, not just in strength?" I persisted. I had to shout each word because the general was all but deaf, the work of a 240 mm. shell that burst near him on Corregidor.

"Yes," he replied with a deepening expression in his eyes. "In the North Luzon campaign when I was ordered to withdraw—it broke me up—to think that I had to withdraw in the face of the enemy. It went against my innermost soul.

"I turned to my chaplain. With tears in my eyes I said to Chaplain John Duffy—he happened to be a Catholic chaplain, I'm an Episcopalian, but it made no difference if he were a Catholic or a rabbi, I didn't care—I said, 'Come out here in the jungle. I want to talk to you.'

"Sure, I turned to God in weakness. I cried. But with Duffy's comforting words I stopped crying and I ordered the withdrawal commencing next morning. He made me see I was merely doing my duty."

In captivity General Wainwright knew what it was to be cuffed and punched by sadistic guards, to be utterly and miserably humiliated even about the natural functions of the body, to be starved to the point where worms were a treat.

"Did you have faith as a prisoner?" I asked him.

"I couldn't have lived otherwise," he replied. "Some gave up the ghost and died. They felt there was nothing to live for, that they would never get out. My faith kept me alive."

"What was that faith?" I inquired.

"Faith in the power of the American armed forces to defeat the Japanese," Wainwright shot back with the pride of an old soldier.

"Was it faith in arms alone?" I pressed.

"Faith in God, sir, with heavy ground, air, and sea support," he replied with a classic line.

He went on, "The most religious man in the world can't take a weak force and defeat a strong one. But where God comes in is—He helps us to raise the force to turn defeat into victory. I prayed in captivity. I prayed that God would give Washington the brains to raise a big force and MacArthur the ability to use it effectively. Both prayers were granted."

So there sat "Skinny" Wainwright, snatched back from defeat, from captivity, from the turning screw of starvation, and as I left him my eye caught a bronze plaque fixed to his desk: "Never Say Die."

But some do die in war, and some are maimed, and innocents are slaughtered, even women and children. Does God okay this carnage? Is this, too, all worked out in advance? Here is how some of the soldiers at Fort Sam felt about it:

"There will always be wars," said a master sergeant. "We're not civilized enough yet. It's not that God wants wars. He doesn't plan them. But if everything was all set, what would we have to do? God lets these things happen to keep us on our toes."

Another master sergeant said, "I think God does plan these wars. He has a purpose—maybe to cut down the population. Even famine and the bombing of women and children have a purpose. We don't know what it is. But that doesn't mean we should sit back and do nothing. That's not part of the plan. The plan is for everyone to do his job."

"No," countered a newly drafted private. "Don't hang it all on God. The only place God comes in is—He forgives us. God forgives us for killing on the battlefield simply because He makes allowances for the stupidity of man."

General Walter Krueger, wartime commander of the Sixth Army in the Pacific, wasn't sure about the "allowances." In his home near Fort Sam he said to me, "If God saw the mess we had made, He'd spew us all out."

I found, as you see, no agreement at all on God's immediate purposes or where, if at all, war fits into them. No one epitomized the quandary better than a B-29 crewman who said, "War may be necessary to prove a point—but why we should have to prove it is more than I can see."

How about the long view? How about ultimate purposes, which may be beyond the sweep of our finite binoculars? Lieutenant Colonel Augusta Short, the nurse, had a hunch on those horizons. Maybe it was womanly intuition. Anyway here's what she said:

"The other night I got thinking—if God is all-powerful why does He let the Commies get away with what they do? After all, they *deny* God. Then I remembered back to a time I visited Versailles, in France, and the guide described the luxuries and excesses of Marie Antoinette when France was in suffering and poverty. The philosophic guide said, 'Maybe it was a good thing. When it got bad enough, the people *had* to do something about it.' So—perhaps God isn't letting the Commies get away with it at all. He's got the whole free world up on its toes."

Colonel Short's hunch was that God, in His mysterious way,

was working out His ultimate purpose with man as His agent. He was doing things *through* us, not *to* us.

I remembered a line in a novel by my friend, Arthur Gordon: "God works through people. It's one of the limitations He placed on Himself—God knows why."

That was what Colonel Short was driving at. God was working things out, not rigidly, not like a Mussolini timetable, "according to plan," but in the freedom and the wisdom of His ultimate purpose. Man was no mechanical marionette. He was, as Colonel Short put it, "God's agent." Without even knowing, sometimes, what God's ultimate purpose was, man was in there pitching—and even fighting when necessary—to help God accomplish it.

And right there I thought again of the Alamo. "Where was God at the Alamo?" I had asked on arriving at San Antonio. I had looked at that line in Travis' own handwriting on the aged mission walls, *"The Lord is on our side."* And I had wondered if it were a cruel joke or a delusion because Travis and his band were defeated, killed, and burned.

Now I felt an inkling of the answer.

God's ultimate purpose . . . Texas won its freedom.

7

WHY DO WE SUFFER?

Where is God in sorrow and adversity?

In a small town in Connecticut a tree surgeon was killed while helping with emergency work after a fierce windstorm which struck on a Thanksgiving week end.

I talked to several of the townspeople who knew him. They described him as a fine man, one of those warm, neighborly people whom everybody loved. They weren't just being respectful. You could read sincerity in their eyes when person after person—the gas-station man, the grocer, the home owner, the postman—called him "a wonderful fellow." One elderly townswoman said, "Just seeing him and exchanging a few words always made you feel good."

This man was killed.

How come? Some of the townspeople frankly wanted to know. When I talked to them about God they told me about the tree surgeon. And they deeply wanted to understand God's ways. One said, "Here was a *good* man. Why did he have to die—while so many crooks, cheats, and scoundrels live on and prosper?"

How about it?

How do we explain some of the things which happen in this world—some of the accidents, tragedies, heart-rending sorrows—for which the victims do not seem at all responsible? . . . A fine, hard-working father of four children is blinded in an automobile accident. A good, charitable woman is stricken with cancer. A devout, wholesome couple lose their only child. An honest businessman is squeezed to the wall by cheats and rascals. A town is wiped out by a flood. An innocent man is sent to jail.

Why? . . . Why?

Where is God in tragedy, in sorrow, in adversity?

As a reporter, I went first to the professionals, the theologians. One of them listened to my questions and replied, "Too many people regard goodness as a bank account and God as the teller. They make deposits of goodness and then want to be able to write out a check and get paid. They overlook entirely the matter of eternity. What about the *eternal* meanings of life and the *eternal* purposes of God?"

Another theologian, a Roman Catholic, put it this way: "Life on earth is but a period of preparation. The obvious answer to material wealth, success, and good fortune is, 'You can't take it with you.' But spiritual wealth has an eternal quality. It becomes part of the soul. It is indestructible."

He drew a comparison to a gang of neighborhood kids playing marbles. Material winnings are "for fun." Spiritual winnings are "for keeps." It makes a big difference when dusk comes and mothers start calling the kids home, and the game is over.

Yes—the good man was killed in the storm. But how do we know how that fits in with purposes far beyond the flicker of earthly existence on this planetary thingumbob which Jesus called "God's footstool"? That's the question the professionals kept raising.

A Protestant theologian insisted, "Only the foolish man gambles all on his own blueprint of life. The wise man stakes his life on God's blueprint."

But I wasn't satisfied. I still wanted to know about the injustices of suffering, about tragedies that hit the *good* people. Where is divine justice here?

A Jewish theologian offered, "That is the theme of the Book of Job: why do the righteous suffer? The answer is that man must not look for reward or punishment in terms of things physical. The good life does not mean riches or good fortune. The bad life does not mean poverty or misfortune. The only *true* compensations are spiritual. As Job finally said, 'Now mine eye seeth Thee.' He had come close to God."

To me, a journalist, such an explanation seemed idealistic and remote, as though it belonged on the pulpit rather than in the humdrum of down-to-earth living.

In fact, when I completed my rounds of the professionals I felt let down. My notebooks were full of platitudes. I felt that most of my questions had been tossed back at me. The theologians had answered one question by asking another.

All right. A reporter expects that. That's why he goes to the "experts" first. He gets it over with. Then he packs up his duffel bag, shoulders his spade, and goes out to dig for himself.

I sought out people who had suffered. Everyone, of course, has suffered some. But we all know special cases, people who seem to have had more than their share—"Poor Dick," "Poor Mrs. Smythe," "Poor Helen." But I was surprised when I found some of them and got close enough to see their real, inner selves beneath the veneer of pity. They weren't "poor" at all.

That veneer of pity, I discovered, often is not theirs; it is something we put on them. All we see is the external evidence: a man who is blind, a mother who is paralyzed, a young girl disfigured in an accident. What we do not see beneath is the transformation which so often takes place in the core of the deep, inner self.

Let me give you an example:

I met a young couple (we'll use the names Bill and Clara) on an airplane trip a few years ago. Bill was an executive in a firm in New York, doing extremely well for a young man, and Clara was vivacious, attractive, a magazine-cover prototype of the modern young wife.

After the airplane trip I saw them intermittently, perhaps twice a year. The picture of a perfect couple persisted without a blotch. They had a beautiful home, three fine children. Bill and Clara themselves seemed a well-matched pair and often I thought of them as having everything to live for.

One day a phone call came out of the blue: Clara was in the hospital. Poliomyelitis.

What a shock! All that happiness ruined. A life blighted in full flower. Here was I, making a search for meaning in the world—a reporter in search of God. I had found out a good deal. But what did it all mean? Was it just academic? Perhaps what happened to Clara was the real thing. Perhaps that, in the last analysis, was life.

Why did it have to happen?

But then that little gong which seems to be built into a reporter's brain began to sound: Did I have all the facts? . . . *Did I have all the facts?* It is a gong no reporter can ignore, any more than a fire horse can stand still when the firehouse alarm starts clanging.

I found Clara in a wheel chair. What a contrast to the young woman I had seen before. I approached her gingerly. My voice was soft and I must have had the expression of a pallbearer on my face. I wanted to be so careful not to say anything—well, embarrassing. I tried not even to notice the thin, limp legs and the arms that could make only irregular, circumscribed movements.

Clara laughed.

"Why so glum?" she asked.

"I'm terribly sorry——" I began.

"Not about me, I hope," said Clara with a joshing twinkle in her eye. "Why, I've found so many things to be happy about."

There it was. Could it be true? Or was it just "stiff upper lip" and "be a good soldier now" and "chin up, old girl" and all the other things we tell people who really want to cry their eyes out?

I talked with Clara for an hour.

"Really, I've gained so much more than I've lost," she told me. She spoke of a new harmony that had come inside her, of finding beauty where many people do not even know it exists, of discovering new meanings and new values and new inner aliveness.

Was this similar to the phenomenon which blind people often experience—losing their sense of sight but gaining a whole new range of senses they never thought existed? I wondered.

Clara spoke to me of a new appreciation of people, how new inner perceptions had, as it were, been awakened and how she could get so much more out of just knowing people and being with people and talking with people than she ever could before. She spoke, too, of new *awareness*.

"That's the key to it," she said. "We go through life, we accept things, we have experiences—and we think that's all there is. We just aren't aware of what we're missing. But most of the time—well, until something puts *awareness* into us, we're like people sitting in a symphony concert wearing ear muffs."

Life had opened wide to Clara. She was getting new joy out of her children, new stimulation from books, new appreciation from the beauty of a summer sky, new interest in her thoughts and the reach of her own mind, new zest from contact with people, new pleasure from laughter, new involvement in the affairs of the world, wondrous new surprises in the growth and outgoingness of her own personality, and a serene feeling of new faith in her inmost heart.

I found myself talking to her more easily. I hardly noticed the wheel chair now and I'm sure the look of the pallbearer had gone away. As I looked into Clara's face I thought what a beautiful face it was. That surprised me a little, for I never had thought of Clara as beautiful. I had thought of her as attractive, but the quality of beauty, mysterious as it is, never had seemed there before.

Before I left I asked Clara, "Would you go back if you could —back to before it happened?"

"No," Clara said. "If I were offered a trade, I'd say no. I wouldn't trade what has come to me for anything in this world."

. . . I thought of Job's line, "Now mine eye seeth Thee."

It wasn't only Clara. In my travels I talked to many people who had suffered the kind of misfortunes which make us want to weep for them. But I found that few were weeping for themselves.

There was a man in St. Louis, a young lawyer who had suffered the agonies of mental illness—a "nervous breakdown," as the layman calls it. He told me what he had been through: the ordeal of a state hospital, the fearful pressures of depression, the urge to suicide. His life had been cut wide open, his career shattered. The questions, "What will people think?" "Will I ever get back?" "Can I start my career again?" were upon him every minute.

And the sheer pain—"Well," he said to me, "if I ever were given the choice between mental pain and physical pain, I'd take the physical every time. There is no pain in the world like mental pain." I knew what he said was true. It is mental pain that brings suicide; rarely does physical pain get that bad.

"Yet," the young lawyer said, "that frightful ordeal was the best thing that ever happened to me."

"I must ask you to explain," I pressed. "You mean the good thing about it is that it's over, don't you? You're like the man who liked to hit himself on the head with a hammer. You like the frightful ordeal—because it felt so good when it stopped."

"No, no," he said thoughtfully. "It is not just a matter of relief. Of course I am relieved now that the illness is over, but that isn't all. Nor is it just a matter of thankfulness—you know, now that I know what suffering can be I'll be thankful for every good moment. It isn't only those things."

He went on, "You know, Carlyle said, 'Grow perfect through suffering.' That's more what I mean. There is a growth process in it, at least there was for me. I think the spirit perhaps needs some tempering, as metal does. And I don't know if there's any substitute for it. You've heard people say, 'Oh well, he—or she—hasn't suffered yet.' They say it of an immature person, one whom they do not expect to have reached the fullness of life. Intuitively they feel that suffering is necessary."

I inquired, "Do you feel it was necessary for you?"

The young lawyer replied, "It seems so. I don't know what else could have changed me so drastically."

"Changed you?"

"So that I hardly recognize myself sometimes. You see, before my 'breakdown' I was a hard-driving, hotheaded, and very rigid sort of person. Remember the play *Margin for Error?* That's the way I was, no margin for error. But that wasn't the worst part. The worst part was that my heart was a fortress trying to shut the whole rest of the world out. I really was afraid of everyone, of the world, without knowing it. That fear made me a miser. I hoarded everything that I had to give to the world, wouldn't let an ounce of it out for fear of being poorer."

"And now?" I asked.

"And now—well, I see myself differently. I am not a fortress, but a—a fountain, a spring with an endless source in all that is infinite about life. All people are. If we open up, let ourselves go, we bubble in a bright stream. We gush out to the world. And inside we are not afraid."

The young lawyer concluded, "Sure I'm glad for my suffering. I am stronger now, happier. Problems? Sure I have them. But I feel more able to deal with them as they come along. Blue moods? Sure, what individual doesn't feel down in the dumps once in a while. Bad temper? Yes, now and then—but not so bad I can't let it out and get over it. Failures? Sure I have them, I make my mistakes—but they don't throw me too badly. You see, I've accepted the margin for error. I've accepted life. I think most of all—I've accepted myself."

Was I supposed to feel sorry for that man?

Was I supposed to feel sorry for Clara?

At first blush perhaps, but not when I knew the facts. The deep, inner facts introduced a new dimension to experience which seemed to contradict the findings of our ordinary measurements. Clara, by ordinary measurement, should have been miserable. The young lawyer should have been bitter, or just relieved that the horror was over.

But in this new dimension, both had profited and both were happier, and both were better off than before: both were blessed.

Kahlil Gibran, the Lebanese poet and artist, once showed a new drawing to his patroness, Mary Haskell, and said, "I have called it 'The Fountain of Pain' and wished it to speak of that hidden power which purifies the soul through pain. Pain is a greater reality than pleasure, and much more effective as a teacher."

A Negro woman I met in Wisconsin put it this way: "I've learned that through every illness there is a glorious experience. I never knew that trouble could bring you closer to God."

But what about death? The other sufferings of life—the sicknesses, the adversities, the plain bad luck—we at least survive. We live through them. Even Job survived his misfortunes; he lived to a ripe old age. But what about the sicknesses, the accidents, which snuff out life itself? We can't accept them in terms of growing to be better people, having new wells of life opened up to us, profiting from misfortune, growing perfect through suffering.

Are tragic deaths, then, just God's mistakes?

Is God caught napping, asleep at the switch?

Let me tell you a tale of two tragedies.

Dolly Vawter, a woman of forty-eight, who lived in Monterey Park, California, died of cancer in the spring of 1951. A columnist in the Monterey Park *Progress* wrote these lines about her:

"Dolly Vawter was a sweet and gracious, gentle woman who

gave herself unsparingly to others. She was a person you meet once in a lifetime, who so lived by the word of God that she could do no harm or speak no word against anyone. [She was] a devoted and faithful wife and mother who affected everyone she met with her goodness and mercy."

Why did she die? Why did cancer take her?

Anyone would wonder. And her devoted husband, Robert A. Vawter wondered most of all. He wrote to me:

"No couple were ever more devoted to one another than Dolly and I. We were never away from one another overnight in our entire married life.

"We neither smoked, drank, nor swore, and we observed to the 'nth degree' the statutes in our Bible, which we taught in the Baptist Sunday school for the past fifteen years. Yes, I have taught that we should not question God's will. It was always, 'Thy will be done.' I taught that we must have courage and faith and accept God's will.

"Yet, after losing our first son, Robert, then our second son, Richard, and now my wife, Dolly, at the age of forty-eight, I told my surviving son, Douglas, age sixteen, that the very pillars and girders of faith were crumbling beneath me. No atom blast or any other phenomenon could dislodge the foundation more acutely than Dolly's passing after six long years courageously fighting cancer and smiling all the way. Her last written words were, 'The Father is doing His perfect work in me,' written in the leaf of one of her many prayer books.

"Where, Oh where, were the miracles of which I had taught in my Sunday-school class? Some were symbolic but there were many actual people who were saved through faith—the blind man, the lame man, the leper, Jarius's daughter, and others—but no help came for us and we had lived as near to perfection as possible.

"I recall the way in which Dolly received great pleasure: it was by visiting sick people and especially the wheel chair patients. That was our form of recreation. We had a large list of such people and some of them were over a hundred-mile drive away in rest homes but never a week passed without our visits. They were so comforting to these unfortunate people and the smiles on their faces when Dolly talked with them were more than ample reward for our efforts.

"Why, then, had Dolly been forsaken in her hour of need? Was this her reward for *doing good?*

"I can't believe it. . . . I cry, 'Why? Why?' and the burden is heavier. Can't someone tell me how to make it lighter?"

Mr. Vawter wrote to me in the hope that somewhere, somewhere he could get, as he put it, "a vision that will help me carry on and restore some portion of that wonderful Christian faith and courage that Dolly always had in abundance."

But I said I would tell you a tale of two tragedies. The tragedy of Dolly Vawter is one. This is the other:

At a religious retreat, a Christian Ashram at Green Lake, Wisconsin (described in Chapter 12, ONE WEEK WITH GOD), I met a young woman named Mary Webster. Like nearly all the others at the Ashram, Mary Webster, a young wife and mother from Toulon, Illinois, was deeply immersed in religious faith. I marveled, in fact, at the quality of her faith. She made enthusiastic professions of belief in God and Christianity. She seemed almost starry-eyed about it. She seemed to wear faith on her sleeve; faith was a passion with her.

Two weeks after the Ashram, Mary Webster and her family were in an automobile accident and her husband was killed.

What about Mary Webster now?—Mary Webster, who in a gathering of *very* religious people had been *super*-religious? Was this her reward for faith? I was shocked when I heard of it because I remembered indelibly Mary Webster's radiant face when she stood up and bore witness to her "conversion to Christ." I remembered her saying, "My life is all different now . . . I just can't explain it . . . It's the most wonderful thing that ever has happened to me . . . God has just come into my heart—I guess that's all I can say."

I remembered the week of prayer and holiness.

And now sudden death.

Was this the answer to Mary Webster's prayers?

Here are her own words:

"At present, I am in Peoria in the hospital with my youngest son. Have been in Kewanee Hospital for a week and the doctor there got a brain specialist in Peoria to operate on Claudie. He has a bad skull fracture and is not too good. . . . How grateful I am that God healed my wounds enough so that I have strength to come to stay with him. My hand has a few fractures and also the ribs on the left side, but my leg wasn't broken nor my jaw as they first thought. I got cut with glass but am still 'on top of the heap.' I'm still very sore and bruised all over but otherwise *just fine!* Am trying hard, with Grace from God, not to *worry* over Claudie's condition but just to *trust* and keep my mind free, so I will be able to help him all I can. He really needs a strong mother now and I know God will help me be strong for he has already done *miracles* for me.

"Ever since a year ago at the Silent Communion Service [at another Ashram in Texas], I've understood what death really is and have tried to tell others in a small degree just how beautiful an experience it will really be. It seemed to me that at the Communion Service, I got a glimpse into eternity and it was so beautiful my heart nearly broke with joy and rapture.

"Well, it is one thing to tell someone else something and another thing to go through it yourself. And I wondered if, when my time came to taste of death, it would hit me as an *evil* thing or if it would still seem the beautiful thing it did then. Now I can tell you with all truthfulness that my original opinion is only strengthened more and more! I can truthfully say that at least for me death really doesn't have any 'sting.'

"This may seem strange to you, as it certainly has to so many others, especially the doctors and nurses. But even when they told me that my husband was killed, I just couldn't feel one bit like crying. I haven't shed a tear over it nor do I feel like crying, for, you see, God has been teaching me so much and he has so transformed my thinking that now I see this accident in its true light and not as a personal issue at all. You must agree *that* is a miracle!

"The truck which caused the accident went to pass another car and saw us coming toward him. He applied his brakes to slow down and get back in line but the wheels of his truck locked and threw him sideways in front of our car and we hit it square in the center. . . . My husband didn't suffer at all as he was killed instantly. It is not tragic just because it happened to *me*. I know that when two cars hit like that it is rather inevitable that some-one get killed. We just happened to be in the path of the truck.

"I certainly *do* know that it was *not* God's will that we be hurt or that my husband be killed, but since He made us 'persons' He made us free and so we have the power to hurt or help one an-other. And because the laws of the universe are truly dependable laws they work the same no matter who uses them or breaks them. How grateful I am that this is so.

"But God was right there all right. I *saw* Him in the faces of those who wanted to help us, out of the compassion in their hearts—in the ambulance driver who was so grieved he could hardly speak, in the doctors who instantly came to help us and worked three hours sewing us up and making us comfortable, in the flowers and cards from people all over, and most of all in that 'still small voice' that said over and over and over again to me, 'Be not afraid for, Lo, I am with you *always*—even unto the end of the world.'

"He has indeed been with me so closely every minute that I feel as though I had wings of an eagle and my heart is singing to the top of its voice the Ashram song, 'I Will Not Be Afraid.' While I thought it possible for me to accept death, little did I dream I could still rejoice and sing in the very face of it. But you know it was not I, but He, who made that possible.

"At the Green Lake Ashram in the prayer room I saw in the Bible on the altar, 'Mary has chosen that good part that shall not be taken from her.' And those words say to me now that I have chosen that 'good part' of my husband that no one can ever take away from me. He is *one* with me now in the spirit of our Lord. It is as if he has just gone 'upstairs' to rest and I'll go, too, when I finish what I am doing and we shall see each other in the morning.

"So please, do not pity me for I find it impossible to pity myself but feel extremely grateful to our precious Lord for standing by me. He really has!"

This is what Mary Webster wrote.

There was a great deal in it for me.

Perhaps there is something in it for Mr. Vawter.

And perhaps there is something in it for you.

It would seem that a good many of our feelings about death and grief could bear revision. We're not a bit consistent.

I was talking about it with Clara Wiktorowsky, a worker in a Detroit factory.

"Do you think that good people—people who lead good lives —get their just rewards after they die?" I asked.

"Of course," she said.

"Well then, why do we grieve when they die?"

"Because we're sad."

"Sad—that someone we love is at last going to collect his just rewards! I don't think that's logical," I pressed.

"Well, maybe they're going to be punished," said Miss Wiktorowsky.

"*Good* people—punished?"

"Well—if they weren't good people they might be punished."

"I see," I said, summing up. "Then to be logical, we ought to feel sad and weepy when *bad* people die because they're going to collect their just punishments. And we ought to be happy and shout hurrah when good people die because they're going to collect their just rewards. Is that it?"

Miss Wiktorowsky couldn't quite answer that. And neither

could a good many other people to whom I posed the question.

Michael Runatz, a steel worker in Clairton, Pennsylvania, made this stab at it: "I guess grief is just a natural feeling. You're going to miss the person. It's like a mother crying when her daughter gets married or her son goes away to college."

But to be logical about that kind of grief, we'd have to call it selfish. Concern for the individual, like concern for the marrying daughter or the college-bound son, would call for joy, or at least acceptance, on our part that the individual we love is moving on toward a new phase in the cycle of existence. Are we going to stand in his way? For whom are we actually grieving? For ourselves?

Runatz shook his head and said, "I don't know what to make of it. I've seen people pray to God to take a cancer sufferer—and then cry like babies when he dies."

What can a mature attitude toward death be?

John Masefield, England's Poet Laureate, reached out for such an attitude when, upon the death of King George VI, he wrote:

O Wisdom, Who, with power infinite,
Utterest death to every creature born,
Grant to us now the mercy of Thy light,
With comfort to beloved Queens who mourn.

Perhaps something of what Masefield was reaching for actually was grasped by the King's Prime Minister, Winston Churchill. Something of his own view of death could be garnered from what Churchill had to say when George VI passed on. He said:

"During these last months the King walked with death as if death were a companion, an acquaintance whom he recognized and did not fear. In the end death came as a friend and after a happy day of sunshine and sport. After 'Good night' to those who loved him best, he fell asleep as every man and woman who strives to fear God and nothing else in the world may hope to do."

I met three people, among the hundreds with whom I talked

of life and death, whose stories I set down in my notebook with a star at the top of the page (a reporter's way of flagging something special).

The first was Mrs. Grace Hume, of Rock Island, Illinois. Mrs. Hume for thirteen years owned and operated a small letter shop, and life must have seemed to her as humdrum and frequently perplexing as it does to many of us. Then a few years ago it dawned upon her that there are such things as love and faith in the world. She retrimmed her sails and the voyage has been entirely different ever since.

"There was a time when I was bored. I didn't care if I lived or died," she told me. "But when my eyes were opened I realized what a wonderful adventure life could be—and actually *is*."

Then Mrs. Hume spoke the lines I starred in my notebook:

"I've told my family not to grieve for me when I die. I told them not to—because I'm sure that what lies ahead will be even *more wonderful*."

. . . A woman without fear.

Then there was Hilda Libby Ives, of Portland, Maine. Mrs. Ives is a minister of the Congregational Christian Church. But she didn't start out in life that way. She started out as a homemaker, wife of a promising young lawyer, mother of four little children. Her marriage was ten years old when her husband died suddenly in the flu epidemic of World War I.

There she was—stranded in life.

"I had no answer to death then," Mrs. Ives told me. "I asked myself, 'Was this God, who sent love into my life only to smash it?' I couldn't understand that kind of God.

"It was like a child saying, 'Father doesn't love me. He makes me take medicine.' Like a child, I had to become aware of Father's larger purpose.

"I had to realize that love does not die with human ashes. It was a process of discovering that God Himself is love."

And so the young widow studied for the ministry. Her first assignment was in a tiny Maine town of four hundred, where an old deacon, irked at seeing a woman minister in the pulpit, grumbled, "Every one they send us is worse than the one before, and this one is the worst of all."

But the town grew to love this woman, and she went on to fruitful decades of service in many parishes. She said to me, "What I have sought is the kind of love that is not perishable with death."

I think she found it.

The third person whose story I starred in my notebook was Master Sergeant Howard Franklin Calloway, whom I met on my visit to Fort Sam Houston, Texas. Calloway had a nine-year-old son, Howard, Jr. His wife had died within the past year.

"Yes, my wife died last December after a three-year illness," Calloway said. "We knew she was going to die. In fact, we even sat around and discussed it—all three of us.

"She'd tell the boy, 'Mommie is going to die and go to heaven. I hope you'll remember all the things I've told you.' "

Calloway wasn't maudlin as he related the story. If any eyes were moistening, they were mine not his. He told factually and calmly how he and his wife, anticipating her death as the doctors predicted, sat around on off evenings and planned how he and their son would carry on after she'd gone.

When I made some casual remark about it being "unfortunate," Calloway corrected me. "No, not *un*fortunate," he said. "I'm *fortunate*—I've got a son to take care of!"

. . . Somewhere among the writings of William Penn you'll find, "They that love beyond the World cannot be separated by it. Death is but Crossing the World, as Friends do the Seas; they live in one another still."

Faith certainly does not guarantee immunity from tragedy. Mary Webster and countless others give proof of that. Yet in my probing and questioning I felt that faith did guarantee immunity from something deeper than tragedy, beyond tragedy. It guaranteed immunity not from death, but from a living death.

It was a farm wife in a small town in Michigan who said to me, "I don't expect that because I have faith in God no misfortune or tragedies will come my way."

"What do you expect?" I asked.

"I expect that—whatever comes—I will be able to accept it," she replied.

A school principal in Bucks County, Pennsylvania—Richard H. McFeely—said in his own personal declaration of faith, "Birth and death, happiness and sorrow, illness and good health, love and loss—these I find are no respecters of persons. They come alike to all. But not all respond alike. Some go to pieces, dissolve in self-pity, become a burden to others, perhaps even take their own lives in their despair and hopelessness. Others have something in them that, in spite of ill fortune, enables them to live constructively and creatively."

This is what I mean by immunity from a living death. It has been said perhaps even simpler: It is not what happens that counts, *but how we take what happens.*

Thus, to some a hard blow of fortune is utterly destructive. Their spirit is snuffed out like an uncertain candle. To others, while the flame may flicker, there is the mysterious fuel of faith to keep it kindled and even to make it glow more brightly.

Job, in the Bible, finally said, "Let come on me what will. . . . Though He slay me, yet will I trust in Him."

Each of us, it has been said, is at the mercy of a falling tile. It is not that God pushes the tile. It is hardly God's will that a child be hit by a truck, that a father fall ill and die, that a mother be stricken with cancer. But it does seem to be God's will that we accept such tragedies, not be thrown by them—even grow spiritually from them. A latter-day Job, a young Catholic worker at the University of Ottawa, in Canada, spoke to me of a tragic affliction of his child, "My wife and I know," he said, "that our suffering is to strengthen us. It will give us growth."

Why do we suffer? This seemed, for one young couple, to answer the question.

And just about the time I was wondering if there couldn't be a pleasanter way—some substitute for suffering—I heard Dr. E. Stanley Jones, the missionary, say with quiet wisdom, "When God waters his flowers he draws a veil across the sun."

And I thought I had better accept it just that way.

8

DOES IT DO ANY GOOD TO PRAY?

A new concept of prayer

But if you go along accepting things, what happens to that central pillar of all religion: *prayer?* It had always seemed to me that prayer was, somehow, a way of changing things. Or at least that's the way it was advertised. I had made up my mind in setting out upon the search for God to do some down-to-earth digging into this business of prayer. Now seemed the time. For in suffering and tragedy people pray more than any other time of their lives.

I realized I had reached something of a dilemma. For, if one is simply to accept suffering and tragedy and to grow perfect out of it, then why all the praying? Or, if prayer actually works, then why all the suffering?

My notebooks were filled, up to this point, mostly with negative evidence. . . .

In New York an aged Jewish man was robbed and murdered as he knelt alone in his synagogue—in the very act of praying. He was not praying to be killed, I'm certain! Also in New York, a police inspector was killed by the most freakish of accidents:

an airplane crashed into the street and hit his car. He was on his way to Catholic Mass at the time, on his way to pray.

In Korea a soldier knelt in meditation in his foxhole with an open Bible in his hands; a bullet crashed through his helmet and he died still clutching the Holy Writ.

In California—remember the little girl who fell in the well? Virtually an entire nation prayed for her (even school children in their classrooms) and the neighbors kept prayer vigils in the fields all day and throughout the night, but when the rescuers finally brought Kathy Fiscus up from the well she was dead.

I was in London when the buzz-bombs began to sputter crazily out of the sky during World War II. One of the first structures demolished was a historic chapel near Buckingham Palace. The bomb struck during a Sunday morning service—and I shall never forget the last words I heard from a friend who attended the service: "God will never let them hurt me while I'm praying." He was blown to bits. . . .

We wonder about prayer. No wonder we wonder.

Does prayer do any good? Are our prayers "heard" at all? Or are we just wasting our breath?

In my reportorial rounds of the nation I found all ranges of attitude toward prayer, from people who thought prayer was all-powerful to those who thought it was nonsense. But the bulk of opinion lay in between.

"Just can't be sure," said a farmer near Waterloo, Iowa. "To be on the safe side, I do a little prayin' now and then. Way I figure is, it can't do no harm."

Many people felt that way. A housewife in Bowling Green, Kentucky, said she prayed "to be on the safe side." A newspaperman in Providence, Rhode Island, remarked, "The way I see it, praying's like crossing your fingers. I do it because—well, if there's really anything to it, I'm covered." Several times I heard the expression, "Can't do any harm, may do some good."

Men of the cloth constantly are bombarded with questions about prayer, some pretty cagey questions, too, such as a Philadelphia lawyer might hurl at a witness. Reverend Tilford T. Swearingen of Kansas City, for example, was asked by a member of his flock, "What about two mothers praying for their sons in wartime? One's son gets killed. The other's doesn't. Is God unfair? Is He partial?"

In Westport, Connecticut, where he formerly had a parish ministry, Reverend H. Lincoln MacKenzie quoted to a World War II veteran the Biblical line, "The very hairs on your head are numbered in the mind of God," only to have the veteran reply, "Yeah, and what about my buddy? I guess the hairs on his head were numbered too. Only maybe God wasn't looking when he got his head blown off on Leyte!"

I was surprised to find that even the serious, spiritually saturated young men who take up religion as a profession have their doubts about prayer. I went to a conference of ministers in Boston and heard Reverend John M. Billinsky, of the Andover Newton Theological School, report that one of the biggest problems with theological students is the *problem of prayer*. Other conferees concurred. They pointed out that many of these young men, whose consecration to life is through religious service, have "tried out" prayer, almost on an experimental basis, as a scientist might try out a formula, and have been disappointed in it. Some have lost faith in it. Some, strangely enough, even in the religiously supercharged atmosphere of the seminary, have virtually come to the point where they *cannot pray*. For these are young men who take prayer seriously and their reactions are stronger than everyday people who can "pray to be on the safe side" or "take it or leave it."

There are times in the lives of all of us when we are as serious as that, or even more serious, about praying. A child is ill. A husband is on the operating table. A wife goes into the delivery room. A plane is late and unreported. A child is late coming home. We hear a fire siren wailing toward our neighborhood. Or perhaps we're waiting—with our fingers crossed—for the results of an election, a court decision, a doctor's diagnosis, or just the list of winners in a contest or the announcement of who gets the scholarship.

"Oh boy, I never prayed so hard in all my life!"

You've heard that phrase. I've heard it. Most of us probably have said it sometime or other.

Prayer, even if some of us secretly think it is bunk, is crucially important in living. It is a line of communication with the vast, imponderable universe outside ourselves. It is easy enough to cut off communication and live in isolation when the going is good. But when the going is tough, really tough, how we strive to get a message through! The prayers that come out of hospitals and foxholes probably outstrip ten to one in intensity most prayers that come out of churches. Why not explore this line of communication? It can't be both hokum and truth at the same time.

I wasn't interested in the platitudes or in those vague notions which are way up at 25,000 feet, where the air is too thin to breathe. I tried to nail down some facts about prayer, just as in my journalistic life I have tried to nail down some facts about migrant farm workers, and judges, and politicians, and crime, and education, and prejudice, and sex, and the raising of children.

The first things I found out about prayer were on the minus side. I found out what prayer *isn't.*

Prayer *isn't* a rabbit's foot. It isn't something to bring you good luck. Otherwise, we could throw it out the window on prima-facie evidence without even hearing the arguments. The boy with the Bible in Korea didn't get any good luck by praying. Nor did the old man who was murdered in the synagogue. If every one of us stopped praying when prayer failed to bring us luck, there would be no prayer left in the world.

Prayer *isn't* an Aladdin's lamp. It isn't something with which to work magic: to turn our slightest wish into God's command.

In Wollaston, Massachusetts, a small boy went up to Reverend William B. Ayers at the Union Congregational Church and complained, "I'm tired of hearing my father tell God how to run the world every morning!" That's what his father's prayers sounded like to him—"God, do this," "God, do that," "God, do the other thing."

"Aren't many of us inclined to give orders to God?" Reverend Ayers wondered.

"Prayer isn't a trick to *change* the mind of God, but a way to *adjust ourselves* to the mind of God," he said.

Even when we pray for peace aren't we assuming that it is God who is responsible for wars and that we can somehow give Him orders to change His mind? If it ever occurred to us that *we* make the wars and that God has been for peace all along, we might pray differently.

One of the finest speeches ever heard in the United States Senate came from Senator Ralph E. Flanders of Vermont on August 2, 1950. It made no eight-column headlines, for there was no genie in it and no magic lamp. But there was this paragraph:

"It has . . . been suggested that bombarding the throne of grace with 50,000,000, 150,000,000 or even 500,000,000 prayers would solve the world's problems. This assumes that with enough prayers God can be persuaded to work a miracle. With regard to this, Mr. President, may I make two suggestions? The first is that no miracle is necessary, for God in His law has already provided the means. The second suggestion is that these prayers would be better addressed to the opening of the blind eyes and closed minds of the petitioners themselves, who have neither understood the law of God nor worked in accordance with it."

Prayer *isn't* "the gimmes." The clergy, I found, are pretty fed up with people whose fundamental idea of prayer is, "God, gimme this," "God, gimme that." Reverend Murray A. Cayley, in Rochester, New York, said, "That's making God into a divine bellhop. I find it absolutely repugnant." Reverend Arthur E. Wilson, of Providence, Rhode Island, called it "pretty pagan."

A psychiatrist would call it infantile. It is like the little child's wish always to be given something, to have all the toys in the store window, to have everything the neighbor children have, to have anything that strikes his fancy from a Shetland pony to the Empire State Building—to have the whole world with a little green fence around it. In little children we understand such egocentricity. It is part of growth. But when grownups try to turn God into a 365-day-a-year Santa Claus that's something else again.

The ancient Greeks had a saying, "When the gods are angry with a man they give him what he asks for." For people with the "gimmes" invariably ask for trash. What they ask of God would do them no more good (and probably as much harm) as all the toys in the store window would do Junior if we heaped them upon him.

I found these lines in a little Catholic tract: "Many complain that their prayers are not heard. This can only be true of their begging for temporal favors. These are sometimes refused because the Lord commutes the temporal blessings into spiritual ones, especially the virtues of patience and fortitude.

"Or again, the Lord forsees injury, for many a child is spoiled by being petted. God will not spoil His generosity by indiscriminate giving, except to His enemies."

A woman in Providence, Rhode Island, gained a rare insight into "the gimmes" during World War II, when her son was overseas. She went up to Reverend Wilson one day and said, "I started out by praying to God to save Jimmy's life. But then I realized it was like asking God to take someone else's son instead of mine."

Prayer *isn't* bargaining. A newspaperman whose daughter was critically ill prayed, "If you spare her, God, I'll never drink again." A businessman, faced with an operation, prayed, "Pull me through, God, and I'll give five hundred dollars to charity." A pilot in a crippled bomber prayed, "Bring me home from this mission, God, and I'll go straight into the ministry when the war is over."

That isn't praying. What would the newspaperman do if his daughter died—become a drunken sot to get even with God? Did the businessman think God needed a five-hundred-dollar bribe? Couldn't an omnipotent God drop five hundred dollars into the lap of His favorite charity any time He wanted to? The pilot, fortunately, never did get into the ministry. He did make the offer, but seminaries are being more careful these days than they used to be. They want to know *why* young men seek the ministry. When this candidate told of his "bargain with God" he was gently informed that God would manage somehow without him. He was sent home for some spiritual and psychological counseling.

"I'll do that for You if You do this for me" is no legitimate part of prayer. It actually puts the petitioner above God. He is going to hold something over God's head. He is going to use bargaining power against God. And if God does not do what he wants Him to do, what then? Is he going to get mad at God? And just how will he wreak his vengeance?

Finally—prayer *isn't* words. When any sentiment, no matter how noble or how tinctured with truth, is set down in words and then handed down through generations and constantly repeated, it runs the risk of turning into gibberish. The words become rote, sounds without meaning. Often they cease to be *words*. For years as a child I thought "tisathee" must be some kind of a word because to me the opening line of *America* was "My country tisathee." Harvard University conducted a study of this phase of semantics. One boy who had said the Pledge of Allegiance scores of times was asked to put down on paper just what he had said. He wrote, "I perjur legens to the Flag of the United States of America and to the Republicans for which it stands, one nation invisible with libbuty and jesters for all." This same descent of noble thoughts into meaninglessness is one of the prime hazards of prayer.

Rabbi Samuel M. Silver, while assistant to Rabbi Barnett R. Brickner at Cleveland's Euclid Avenue Temple, turned to the mothers of the congregation and asked them to send in any new, fresh prayers for children which they had composed. He knew that many a child was saying lines which had turned into mere rhythmical rote. "The old prayers have lost their force, and the new ones are missing," Rabbi Silver said.

Even in Catholicism, where ritual rates high indeed, Father George J. Haye, writing on "The Art of Prayer," reminded his readers, ". . . it is better to say one vocal prayer slowly and full of meaning, than to rush through many meaningless prayers. (Some nervous people today are hurrying through five novena booklets at bedtime; it would be better to make only one novena, well-made.)"

I had little difficulty in finding out what prayer *isn't.* It was much harder to find out what prayer *is.* The first real inkling came to me on a freezing cold night in a little town you've probably never heard of: Beaver Meadows, Pennsylvania. It is a tiny farming hamlet in the wilds of the Allegheny Mountains, the kind of place you might look down on from an airplane and think to yourself, "What a Godforsaken little place."

Little, yes. But not Godforsaken.

I drove up in a jeep with a minister from down in the valley. The dirt road was frozen into implacable ruts. The jeep argued its way over them. Beaver Pond, across from the Methodist Church, was frozen solid and in the night light looked like a giant's looking glass dropped in the woods.

We went into the church and saw children standing over the hot-air registers, singing hymns with their coats on. This was a young people's meeting. I wanted to go to it because a farmer in the valley had told me what the subject was: "The Importance of Prayer." I had talked to a good many grownups so far in my travels and had yet to find out just what prayer really *is.*

Perhaps the children could lead me.

There were eight girls and one boy. Some of them gave reports. They read things they had looked up, things people had told them, and things they just figured out for themselves.

Norma Sharer, who lived on Clapper Hill, was just thirteen, a farm child. When she read her report I started writing in my notebook.

"Prayer," she said, *"is not overcoming God's reluctance. It is taking hold of God's willingness."*

Norma kept talking and some of the kids asked questions.

Then Norma turned back to her report.

"Prayer does not change God, but it does change us," she read. And I wrote that down too.

There were goodies and movies in the basement of the church after the meeting. The minister and I waited until all the children were called for and then jogged down into the valley again in the jeep.

He asked me, "Did you get anything out of it?"

I said yes; I knew I was on the right trail now.

Two weeks later I was talking to a young Negro flier in Texas, Aviation Cadet Lieutenant Gordon Walls. He told me about the day he was shooting landings with his instructor, before he had ever soloed.

"The instructor said, 'Taxi over to the control truck.' Then he got out and asked, 'How about going up yourself?' " Walls related.

"What did you do?" I asked.

"I started praying right away."

"What prayer did you say?"

"The *best prayer,"* said the young flier.

I asked him what the "best prayer" was and he replied, "You've heard it many times—*'Not my will but Thine be done.'* "

"But how would you expect that to help you?" I asked.

"Just by putting me in tune with God," he said.

Here was another intimation of what prayer *is*. No "gimmes" here. No divine bellhop. No bargains. Just a simple turning over of one's self to the God force of the universe.

"This doesn't mean," Reverend Cayley later explained as we talked about it in Rochester, "that a person can't state his case before God. Why not? He can say, in effect, 'Now look, Boss, this is the way I feel about it. . . . But nevertheless, let not my will but Thine be done.' "

Then Reverend Cayley, a straight-from-the-shoulder preacher, started talking about "God's leadership." He said the purpose of prayer was "to put yourself in a position where you can be led by God."

"Take myself," he observed. "For me, prayer brings on a sense of God's leadership. I become more aware of His design and plan of the universe. It is a good plan and a good design. There is nothing vicious or vindictive about it."

The expression in Cayley's eyes seemed to say, "You see, I know all this because the Boss and I have talked it over many times."

He likes to talk about God in warm, everyday terms. "Prayer is a thought relationship with the Diety. I don't see why it should be so formal," he remarked. "I'd like to say to my congregation, 'Now just sit back and let's pray. Close your eyes if you want to. We're going to talk to God.' "

"Just how does this kind of 'talk' go?" I inquired.

"For me, something like this," Cayley replied, " 'Hi. It's been a grand week. I want to thank You for lots of undeserved generosity. Quite a lot got accomplished. But, you know, Boss, some of it I did myself. I hope to keep trying.' "

The further I dug into what prayer really *is,* the less the extremes of magic and nonsense obtruded themselves. Where there was no infantile belief in a genie there was no need to debunk the genie because it failed to appear at the rub of the lamp.

Prayer began to take on a new garb, too. It wasn't just an asking of favors. It wasn't being a special pleader. It was a *two-way* communication. What you did was clear the wires so that you could address yourself to the spiritual force of creation—but not only that; you also cleared the wires so that this force could address itself to you. I began to see prayer as not so much a set of the mind so that you could talk to God, but a set of the mind so that God could talk with you.

Here's how Reverend Wilson put it: "You can state your case. You may say, for example, 'Heavenly Father, this is the situation. I'm worried about it. Frankly, I don't know just which way to turn, which decision to make. These are the facts as I see them. . . .' Then just be quiet for a bit. Wait and see if some answer doesn't come to you. You may actually *feel* the answer within you."

I began now to understand more richly what the young flying cadet in Texas meant when he spoke of getting "in tune with God."

How many different forms can prayer take?

You answer it. I can't. How many different forms can love take? How many smiles can you see on the face of a child? How many different skies do the sun and clouds make?

"A poor laborer in the parish of Ars used to spend hours on his knees before the Blessed Sacrament, his eyes fixed on the Tabernacle, but his lips never moving. The Curé asked him one day, 'What do you say to Our Lord all the time, my friend?' The simple soul replied, 'I say just nothing at all. I only look at Him and He looks at me.' "

The story was told by Reverend Walter Elliott, of the Paulist Fathers. Can you think of a purer form of prayer?

I met a woman factory worker in a Detroit plant, Mrs. Hazel Vollmar, who told me, "Lots of people have the idea that you only *say* your prayers. I *feel* mine. I often pray while I'm working. Especially if there is something on my mind, if I feel troubled—it brings peace of mind."

Mrs. Vollmar is just an everyday American woman. But what she said was pretty much what Norman Vincent Peale meant in his statement, "When we speak of praying, we do not necessarily mean that a man goes into a room, gets down on his knees, and indulges in formalized expressions of petition to God. What we *do* mean by prayer is the turning of men's minds to God."

It's not the form; it's the content. I began to see that a man could truly pray in a cathedral, but he could also truly pray walking along a country road. He could pray by repeating the words of a liturgy, or just by a deep feeling which might pervade him at the view of a sunset. He could pray alone in his bed with his silent thoughts, or just looking into the faces of his children and really *seeing* them.

"Prayer doesn't need to have words. It can be a feeling," Reverend J. T. Morrow, of Tulsa, Oklahoma, told me. "When a man is walking along on a beautiful day and is overwhelmed with appreciation—that's prayer. It's prayer when he drives up his driveway at home and catches a first glimpse of his wife and children in the yard and a feeling of love wells up inside him. And when a man gives up something—even a little something like a place in line, or an honor, or a privilege—to someone who needs it more than he does, that's prayer too."

There I could see another widening glimpse of what prayer *is*. Prayer is action. It was a form of prayer when the neighbors in a New Jersey community got together and built a house for a family whose home had burned down. It was a form of prayer when a society woman in New Haven, Connecticut, gave up the social whirl to devote herself to improving race relations. It was a form of prayer when a man driving down a road in my town stopped his car to pick up a baby robin and put it back in its nest. And what a form of prayer it was when Albert Schweitzer turned his back on worldly fame and went to French Equitorial Africa to start a hospital for the natives!

In prayer, as in life, actions speak louder than words.

Reverend John S. Higgins, rector of St. Martin's Church in Providence, Rhode Island, listed the five formal categories of prayer: 1. Adoration. 2. Thanksgiving. 3. Confession. 4. Intercession (prayers for others). 5. Petition (prayers for ourselves).

"Note," he said, "that petition comes last. The higher one goes in the levels of prayer; the less he is concerned with petition, the less he asks for himself."

But, certainly, a person wants to ask God for something once in a while. People are only human. They can adore, and thank, and confess, and ask good for others—but don't they get a break once in a while? Can't they throw in a purely personal request now and then and feel that they are *really* praying?

Sure they can. Rabbi Abba Hillel Silver, of The Temple in Cleveland, suggested to me a purely personal prayer which seemed to reach into the highest realm of communication with God.

"Pray," he said, "to *be* more, not to *have* more."

I came to a point, after talking to scores of everyday people and scores of ministers, priests, and rabbis, when a question kept nudging its way to the front of my mind—"That's all very well about prayer, but does it *work?* Does prayer *really work?*" All journalists, I think, must trace their spiritual birthplace to Missouri. It's in their blood to want to be shown, to see for themselves. So I started on the trek again with an empty notebook.

I wanted the evidence.

At an army base in the Southwest I found Lieutenant Colonel William F. Kernan, just before he left for Korea. We sat down together beside a window with sunlight streaming in and we talked of prayer and battle. Kernan was a Catholic. He had been a major in World War II.

"I had my battalion at Brest," he said. "We had a tough position; we couldn't bust through. The enemy was giving it to us in spades.

"I had always had my misgivings about somebody getting killed because of my ignorance or stupidity. I remember walking out at twilight and the field was full of dead men. I didn't see how we'd ever get the enemy out of there. I walked out alone and took my rosary in my hand. I started praying. I squeezed the rosary so hard I broke the beads.

"I was on the verge of breaking then. In similar circumstances I had heard men say, 'Cry, go ahead and cry. Get it out of your system.' I knew I was going to pray or cry. I prayed instead."

"Any results?" I questioned.

"Next morning the enemy was gone. They had pulled out during the night," Kernan replied.

"But," I pressed, "suppose they hadn't pulled out? Could you still say your prayers had been answered?"

Kernan looked straight at me and the sun streaked across his face. He replied:

"Yes. Prayer produced three immediate results—even before I knew we'd ever get out of there alive."

He listed them.

"One. Prayer relieved the feeling that I was responsible for those dead men. It put at rest my feeling that I'd killed someone through ignorance or stupidity. I realized I had done all I could.

"Two. Prayer made me feel prepared to die. I had made my peace. If my time was up—okay.

"Three. Prayer saved me from breaking."

Kernan paused, then added, "You see, I believe in prayer for a very simple reason—*because it works.*"

Life under fire is an ordeal in many respects. But primarily, I believe, it is an ordeal of loneliness. There is no feeling of aloneness quite as cutting as the aloneness of a man in a wilderness of death. I know this from firsthand experience as a war correspondent during World War II. The very core of a man feels nude and abandoned and alone. His heart of hearts cries out for company. That's why there is so much to-do over "buddies" in a war zone, so much emphasis on the "outfit," on *esprit de corps.*

But there is a still deeper aloneness. It is an emptiness way down in the profound well of a man, and only one kind of company really can fill it. A little while after I spoke with Colonel

Kernan, I met Master Sergeant James A. Gorsuch, who told me this:

"I've had nearly twenty-nine years in the Army. I'm a family man with four children. It was in 1940 that I started praying, morning and night. That was the first separation from my family. I went on those 'sewer-pipe maneuvers' in Louisiana.

"Then came World War II and eighteen months of combat in the Pacific. I had plenty of close calls, but my prayers got me through. I can't explain why other fellows got it—but I'm sure my prayers got me through.

"When I prayed I always felt someone was with me.

"On an escarpment in Okinawa I heard men yell, 'Oh my God! My God! My God!' But I always felt, 'As long as I continue to pray I can get through, I'm all right.'

"Once a shell landed nine feet away—a dud! Then I knew there was a God."

I interrupted with a question, "What if you had been hit?"

"I'd still believe—I'd believe it was just that my time had come."

He continued, "When I heard soldiers groaning and screaming I'd pray they'd be taken into God's fold. Sometimes I prayed all night when shells were coming over. I'd say so many prayers it's a wonder they didn't make me a preacher."

I asked, "Isn't that a lot of prayers for Someone to listen to?"

"Yes," said Sergeant Gorsuch, "but I think God has His own system. If He didn't, He wouldn't be the Supreme Being."

I remembered the talk with Gorsuch a long time and kept coming back to the line he said so casually, *"When I prayed I always felt someone was with me."* Sure, he wanted to "get through." All people want to live. But with God as his buddy, he was prepared to die, too. He had, somehow, a sense of a bigger plan. Unlike the men on the escarpment he wouldn't have to cry out in the despair of utter aloneness, for Gorsuch had company from the word go.

Still, I wanted more evidence to confirm or deny a simple

down-to-earth proposition: Can prayer actually bring you back alive? Prayer might calm your spirit, and it might quell the choking sense of aloneness, and it might prepare you for death or whatever happens—in other words, it might be good therapy, good medicine—but can it get you through?

On the outskirts of San Antonio, Texas, I went to the peaceful, flower-decked ranch house where General Courtney H. Hodges, commander of the First Army in World War II, was living in retirement. He told me, "Stonewall Jackson, Montgomery, Patton—many a great fighter—prayed before going into battle. Soldiers, you see, don't believe in the miraculous, but they do turn to God."

"Does it do any good?"

"The fellow who prays isn't running away—he's fighting!" the general said.

Then I remembered those nightmarish mornings at an Eighth Air Force Base in East Anglia, England . . . how the fliers would come to briefing in the middle of the night and how they sat down to a breakfast of fried eggs and what a treat it was, even before a rendezvous with death, to have *real* eggs, not dried ones . . . and how they were promised bananas if they clobbered the target—when, and if, they got back.

And I remembered the chaplain who would get together with the boys before they took off. One morning a new crew, fresh from the States, was going up. The chaplain let them have it straight from the shoulder. I remember just how he put it: "Prayers won't hold your planes up, boys. Only aerodynamics will."

A scared young pilot said, "You mean we shouldn't pray? You mean prayers aren't worth a hoot?"

"I don't mean that at all, Lieutenant," said the chaplain. "Prayer has brought many a plane home safely. Not because it gave magical immunity—but because it gave the crew peace and calm and courage, and enabled *them* to bring the plane home safely!

"Prayer isn't a rabbit's foot, Lieutenant. It won't draw a magic ring around your plane and post a sign in the sky, 'All flak detour here.' But prayer will give you inner peace—another name for courage—and you'll handle that plane right. You'll make the right decisions, you'll take the right evasive action, you'll be alert, you'll do right by your instruments. There's no better way to get aerodynamics on your side."

And so the plane comes home.

Does prayer do any good before an operation? I couldn't quite see it guiding the surgeon's knife, and the patient was under anesthesia anyway—so I didn't expect to find much evidence there. I was surprised when I visited one of New York's most famous hospitals, the Columbia Presbyterian Medical Center, and found that prayer was one of the things the doctors depended upon most in preparing a patient for surgery. Chaplain Lyman R. Hartley was one of the busiest men in the hospital.

Perhaps this was just a kind of routine, I thought. I still wanted evidence that prayer *did some good.*

I got it from a noted surgeon. He explained:

"In operative cases, prayer reduces muscular tension. It lowers the blood pressure and lessens the danger of heart strain, which might otherwise be induced by a tense and fearful state of mind. The patient responds much more favorably to anesthesia. For a patient calmed by prayer, in contrast to one inwardly riled up by dread and anxiety, the chances of successful surgery are greatly increased. Post-operative recovery likewise is more rapid and more successful."

What about less dramatic forms of medical care? Surgery always has an edge-of-the-cliff feeling about it. How about everyday sickness, the kind of thing that brings the doctor out to the house a few times a year?

"I can't exactly say that prayer is medicine," a physician told me. "But I know this—it certainly helps medicine do its job. Prayer is a manifestation of a will to get well and, as such, galvanizes the resources of the body and mind into a maximum effort towards recovery. This makes any medicine I prescribe twice as effective."

How about the field of medicine which deals with sick emotions? Dr. Edward A. Strecker, professor of psychiatry at the University of Pennsylvania, has stated, ". . . prayer has an important place in psychiatric treatment. Often the psychiatrist finds it necessary to help the patient relinquish excessive and childish emotional dependencies upon others. Through prayer, the patient can take his troubles to God and find the support and strength he needs."

I got the final evidence I needed from just everyday people. You don't have to be a big shot or an expert to know whether prayer does you any good. So I asked lots of people I met across this broad land of ours, and here are three samples of what I collected:

A store manager in San Francisco—"Does it do any good to pray? For me it sure does. It gives me a good feeling inside. I get a sense of satisfaction. It makes me feel good."

A confirmation-class student at the Euclid Avenue Temple in Cleveland—"Praying helps because it makes us think out our problems and ideas."

A woman government worker in Washington—"My marriage was breaking up and I prayed a lot. Well, praying didn't stop my divorce—but it sure helped me to weather it!"

From all the probing, the thing that is going to stick to my ribs about prayer is that it is a rare, unduplicable kind of experience. It is the art and act of putting yourself in communication with the essence of the universe. Playwright Arthur Miller wrote "Death of a Salesman" to drive home the need all of us have to find out, as he put it, "who we are." I think there is as great a need to find out, "where we are."

Prayer, it seems to me, relates us to all that is mysterious and unknown and imponderable in creation. It is an affirmation that we are, somehow, a part of all there is. I like what Rabbi Abba

Hillel Silver said to me, "In prayer you link yourself up with the source of all spiritual strength. You are not alone in the world. You dwell where God is." I also like what the Catholic priest, Reverend Walter Elliott, said, "No man is fit to deal with other men who has not learned how to deal with God."

Prayer is a channel of communication, like a telephone line to the forces of creation. It is a wonderful thing to keep in touch. Just being "in communication"—whether through the heart of a poet, the eyes of an artist, the liturgy of a priest, the love of a parent, the thought of a philosopher—is a wonderful thing.

No, we don't get what we want every time we pick up the spiritual telephone, any more than we get what we want any time we pick up the phone in our office. But if we telephone J.B. and he says he won't sign the contract we don't hurl our office phone out the window. No more should we throw out our spiritual telephone, tear down our lines of communication with the God force of creation, just because we don't get what we want—or think we want—every time we pick up the phone.

One thing we *are* sure to get every time we pick up the phone: *help*. It may come in the form of a strengthened will, a lighter heart, a clearer head, the courage to do what we have to do, the steadiness to carry us through, the ability to face up to life.

As to material results—who knows what is good for us anyway? Remember the Greeks and their gods who got angry and gave men what they asked for, figuring it would serve them right?

Who knows when a prayer is answered?

There is an old folk tale out of Europe about a family of peasants. They were in their hut one stormy night, with the snow blustering outside and the wind shrieking, when two men from the village came by. The men looked in the window and saw the family of peasants kneeling in a circle by the fireplace.

Flinging open the door, the men asked, "What are you doing?"

"We are praying for bread," said the father of the family.

"Ho! Ho!" roared the men from the village. "You think you are going to get bread *that way!*"

After warming themselves the men departed. One said to the other, "Let's have some fun with those peasants. Let's get some loaves of bread and come back later when they've gone to sleep and drop the loaves down the chimney!"

This they did.

Next morning the men from the village stopped back at the peasants' hut to enjoy the fruit of their joke. Sure enough, the peasant family was radiant with smiles, and the father eagerly told how the bread they had prayed for had been given them. It had dropped right down the chimney in the middle of the night.

Then the men from the village blurted, "Go on, you stupid peasants! You think your prayers brought that bread! Why, we brought that bread ourselves. We climbed up on your roof and we dropped that bread down your chimney! Ho! Ho! Ho!"

The peasant father looked up at them with a luminous smile and said, "Well, we got it, didn't we?"

9

PEOPLE WANT TO BE GOOD

The business of sin

You get the creeps a lot down there. When you're bent over in that black void and the rock is cracking and groaning, you hope God won't lose track of you. . . ."

The speaker was young Charlie Semko, a mine worker. I knew what he meant by "down there" because I had just been *down there*—426 feet below the surface of the earth in the narrow black vein of Colver Number 1, a mine of the Ebensburg Coal Company, at Colver, Pennsylvania. Going down in the cage was like riding the express elevator in a skyscraper—in reverse. "Hellscraper," one of the men called it.

"You get the creeps," Charlie continued, "when you're 're-treating.' That means you've cut out the last of the coal in a certain area—a 'room' we call it—and you're backing up into the side headings and letting the roof cave down in front of you."

Here's what it's like:

You are in a little slit in the earth. The coal vein is only three feet, eight inches thick; you work stooping over. Yes, it's black down there, so black that if your lamp goes out you can't see your finger. Now you hear a creaking, cracking. You hear the roof "working," as they say, and you back up. The rock in the roof starts cracking up because you've cut out the last pillars of coal in the "room" and there's nothing left to hold the roof up. The weight of 426 feet of earth is on it. It groans and rumbles and crunches downward, straining.

You are on all fours. You feel that power. The floor heaves under you. You hear the props and timbers snap in that mined out slit of earth. They are big, heavy timbers, but they go tick, tick, tick, as though some great thumb were running over piano keys. Then the rumble, and the rock comes down. Dust puffs out and a rush of air comes at you.

"That," said Charlie, "is when you hope God's eye can penetrate 426 feet of earth and rock. You hope He won't overlook *our world*—way down there."

The world of twenty-six-year-old, redheaded Charlie Semko and his fellow miners appeared, almost literally, as different from the world of most Americans as night from day. But viewed more profoundly it was quite the same. I went down into the mine prompted by a reporter's hankering to see how the other half lives, or, in this particular quest of mine, to find out what the other half believes. I found that Charlie and his fellow miners, no less than the big-city sophisticates and the plain farm folk, were reaching out for God in a world which seemed to need God more than it had needed Him for ever so long.

Charlie spoke about the fear of cave-in. But when I got to know the men of the mines I found that the cave-in they really were worried about was more than a crush of rock from the roof of a vein. They were worried about our moral and ethical ceilings. What about the crumbling there?

There was Earl Tyson, whom I first met at the top of a coal-coated stairway in the tipple. He was operating the coal washer and was coated with coal himself. I hardly recognized him later when I went to his house in the mining village and met his family. At thirty-four, Tyson was the father of three boys and a baby girl. As he bounced the girl, Carolyn, on his knee, he said, "One thing I've got to do is teach these kids that there's a *right way* and a *wrong way* of living."

"How do you propose to do it?" I inquired.

"The only way I know—by example," Tyson replied. "That's the way I learned it."

He then talked of his father, Chauncey Tyson, who had been watchman at the mine and died of a heart attack a year before. Chauncey had been well known in Cambria County, and folks still talked of the crowd that turned out for his funeral. They remembered Chauncey as an upright man. But his son, Earl, particularly remembered him for something that happened a long time ago.

It was in the little town of South Fork, where the family lived at the time, and Chauncey was town constable. It was during Prohibition. Earl was just nine. "I remember it like yesterday," he said. "We were in the kitchen and this man came in and planked a thousand dollars on the kitchen table and he said, 'Here, Chauncey, you take this. It's clean money. It's not marked. Just forget all about that still.' I never saw my father get such a cold look in his eyes. I'll never forget his face. He said to the man, 'You take your money and get the hell out of my house!'

". . . I've carried that lesson with me ever since. Was there any better way to teach a kid?" Earl concluded.

As I went from house to house in the tiny mining town, set on a gently sloping hill like a cardboard town made out of cut-outs, I wondered why these people were so concerned with goodness. Toward evening I wandered over to the lamp house of the mine, atop the shaft. I looked into the faces of the men, some coming up in the cage, hanging their cap lamps on the big rack, heading for the showers; others going down, stopping to take with them their flame-safety lamps to detect gas underground. I rode down in the cage with William McHenry, who had spent twenty-one of his thirty-seven years in the black world of the mine. We strolled through the headings, under the propped up ceilings of rock. A whole world was up over us, pressing down upon us, squeezing out drops of water which glistened along the rock.

What kind of world? A world like Noah's before the deluge? Like Sodom and Gomorrah? Like Nero's Rome?

Or a world of yearning? Charlie Semko hoped God would not lose track of him *down there*. Earl Tyson wanted to teach his kids the *right way* of life. And William McHenry said, as we padded our way through the black vein, *"People want to be good."*

These mining folk opened my eyes to something which I had seen only dimly in my exploits so far. I got from them a salt-of-the-earth feeling, as though life were basic to them, stripped of its false faces and furbelows. Their concern over the state of the world went right to the heart of things: good versus evil. For high-flown philosophical concepts or the dialectics of the theologians they had little appreciation. Their concern flew like a rifle bullet toward the bull's-eye of the broad target: that tiny black dot labeled *how-to-live-here-and-now*.

From the depths of the Colver mine I carried my new curiosity to other settings. At the Cadillac plant in Detroit I sought to explore further this new avenue opened up by William McHenry, whose phrase was doubly underscored in my notebook: *"People want to be good."*

. . . It was night at the big auto factory. The die presses were stamping hoods out of sheet steel, and in the din, at the controls of one great press, I met a sandy-haired, gray-eyed, youth of twenty-four. He already had been stung by life: married at twenty-one, divorced at twenty-three. Now (an old man of twenty-four) all he wanted was to marry again, settle down with a girl who was, as he put it, "respectable, not a bar fly, not quarrelsome."

We talked a long time in the feelingful lull of after midnight, away from the din of the press room. The young man said, "This world is in about as bad a shape as it's ever been in. I think the world is getting worse—actually worse. There is so much more evil today than in years before. My explanation of it is one word —*greed.*"

"Do you feel there is any hope?" I asked.

"Not unless some miracle happens, like Jesus Christ coming back," he replied. "As things stand, there are too many atheists in this world, too many people who don't believe in God or Jesus Christ or anything."

Next day I strolled along the assembly line. The air was a potpourri of sound: the wirrump of the air wrenches, the high-pitched scream of a nut whirling tight against steel, the clank of the ball-peen hammers, the hiss of air hoses. Engines, then engines and chassis, then engines and chassis and bodies moving along, steadily, fifty-two an hour, moving like time itself. Busy hands reached out at them, a pull here, a turn there, a shot of the air gun. Cars going to market.

I talked with a woman on this amazing technological treadmill, a woman of fifty, a former high school teacher from Carson City, Michigan. She was a soft-voiced woman with silver-gray hair and warmth behind her hazel eyes.

"Our trouble is this," she said. "We aren't putting first things first. We've got to get back to the principles of Christianity. We're more interested in making money than in the principles of right living. Look at our corrupt officials! The mayor of one of our neighboring communities just got out of jail for black marketing during the war. That's the things we do red-handed. But we do a great deal more just by omission. Look at all the things we *don't do* that could make the world right if we did them!"

"People today are like kids in a toy shop," said another worker, Hugo Yatzek. "They don't know what they want. They always want what they haven't got." I found Yatzek in the paint line, spraying hoods and fenders with their second coat of lacquer. He had been on the paint line for twenty-five years. "Maybe things come too easy for some people," he went on. "I say—the only time you appreciate a dollar is when you've earned it."

A pretty eighteen-year-old, Vivian Tegels, was tightening manifold and tail-pipe bolts as the cars moved by. "I'm earning money to go to modeling school," she told me. "I want to be a Powers model." She wiped her hands on her overalls—"I think if you go after something long enough and hard enough you'll get it. Too many people nowadays want things dropped in their laps. They want everything on a silver platter but don't do anything about it. Believe me, if people in the United States had gone through what some of the rest of the world has gone through, we'd be more satisfied with what we've got."

Steel workers I met along the fire-breathing shores of the Monongahela felt much the same. I talked with them in Clairton, Homestead, McKeesport, and Duquesne. They felt we were going soft, unappreciative. We were too keen on the easy way. Our morals were shot. I sat in the union hall of Local 1557 of the United Steel Workers at Clairton, Pennsylvania, and talked with some of the men from the United States Steel Corporation's big Clairton works.

Joseph Urbanik, a millwright helper, threw up his hands. "The things that go on in South Park!" he said. "It's hard to explain to my boys, seven and a half and thirteen, what we see in the park. People don't care any more about right and wrong. Before, people used to raise families and take care of their kids. Now they get married, they have kids—then they split up and put the kids in a home."

"They don't teach kids right in school any more," declared Clenard Lewis, who was working on the big blast furnaces. "I went to a school play the other day and three fourths of the boys sat with their hats on."

Michael Runatz, a rolling-mill worker, added, "When I was a kid I was tickled to death to get an ice-cream cone. When we wore out a baseball we'd tape it up. We'd tape it again. Not today. Today the kids get too much. They're spoiled."

But Runatz didn't blame it all on the kids. Too many grown-ups, he felt, had no values of their own to pass on to children. He railed at all the hypocrites. "Why," he said, "one friend of mine asked me to join a religious society and then wanted me to steal stuff out of the plant!"

But why be ethical anyway? Why be moral? Why this yearning to be good which I found among our working people? The answer, I learned, was that most of them have a deeply ingrained moral sense. Some didn't know where it came from. But it was there. Some attributed it to religion, to the Bible, to the teachings of parents. Some attributed it simply to "what's inside you."

At one of the steel mills I met Robert Elmgren, a soaking-pit heater, age forty-eight, a bachelor. When he was just a boy of fourteen Elmgren went to work to help care for his family. His father had taken ill. Later he dreamed of being a doctor, but hard times of the early twenties shattered that. He stayed in the steel mill. He went to night school at Carnegie Tech for eleven years, working in the mill by day. He finally had to give up the night school to look after his mother and an aged aunt. For nineteen years he cared for his mother, until her death. Now he was thinking he might go back to night school and get his degree in metallurgy.

"You've made a lot of sacrifices," I observed.

"I don't know," he said. "My parents always did right by me. It seemed only proper for me to do right by them. I've always had the feeling that if I took care of my elders the good Lord would take care of me when the time came."

"Do you mean you expect some kind of reward?" I asked.

"No," he replied. "I've had the reward all along. I know that if I do justice, if I do right, I'll have a good feeling inside. That's reward aplenty."

It seemed a long way from factory, mine, and mill to Washington, D.C.—long in more than miles. But how could one seek out the moral inclination of a nation without putting an ear to its heart, its capital? It seemed so long a way because of the contrast between the yearning of the working people for goodness in the world and the fetid vapors of mink coat scandals and influence peddling and tax briberies which had risen from Washington in the recent past.

But even Washington I found like a man in a strait-jacket struggling to get free. The confused capital, aware of its ethical failures and moral vacuity, was struggling in its confusion to restore goodness somehow.

I cannot report that I found goodness fully re-enthroned. But I can report that even while corruption was getting the front-page headlines, a fight for good was quietly under way.

One leader of it was Senator J. William Fulbright of Arkansas. He was the author of the famous "Fulbright Resolution" to set up a Commission on Ethics in Government. He envisioned, the senator told me, a permanent kind of commission which would always be in the background, not meddling, but studying and probing the problems of ethics and evolving standards for the legislator and other members of the government to live by. Though he didn't get it, extensive hearings were held and Congress was at least exposed to a thorough airing of the problem. This may have had, in itself, an effect nearly as salubrious as the kind of commission Fulbright wanted.

Among those heard at the Washington hearings were the outstanding Protestant theologian Reinhold Niebuhr, the Catholic professor of political science Reverend Wilfrid Parsons, and the noted Jewish leader Rabbi Philip Bernstein.

Niebuhr told the senators: "We do not need a new moral code so much as the recognition that a very old code has become more and more imperative as modern society becomes more and more complex. The moral standards of the civilized nations contain many elements, some of which transcend politics. I think, for instance, the standard of love in the Christian faith . . . is in many respects beyond the standards of public business."

Father Parsons told them: "The holder of public office wields a power which is ultimately derived from God and which he holds and can hold over his fellow men only as a minister of the Creator. . . . The unfaithful official, therefore, in any of our three branches of government incurs a double infamy which much transcends the mere legal guilt involved. . . . Such an official has, by using a public office for private interests, his own or that of his intimates, betrayed something infinitely more precious than the laws of the land; namely, his Creator and his own people."

Rabbi Bernstein told them: "Too often religion has been silent in the face of crying public wrong. If religious leadership does not speak out against crime and corruption, how can we expect the average layman to become articulate? The ancient prophet said even to the king who had done wrong, 'Thou art the man.' Jesus did not hesitate to overturn the tables of those who were corrupting the temple courtyard. . . ."

The senators listened in earnest. For one of the few times in history they sat back, some quite humbly, and listened to simple men of God roll the drums of moral thunder. But more important—they faced the facts which few politicians ever like to face: that there is a higher law than the law on the statute books, that there is a measure of morality that goes beyond legality, that there is, in short, a God above politics.

Senator Fulbright flashed this rapier in a speech on the Senate floor:

"Much of the evil of the world is beyond the reach of the law. The law cannot prevent gossip. It cannot prevent men from bearing false witness against their neighbors. It cannot restrain men from avarice and gluttony. It cannot restrain a man from betraying his friends. In short, it cannot prevent much of the evil to which men are, unfortunately, too prone. . . . Underlying the law are the codes of ethics promulgated by the great religions and recognized by all civilized men as being essential to a humane and enlightened existence."

There were others besides Fulbright who were reaching into the realm of ethics. They knew Washington was inching downward into a bog. But, more than that, they were uncomfortably aware that corruption in the capital was but the outward symptom of ethical confusion in the hearts of the people. Like the miners and factory workers and mill hands, they saw the moral emptiness on every hand and yet they knew that in the profound depths of people there was a different yearning. They knew, just as William McHenry in the Colver mine knew, that *"people want to be good."*

Former Senator William Benton of Connecticut went so far as to draw up Ten Commandments for Congress. In introducing them, he said, "Modern Communist leaders reserve their bitterest scorn for what they call bourgeois morality. They know that the real chasm which separates us from them is not our stockpile of atom bombs or our industrial genius, but our dim ancestral reverence for a few great ideas—ideas which reach back more than three thousand years to the ancient prophet Amos: 'Let justice roll down as waters, and righteousness as a mighty stream.' "

If the mighty stream seemed a bit muddied, Senator Benton proposed his Ten Commandments as a way of restoring its pristine sparkle.

Here is his Decalogue for members of Congress:

I. In the same sense in which a judge debars himself from decisions in which he has a direct personal financial stake, so I shall debar myself from legislative decisions, or, if I take action or choose to vote, I shall fully disclose the nature of my interest.

II. I shall never use my office to exert extra-legal pressure over the decisions of executive or administrative agencies.

III. I shall treat witnesses who testify before committees on which I sit with courtesy and fairness, following self-imposed limitations which for centuries have been the hallmark of the judicial process.

IV. I shall not abuse my privilege of Congressional immunity; I shall not say things on the floors of Congress that I am not prepared to say outside, nor shall I betray the official confidence of the Congress, or of any committee thereof.

V. I shall not indulge in personal vilification of any kind, but I shall not hesitate to criticize public figures and public policies with determination and courage whenever facts of a public nature justify such criticism.

VI. I shall not vote on any issue without an attempt to consider the voiceless interest of the unorganized in our society.

VII. I shall strive constantly to interpret the interests of my constituents in the perspective of the total national interest.

VIII. I shall try to be loyal to the promises of my political party, and thus to strengthen party teamwork and party responsibility in the Congress.

IX. I shall not waste my own or my colleagues' time with irrelevant and inconsequential talk in committee or on the floor.

X. Whether as a member of the majority or the minority, I shall attempt in all my actions and words to educate and clarify, never to obscure or confuse.

Senator Benton's Ten Commandments were, perhaps, the conscience of Congress crying to be heard. I was aware of a resurgent conscience throughout the marble capital. Members of the House of Representatives were sick of being identified with charlatans, political hacks, and even downright crooks—two of whom had gone from the Halls of Congress to prison cells for bribery and kickbacks. In the executive offices of the government there was not only nausea, but anger, at the cheapness and dishonesty which had made Washington virtually a synonym for scandal on our front pages.

Senator Benton, eyes flashing like an old-time prophet, said to me, as I saw him off in the private elevator to the Senate floor, "We need two things—give 'em the hope for heaven and the fear of hell!" Unfortunately Benton lost the chance to deliver either of these in person, being defeated in the 1952 election—an election which was in many ways a popular revolt against shabby morals in Washington.

Why do people want to be good anyway? Why, I began to wonder, should there be so much concern over evil? Hasn't this business of sin been greatly overplayed, and wouldn't mankind be better off if, as the saying goes, he just relaxed and enjoyed it?

I went around asking questions. At a little country carnival outside Greenville, South Carolina, I asked a pitch man, "Do people really *want* to be good?"

"Yes, of course they do," he answered unequivocally.

"Then why aren't they good?" I pressed.

"Because they have so darned much fun being bad!" he replied with a flourish of his candy-striped cane.

In San Francisco I put the same questions to an earnest young high school teacher. He looked me squarely in the eye and said, "Don't you know that to live the life of a Christian today would be hell?"

"In what way?" I inquired.

"You'd be exploited to death, you couldn't earn a living because you'd refuse to exploit others, you'd lose all your friends because you'd refuse to tell lies, you'd be penniless and ragged and starving because you'd deny materialism and give away your goods, and on top of it all you'd probably be hailed before a congressional committee!"

The final word in cynicism came from a leaflet I was handed at a meeting of atheists in Illinois. It was drawn up as a burlesque advertisement for Asbestosin, described as a new and wondrous product which "fire-proofs the soul."

"What penicillin and the sulpha drugs are to certain diseases of the physical body, Asbestosin is to the diseases of the spiritual body," the advertisement set forth.

"Rubbed briskly on the chest, Asbestosin penetrates the entire body and renders the soul of even the most hardened sinner immune to Hell's hottest flames. . . . One application is sufficient for all eternity. Money back guaranteed, if not as advertised."

It was explained that the name Asbestosin was derived from two sources: from the word "asbestos" and from the phrase "as best to sin." And with a final flourish the ad declared, "It fireproofs what the Devil intends to burn—the soul—and, at the expected rate of sale, bids fair to do His Satanic Majesty out of the job of eternally roasting sinners, and may cause that bachelor gentleman to enter another profession."

. . . All right. Kid as we will, and be as cynical as we like, the fact still remains: people *do* want to be good. In my years studying crime and criminals I never met one wrongdoer, from petty shoplifter to first-degree murderer, who didn't in some pathetic, if confused, manner yearn to exorcise the evil (the psychological compulsion, if you will) which had driven him. Robert Irwin, the "mad sculptor" slayer of the 1930's, in a primitive and totally erroneous notion of what caused his weird behavior wanted—and actually attempted—to amputate his genitalia. Old Grandpa Fred Stroble, the Los Angeles child-murderer, pleaded to me in his cell in death row, "Oh, why can't they operate on me! Can't they cut the badness out of me!"

For years criminologists followed the case of Millard Wright, a habitual, or compulsive, burglar. In 1947, Wright, then a prisoner in Western Penitentiary, in Pennsylvania, volunteered to undergo an operation in the hope it would cure him of stealing. He was given a prefrontal lobotomy, one of the types of psychiatric surgery in which nerve tracks connecting the frontal lobe of the brain and the more primitive emotional brain centers are severed.

After the operation Wright emerged a model prisoner and he was released in 1949. His life seemed outwardly normal, even exemplary. But three years later, in 1952, Wright was dead—a suicide. It was discovered that his apartment in Butler, Pennsylvania, was crammed with the loot of twenty-eight burglaries, all committed after he was supposed to have been "reformed by science."

But the key to Wright's inner torment was revealed not in the "reformation" nor in its failure, but in the suicide note he left behind after slashing his wrists with a piece of glass:

"I am sentencing myself to death for my evil misdeeds."

What is it in us which impels us to judge ourselves?

If being bad, as the pitch man put it, is "so darned much fun," then why do we have any truck at all with being good?

At one of the steel mills in McKeesport, a grimy worker with the sweat of the furnace on his brow, shook his head as he related, "Five or six years ago I picked up two bolts in the plant. I was going to carry them off. I got to the gate. Something hit me. I turned around and put them back. I tried it again. Something hit me again. I don't know what it was. I just couldn't swipe those bolts."

As he walked away he added, "I guess I felt better afterwards for not takin' 'em."

What will we call it? Conscience? Super-ego? The eternal law? The God within us?

A Wac I met at Fort Belvoir, Virginia, remarked, "I can't explain it, but when I do something good I just feel good all over." Another American, Abraham Lincoln, who perhaps couldn't explain it either, had said, "When I do good I feel good, when I do bad I feel bad, and that's my religion."

In the hopes of finding some glimmer, at least, of where the impulse for good comes from, I turned to the professors. Dr. George Lechler, professor of history and anthropology at Wayne University, had been studying mankind from the earliest beginning. I asked him: Has mankind always striven—or been driven—toward the good? Or is this just some new wrinkle, some conditioned reflex, some excrescence of latter-day culture?

"At one time we did believe that mankind's conflict over good and evil was a fairly recent acquisition," Professor Lechler explained. "We believed that the pagan of ancient Greece and ancient Rome lived in a state of peace of mind until Christianity came along and gave him a sense of penitence and atonement.

"But now we have learned that this was not the case. Our anthropological discoveries have proven to us that even Neanderthal Man was plagued by guilt."

Professor Lechler told of the discovery of remains of the "Bear Cult" of Neanderthal Man in the snowy ranges of the Alps. This was a cult of early man which hunted and feasted on bears. But, as the skilled anthropologist reads the evidence of the fossilized remains, the hunters and feasters did not simply enjoy their fare without a qualm. There is evidence that they also offered up sacrificial meals. Apparently they wished to appease, or make amends to, or stay on the good side of some great power. They are known, too, to have placed the skulls of bears in stone boxes, perhaps a form of atonement or even a totem worship of that which they had killed.

"It seems that there was a great mental impact upon man when he began to kill—when he ceased to be a vegetable eater," Professor Lechler explained. "The cave paintings of early Homo sapiens show a great concern over the extinction of the species and an emphasis on fertility."

Could this, then, be the origin of a moral sense? Was the overwhelming urge toward self-preservation—the fear of being killed and its reciprocal guilt over killing—the bedrock of man's conscience?

I found a different explanation at the Carnegie Institute of Technology. Here I put to six professors, all experts in some branch of science, the central question, "Where do moral values come from?"

There was much hemming and hawing. Finally I received from the group two answers:

"We get our sense of right and wrong from teaching, mainly from what our parents teach us," one professor said.

"Each of us develops his own moral sense. It is a purely subjective thing," said another.

I raised a reporter's objection, "If we get it from our parents, where did *they* get it?" and "If we develop it ourselves, how come *good* always wins? Why don't some of us have a conscience which exhorts us to evil?"

No answers were forthcoming.

Flying back to New York, I read over the notes I had taken on this leg of my journey. I came upon a conversation I had had with Dr. Katherine M. Chamberlain in the physics department at Wayne. These words stood out boldly: "I never knew a student who didn't aspire to be better than he was," she had said. "I never knew a person who didn't want to be good."

To my question on the source of it all, she had replied, "Read the story of Adam and Eve in the Bible. The ultimate significance of it is that *man has a sense of right and wrong*. Man is born with a moral sense. It is innate."

I felt satisfied to accept that. It is *because it is.*

In the days of colonial New England, Jonathan Edwards stood dourly in the pulpit and warned his flock, "You cannot stand before an infuriated tiger. What will you do when God rushes upon you in His wrath?"

This was Edwards' implementation of the New England conscience. It was thoroughly consonant with the moral philosophy of the time: a rigorous belief in bitter punishment for sin. Being *good* was, as it were, the alternative to hell-fire and brimstone. Being *bad* was to invite the retributive tiger to rush upon you.

I found, in my reportorial rounds, occasional evidence that such a philosophy not only persists but is carried to fantastic extremes. In St. Paul, Minnesota, a frail little woman of forty-seven was horsewhipped into unconsciousness by her co-members of a religious cult because they felt she had been "disobedient to God." Revived in Ancker Hospital, she told the doctors that such whippings were routine in the cult. The purpose, she said, was "to drive the devil from my soul."

The woman, suffering bruises and welts all over her body, said her husband and two sons also were members. "About twenty of us formed the group because we were sick and tired of the junk they were feeding us in our regular churches," she related. The horsewhipping rite was regarded by the members as cleansing their souls of sin. They flogged one another as and when a cleansing was needed.

"I asked for one beating myself," the woman said. "My husband handled the whip."

One of her sons, a youth of twenty-four, was present at the flogging which left her unconscious. "How could you stand by and watch your mother beaten like that?" a local sheriff asked him.

He replied, "Which comes first—your mother or God? She needed the whipping to clean her soul of the devil."

In Los Angeles, I came across a case which a police lieutenant had put down as "Bible suicide." I wondered what possibly could be behind such a label. A salesman, forty-seven years old, living in Highland Park, had shot himself. He had done it, I learned, with a rifle he had rented from a sporting-goods store.

How did the Bible enter the picture?

When police found his body an open Bible lay beside it. The page was Romans, Chapter 3. Verse 23 had been outlined with bold strokes of a pencil: "For all have sinned, and come short of the glory of God."

This man had been his own tiger.

But, by and large, I found that the wish to be good in our world today was something more tinged with positive aspiration and the upward look than with the fear of tigers' fangs. The clergymen I met, of all faiths, were not preaching hell-fire and brimstone. One, for example, said, "It is not our task to make the sinner wretched, but rather to make him righteous."

Another declared, "I denounce guilt-ridden piety. I denounce imposed discipline and the unnatural suppressing of human nature." He told of a parishioner who, feeling he had committed sins, would lash his arm to the bedpost when he went to sleep at night. By having a horribly uncomfortable night's sleep he hoped to atone for his sins.

"Stupid, ridiculous," the clergyman said. "The center of discipline is through self-surrender to God, not through self-laceration. It is foolish to try to lop off this sin, and that sin, and the other sin; one must go to the center of all sin, the self, and offer it up in surrender."

When a conscience-stricken woman told this clergyman, "I am going to declare a full-scale war on myself!" he smiled at her and said, "Don't fight. Surrender. Once you give up to God, self-discipline comes automatically."

The tiger school of sin and retribution has probably been responsible for a good deal of the neuroses of our time. Not all of the guilt-ridden bare their backs for flogging or put bullets through their heads; far more simply rip themselves apart inside. They heap upon themselves the tortures of emotional masochism.

The Canadian psychiatrist, Dr. G. Brock Chisholm, first head of the World Health Organization of the United Nations, has stated: "We have been very slow . . . to recognize the unnecessary and artificially imposed inferiority, guilt and fear, commonly known as sin, under which we have almost all labored and which produces so much of the social maladjustment and unhappiness in the world. For many generations we have bowed our necks to the yoke of the conviction of sin. . . . The results, the inevitable results, are frustration, inferiority, neurosis, and inability to enjoy living, to reason clearly or to make a world fit to live in."

Religion, which has been eager in recent years to take up the challenge of mental illness, has slowly swung toward the acceptance of a more healthful and psychologically sound view of good and evil. But actually it is no new departure. Reverend Maurice A. Riseling, while chaplain at the Norristown State Hospital, in Pennsylvania, said to me, "It is a basic tenet of Christianity that human beings must be understood, not condemned. It was Jesus who was called the 'friend of sinners' and Jesus who said, 'He that is without sin, let him cast the first stone.' "

Riseling had little use for the fire-breathing preacher whose stock in trade is condemnation. "Such a clergyman," he said, "produces more guilt neurosis than is compatible either with good theology or good medicine. He has missed the meaning of religion."

The old idea of piling up guilt, heap upon heap, has given way to a new attitude toward the moral law: *understanding and acceptance*. By understanding the moral law we can see that it is no onrushing tiger. By accepting it (or "surrendering ourselves") we can live in harmony with it.

There has been in our generation an understandable rebellion against authoritarianism. We saw authoritarianism take root in the field of government and grow into the poison vines of fascism and nazism. We didn't want to see moral authoritarianism spread the same way. Moreover, we were the generation of the new light. We had learned more about human behavior in the scant decades since Freud than in a dozen centuries before him. Understandably, we were not going to cower beneath the whip hand of reactionary, authoritarian morality.

Now we have had our progressivism and our moral relativism, and we have learned a lot. It may be time for a synthesis: the acceptance of basic God-given morality together with a loving, aspirational approach toward it. Authoritarianism and the whip hand can well be thrown away. In its place we are ready for understanding and the open heart. We are ready to *help* people to live by the essential laws of God and nature.

Senator Ralph E. Flanders of Vermont, in the remarkable speech referred to in Chapter 8, set forth the nature of the moral law as follows:

"The moral law is unlike statute law, which can be broken. It is unlike statute law in that punishment is not inflicted after indictment, trial, and judgment. The punishment is an indissoluble part of the law itself. The unlawful act carries its own punishment with it.

"In these respects the moral law established by God for the ordering of the moral universe more nearly resembles the physical law for the ordering of the physical universe. If we decide to walk on the air and for that purpose step out of the tenth-story window, we are punished by a swift fall to the ground and sudden death therefrom. We are not punished after indictment, trial, and conviction. The punishment is part of the act. There are no indulgences or judicial pardons. Results are inescapable. The same is the case with the moral law."

In my talks with theologians I many times heard the line: "You don't break the laws of the universe. You only break yourself upon them."

One had a more concrete way of putting it: "He who spits into the wind spits in his own face."

It wasn't only the theologians and philosophers who took this view of morality. I sat down one March afternoon with a tough old soldier, as practical and down-to-earth a man as you could meet—General Walter Krueger, commander of the Sixth Army in the Pacific during World War II.

"Wrongdoing has its own punishment. You can't go against the laws of the universe," he said as we talked of war and peace. "If a nation does wrong, it will pay. Just look at the world around you. And if that isn't enough, look at the pages of history. The decay and fall of old civilizations prove the point irrefutably. Chaldea, Babylonia—where once they flowered there is nothing today but a sandhill and a silence."

The old soldier added, "It is the same with a man. If he does wrong, he will pay. If a man turns to wrongdoing, no one need punish him. The law of the universe punishes him."

Many of us have a built-in awareness that this is so. Isn't it common experience to desist from doing something which we know is wrong because we'll "feel awful about it later"? I remember a friend in business who refused to engage in a shady deal, though it would have brought him enormous advantage. "I don't want to burn my own house down," he said.

No wonder the physicians of the body and the physicians of the mind and the physicians of the soul, though they squabble over terms and formulations, agree on the very first principle. The surgeon says, "The right thing morally is the healthy thing."

The psychiatrist says, "The well-adjusted man is also the moral man." The clergyman says, "The moral man is the happy man."

Hence the new emphasis, which I found on every hand: People want to be good. Let's help them be good. Let's help them say "yes" to the moral law of God.

Dr. Andras Angyal, Boston psychiatrist, drew the line quite clearly at a professional meeting I attended. "The non-punitive attitude of the psychotherapist is not based upon moral indifference," he said. "He sees the problem of immorality in an even more serious light. He sees the destructiveness of it to the individual himself. But, as with religious 'forgiveness,' he sees the patient as outwardly a sinner but inwardly a child of God."

Therefore, he tries to help him.

To help him do what? In one terminology, to make an "adjustment"; in another terminology, to accept the law of God. In either case he helps him; he does not browbeat or oppress him. This actually is the more difficult way, though for free man it is the only way. Professor Harry C. Munro, of Texas Christian University, once wrote, "A code of regulations clearly written down in terms of 'Thou shalt' and 'Thou shalt not' is far easier to follow than God's 'law written in the heart.' "

But once God's law is accepted, moral living is inevitable. This is the kernel of the Christian idea of "surrendering to God," of letting God "work through you." When man becomes a channel for the expression of God he can do no wrong.

That's why St. Augustine said, "Love God and do as you please."

10

THE TYRANNY OF THINGS

"Materio-sclerosis," a new disease

When I was a boy I heard a preacher tell of a woman whose entire life was geared to acquiring *things*. There was always something she wanted—a new coat, a new car, diamond earrings, new hats, new dresses, new silverware, new bedroom set, new wrist watch, silver bangles, diamond bracelet, pearls, furs and baubles without end. Her husband was a money-making businessman and managed to gratify these desires almost as fast as they beset her. Being a man of foresight he also bought burial plots for himself and his wife against the eventual day of their passing. He even selected tombstones and ordered the inscriptions.

"On my wife's just put, 'She Died of Things,' " he told the engraver.

"And on yours?" the engraver said.

"Put, 'He Died Providing Them,' " the man replied.

I was not long upon the search for God when the hurdle of materialism loomed across the trail. I expected it. The literature and philosophy of the ages is full of the poignant and perplexing lament of man's enslavement by matter. In school days we heard it in Wordsworth's, "The world is too much with us . . . Getting and spending, we lay waste our powers." Later we came upon it in T. S. Eliot, who wrote of a culture "Whose only monument is the asphalt road, And a thousand lost golf balls." And almost any Sunday we can hear it echoing from thousands of pulpits across the land.

In the era of the cold war one often heard the phrase "communist materialism," and orators referred to Russian culture as "the great materialism" which had to be checked lest spiritual values were totally suffocated. Other orators, recognizing that in the sheer production of "things" nothing holds a candle to capitalism, warned that "the two great materialisms" would knock each other out unless spiritual forces came to the rescue.

The atomic age seemed to bring to the world a fey warning. It conjured up Thoreau wrapping on the knuckles of civilization for everlastingly seeking "improved means to unimproved ends." Inadvertently, a San Francisco newspaper at the turn of the century had sounded the same philosophic note when the first electric trolley line was opened, providing service to a suburban cemetery. "By Electricity to the Crypt" the newspaper headline read.

By electricity, by atomic energy, by advertising, by "getting and spending"—are we simply heading for the same old "unimproved ends"? Is that what some of the people I met meant when they called life a "rat race"?

Is that what the sociologists meant when they said our cultural goal is "more"? More what? More everything—more products, more possessions, more clothes, more cars, more super-duper, electro-magic, self-defrosting, miracle-tuning, rocket-zooming, wonder-rinsing, marvel-making gadgets and contraptions to take the place, for a small down payment, of last year's models of the very same things.

"The goal of 'more' is a strange one. It is *impossible by definition,"* one sociologist remarked. "If what you really want is 'more,' you obviously never can achieve it." The picture which came into my mind was one I had seen in a comic strip: a poor, harried puppy dog chasing a sausage that was dangling from a stick tied to his collar.

At a Cana Conference of the Summer School of Catholic Action, in Detroit, Reverend Edward Dowling told young couples that materialism in our day even was casting a blight upon the marriage ceremony. Weddings, instead of being joyous affairs full of "psychic and spiritual luxury," were becoming grim, he said. Why? Because materialism has taken over—"There is the spending for engagement rings, honeymoons, and other material things, whose cost frightens the husband and whose shabbiness disappoints the bride," he told them.

Another Catholic priest, Reverend Timothy J. Flynn, said at St. Patrick's Cathedral, in New York: "We are so caught up in the whirlpool of earning a livelihood, of acquiring the accessories for comfortable living, and of providing against every doleful physical calamity that we have become what we profess we are not—practicing materialists."

Well, what are we supposed to be—ascetics? Are we supposed to go around as did Mahatma Gandhi in a sheet and safety pin, and leave behind us as our sole concession to the materialism of the world a pair of sandals, eyeglasses, and a book?

No, Father Flynn did not ask a renunciation of all things material. Nor does his church. He clearly stated that day at St. Patrick's that it was not a teaching of Jesus, nor has it ever been a tenet of the Catholic Church, that all things material are to be despised. On the contrary, he said—"The Church well realizes that a virtuous life is scarcely possible without an adequate share of this world's goods."

It is a matter of emphasis. Things and gadgets may be a *means* of living, but they are not an *end* of living. That seemed to be the heart of it.

When I talked with Reverend Willis H. Porter, of the First Baptist Church of Nashua, New Hampshire, he pointed to the line from the Lord's Prayer "Give us this day our daily bread" as symbolic of the rightful place of material values in this world. Daily bread, necessities, material things which are stepping stones to the life of creativity and spiritual growth, are certainly not to be spurned. But when you come to a surfeit of material things, a bloatedness with objects, that's quite another matter.

Reverend Porter referred again to Jesus, this time not on "our daily bread" but on the "deceitfulness of riches." Explaining the phrase, he said, "Riches deceive us in two ways: First, they fail to give what they promise. Second, they deprive and crowd out any higher values we might already have."

I asked him, "Do you mean we shouldn't strive for success in the world?"

"Not at all," he replied. "I mean we must re-think our values. We must strive for *real* success, not the materialistic illusion of it."

Not long after I talked with Reverend Porter a famous and much-admired literary figure died in New England Baptist Hospital in Boston. He was Harold Wallace Ross, editor and founder of the *New Yorker* magazine. At the funeral service in New York, Dr. Sidney Lovett, chaplain of Yale University, said of Ross:

"[He] hated all tyrannies, not least the insidious tyranny of things, and he made us feel that the world of matter or even of atoms is somehow too narrow for any one of us."

That was the feeling which a good many of the people I talked with and listened to were trying to get across.

Yet there was something platitudinous and churchy about what I had learned of materialism so far. Reverend Porter's homiletics on the "deceitfulness of riches" sounded all right in words, but I was after something more than words. I suppose it was the old journalistic hankering for something to sink your teeth into.

I found it at the Mayo Clinic in Rochester, Minnesota. The handsome diagnosis tower dominates the town like a beacon, and for me, after I had been there a few days, it rapidly became a symbol of the finish line of the great American rat race. It became the steel and masonry version of Justice Oliver Wendell Holmes' famous line, "A man begins a pursuit as a means of keeping alive—he ends by following it at the cost of his life."

What prompted me to look in on the Mayo Clinic was a statement of one of its staff members, Dr. Harold C. Habein. He declared, referring to modern medicine's much-vaunted increase in life expectancy, "The reduction in the death rate has taken place almost exclusively among persons less than fifty years old. There has been practically no saving of life among persons past this age.

"Moreover, among those persons who earn their living with their minds rather than their bodies, hypertension, arteriosclerosis, and coronary thrombosis are not only a *more frequent cause of death* than formerly, but they are causing disabilities in a *younger age group* than ever before."

By way of illustration, Dr. Habein told of the head of a large corporation, who remarked, "When I hire an executive I pay him $100,000 a year on the theory that he'll kill himself working in ten years."

Trains, planes, and big black limousines have over the years carried a constant flow of high-pressure executives to the Mayo Clinic to be patched up. They come with their wounds from the materialistic wars. Some corporations have kept standing reservations, year in and year out, so that their battle-scarred executives could rotate through the clinic on a systematic basis.

In Chicago, before I entrained for Rochester, I saw a special railroad car fitted out for the run with every convenience for the hard-driving businessman who had driven himself onto stretchers. I was reminded of the Plaza de Toros in Madrid, where I had seen the weary old horses of the picadors gored and ripped repeatedly, only to be dragged from the ring and patched up so they could return to face some more bulls.

Patching up hard-driving businessmen who were trying to succeed themselves to death was, of course, just a part of the work of the renowned clinic. But it was the part I was interested in. It seemed to me the concrete answer to the rat race of materialism.

Here, for example, was a score sheet: the medical record of a group of 142 executives of one of America's largest corporations who had gone through Mayo's on the regular checkup-and-repair plan. Fifty-three had cardiovascular diseases, fifteen had serious heart conditions, eight had ulcers, thirty-five had digestive diseases, fifty-two had nervous and mental disorders, twenty-three were psychoneurotic, twenty-two had eye diseases, ten had genitourinary diseases, twenty had skin diseases, and twenty-eight had diseases of the bones and organs of movement. Several spilled over into two or three categories. Only twelve—out of 142—bore no detectable wounds.

Certainly the explanation of much of this carnage was in Dr. Habein's statement: "The average executive . . . is frequently nervously and physically fatigued and emotionally tense, and his working hours are not governed by union rules, but by an inward drive which we call 'ambition' and by intense competition. . . . Even in recreation the executive frequently retains his competitive instincts. He must be beating something or somebody. . . ."

Why?

I checked the case histories of a few of these dynamos who had burned out their fuses.

One came to the Mayo Clinic in a blue funk. He lamented to the doctors, "I've gone to pieces. I can't work any more. I can't even write a letter." The man was completely gray. He was only forty-six, but he looked at least sixty-six.

"Tell me about yourself," one doctor asked him.

The patient, with what remnant of pride he had, boasted that he had been a "terrific worker," had "tremendous capacity." As head of a chain of retail stores, he had worked day and night during peak seasons. "Sometimes I didn't have my clothes off for three days," he said.

The man was intelligent. He knew all about the business world. He could have told you what was wrong with any store operation, with any sales campaign, or—if you asked him—with the United States Government or the world. About the only thing he didn't understand was himself. He had no idea what his goal in life was, except possibly a narrow six-foot excavation.

Another hero of the melee of materialism was told, as he took the train back to Chicago after being patched up, "You'll have to take it easier from now on." This man already was the head of four corporations. Shortly after his return a fifth corporation was offered to him. His doctor, hearing the news, asked, "Well, did you take it?" Red-faced, the big executive admitted, "I'm afraid I did."

One patient, a department manager for a large firm, was even more assiduous in his pursuit of a cemetery plot. When told he would die in three years if he kept on being a department manager, while he might live another twenty if he would step down and be a clerk, he replied, "No, Doctor, I wouldn't want to live twenty years under those circumstances."

There's materialistic culture for you—men who must succeed if it kills them. Of course they collect some trophies along the way. Perhaps a big house on Moneybags Street . . . some square-cut diamonds to hang on Mrs. Dynamo . . . a posh country club . . . a town automobile . . . a country automobile . . . a town-and-country automobile.

But actually, such men are the prisoners of their trophies. I had a talk with Dr. Howard P. Rome, of the clinic's psychiatric section. He spoke of these men as "rigid," "unadaptable." "They live," he said, "under a kind of personal bureaucracy." They are police states unto themselves. They make themselves toe the line, goose-step more severely than any tyrant could. They are, in short, their own worst enemies.

The Mayo Clinic has no monopoly on them. Every doctor knows the type. Hospitals all over the country recognize them at the admitting office: men who get *less* out of life because they incessantly seek *more*.

Johns Hopkins Hospital in Baltimore, for example, had a patient who came in worked to a frazzle, a physical and emotional wreck, with just about enough energy left to tell the doctors, "I swore I'd live to make $50,000 a year—and by crackie I did it!"

The man displayed a dozen medals he had won from his corporation for breaking production records. But there was one big drawback to winning medals, he confessed. Each year the medal he won would throw him into a terrible state of anxiety—he'd lie awake worrying lest he fail to win another medal next year. He developed a compulsive work habit which spiraled like drug addiction until he was grinding away ninety hours a week.

"When we got him into the hospital, we had to confine him to his room for ten days—almost forcibly—to break the compulsive cycle," said one of the Johns Hopkins staff.

There was the medal winner. At fifty-one, he was racked by aches and pains. He couldn't work any more. At an age when many men begin to reach their true heights of productivity and creativity, powered by true motives, aiming toward true goals—this man was ready to be junked.

All he had left was his battle cry—"I swore I'd live to make $50,000 a year—and by crackie I did it!"

When I repeated the story to a philosophic delicatessen man I know on Second Avenue, New York, he remarked, "What would a fellow like that want to be—the richest man in the cemetery?"

Perhaps that's it—a delicatessen man's version of the Freudian theory of the death instinct, the race to the grave.

The further I explored the Stygian caverns of materialism, the more a wise and ancient dictum impressed itself upon me: man should concentrate less on *making a living* and more on *making a life*.

I was glad to find some people who had succeeded in doing so.

Let me tell you about Louis Lurie, one of the most successful businessmen in San Francisco. Financier and real-estate operator, he had piled up a most agreeable living—and he also had piled up a most agreeable life.

I met Lurie at one of his famous "lunches at Jack's." These were a San Francisco institution. Every day at noon Lurie would meet a group of his cronies—a banker, a judge, a merchant, perhaps a visiting actor from New York, a lawyer, a few vice-presidents—and together they would eat at Lurie's big, specially reserved round table at Jack's restaurant. They never regarded it as a businessman's lunch. It was an occasion, an event. Lurie and his pals would chat and dawdle. They'd talk about people and places. They'd try a new salad dressing of tarragon vinegar (Lurie always would do the mixing himself). They'd enthuse over a new kind of omelet, or a schnitzel sauce.

"Up to ten years ago I used to get the gang out as fast as possible—now I keep them here as *long as possible,*" Lurie said to me.

"From the time I was twelve years old up to the time I was fifty (in 1939), I worked from twelve to sixteen hours a day, seven days a week," he related.

"Then came the old coronary thrombosis.

"After I had been in bed flat on my back for about a month, the doctor, following his usual daily examination, said, 'Well, Louis, you're fine this morning. God certainly was good to you.'

"I yelled out, 'What do you mean, Doc—*good to me!* I had a heart attack, didn't I?'

"And he said, 'Yes, that's correct. But now you can live as long as you want to live. All you have to do is change your mode of living. . . .' "

So Lurie changed his mode, his pace, and his goals of living. More than a decade had passed when I met him at Jack's. "I've had more fun than in all the previous fifty years combined," he said. "I've really come of age."

As I left him I wondered if perhaps that's what we all need to do in a culture which has turned into a rat race. Perhaps we need to *grow up*. There is much that is pathetically childish about our rush to keep up with the Joneses, to barricade ourselves with possessions, to race one another to the grave.

I could see that it is not *arteriosclerosis* many men die of.

It is *materio-sclerosis.*

Still, the trek to Mayo's and even the talk with Lurie had left me up in the air. After all, Lurie already had made his pile and it was all very well to talk about changing one's mode of living *then,* and adopting new goals. And as to the human dynamos who burned themselves out—weren't they the very epitome of the American age? They were Horatio Algers come to glory, with a slight mishap at the end of the glory road. They were the American virtues incarnate: work hard, keep plugging, do it now, time is money, business is business, nose to the grindstone. Where could I go from here? Certainly I could not subscribe to laziness, sloth, indifference, and parasitism.

From my perch on the horns of the dilemma I riffled through my notes once more and my eye lighted upon the line the man in Nashua, New Hampshire—Reverend Porter—had said to me: "We must strive for *real* success, not the materialistic illusion of it."

Real success. With its clear implication that success, after all, is but a matter of definition, this line took me down from the horns and turned my feet in a new direction.

I would search for a definition of *real* success.

In a speech at the Washington Conference on Children in 1950, Reverend George A. Buttrick of the Madison Avenue Presbyterian Church, in New York, had defined success in our modern world as "a fairly nasty mixture of cash and gadgets."

Kahlil Gibran, the poet, had asked the question, "What is glory?" and answered it, "It is to drink cod-liver oil mixed with carbolic acid and not to vomit."

It was easy to collect the negative definitions, to delineate what *real* success *was not,* but quite another matter to set forth just what it *was.* I found myself up to my ears in platitudes—"Common things, uncommonly well done, pave the way to success," "Success comes in cans, failures in can'ts," "Success is a matter of buying experience and selling it at a profit," "Success doesn't come from lying awake nights, but from keeping awake in the daytime."

All these platitudes begged the question. They were hortatory short cuts to success, but they didn't say what it was when you got there.

Finally I found what to me was a good answer. It was no pat platitude or easy epigram. I found it at the University of Chicago, in the psychological laboratory of Dr. Mandel Sherman, professor of educational psychology.

Professor Sherman had taken "success" into the laboratory and had been disassembling, examining, and assaying it for two years. He had begun with studies of frustration. He wanted to learn something more about what caused this reaction in human beings and how they could deal with it.

Frustration was measured by such devices as the electroencephalograph, popularly called the "brain-wave machine," and the photopolygraph, which records changes in blood pressure, heart rate, sweating, and hand tremors. It was discovered that *success* was the greatest conflict factor. Lack of success caused the maximum frustration, the greatest feeling of defeat.

One can demonstrate the principle involved here quite simply. Just ask someone "What is the fourth dimension?" and you get no frustration reaction at all. He doesn't think he ought to know the answer and consequently doesn't consider himself a failure. But ask him "What is the capital of Illinois?" and if he cannot answer, he shows considerable frustration. He feels he ought to know and he considers himself a failure because he doesn't.

On the other hand, the kick which radio and television fans get out of quiz shows, Professor Sherman pointed out, stems from the superiority—or success—they can demonstrate by answering the questions. They race to give the answers before the participants do. It is not because the producers are naïve, but rather because they are well up on their psychology, that these quizzes often are so blatantly simple. They give the fans success in huge portions. How happy and superior they make the audience feel!

"The trouble with *success* as we know it is that we have entwined it with *superiority*," Professor Sherman remarked. "To be successful, a man must be superior to others in riches, in power, in social position. This automatically restricts success to a few. It means that the majority of people—simply because they do not demonstrate superiority—must look upon themselves as mediocrities, or failures. Inability to accept *failure,* in this sense, causes about half of our acute cases of unhappiness—our personality breakdowns."

The American penchant for entwining superiority with success is caricatured in the number of "champions" we produce. We have at one time or another acclaimed champion beer drinkers, oyster eaters, flag-pole sitters, hog callers, and marathon dancers. Almost anything at all, no matter how ridiculous, will make you a champion—a *success*—so long as you are superior.

In place of this dismal view of success, Professor Sherman offered a new definition stemming from his work in the laboratory. It was a definition based upon sound psychological values. It was a scientist's view of *real* success.

The definition rests upon three pillars:

1. You must be inwardly stimulated, from your own love of doing and creating, to achieve the maximum of which you are capable in your chosen field.

2. You must not be upset emotionally by the competition of others. Your success *as a person* has no relation to the success or failure of anyone else.

3. Your interest in what you are doing must stem, in equal measure, from the value of your work to society and its personal value to you.

In the light of this definition, success is not restricted to the few who demonstrate superiority. It is available to one and all, like the free air. Success becomes a personal thing, like a man's inner contentment or the love he can give to his family. The millionaire steel magnate may be outshone by his lowliest puddler.

The man at the top of the competitive mountain is not necessarily a success. Superior he most definitely is, but he may not be successful—not always. Take him apart psychologically and often you find a hard-driving automaton, working out of inner compulsion rather than joy, constantly dreading that he may lose what he has amassed, unable to extract an ounce of happiness from his piles of wealth.

By contrast, let's look at the man who has achieved real success:

Mr. A is a man of executive ability, a "natural-born leader." He has realized this capability by becoming the president of a manufacturing company, which is his chief interest outside his family. Friends hear him remark, "My work is really play. I love it." He tries to produce as much as he can at his plant, to sell it at a fair price, to treat his workers well. When his general manager frets about the competition, he says, "We don't want the entire pie, George. We just want one slice of it."

Mr. B is another type of success. Intellect is his strong point. He has made the most of it by becoming a college instructor. His work gives him continuing pleasure and his $6,000-a-year income makes him, in his own terms, a rich man. His little house and the garden in which he putters are full of contentment for him. His library is full of books. He loves his family, loves people in general, loves life.

Mr. C is also a success. He is a sewer digger. Many sewer diggers consider themselves failures, but not Mr. C. He has a flock of friends, a good sense of humor, a wife who values the warm sparkle in his eyes more than large figures on a pay check. No giant intellect, Mr. C is doing the best he can do. Far from being grieved at his status, he takes pride in being a darned good sewer digger. He knows that sewer digging is a vital part of public health. Instead of considering himself a failure he takes pride that his digging may prevent an epidemic, may save a hundred lives.

I couldn't help comparing these *successful men* to the human dynamos I had encountered at Mayo's.

As I left the University of Chicago I felt that in Professor Sherman's laboratory had been found a miracle drug for *materiosclerosis.*

But the really striking thing was that here again, as in so many other aspects of the search for God, the oldest truths of religion and the newest insights of science walked hand in hand. I had started out with religion's adjurations on materialism and ended up with psychology's latest findings, and I had found them perfectly in step. I found that the "deceitfulness of riches" had just as much validity in Professor Sherman's laboratory in Chicago as in Reverend Porter's church in Nashua, New Hampshire.

Scientist and clergyman both seemed to be telling us to fight free from *the tyranny of things.* Both wanted us to take hold of the verities of living which are not material and cannot be bought: the giving of one's self in productive and creative work, the growth of the personality, love for all of humanity, and attunement to God.

As a chaplain back from service in the South Pacific said to his people—"We put our faith in *things.* And then war showed us that you could bomb, burn, and sink *things*—and what were we left with? Practically no faith at all. Today, some people would have us reclaim ourselves with *things*—the same old rat race. Oh, no. The only faith that is worth having is pegged to that which is indestructible. You can't bomb love and compassion. You can't sink it, or burn it."

We talk of security. How secure can man be with only material props holding him up? Reverend John Arthur Visser, of Detroit, remarked to me, "I know a millionaire who is killing himself by economic security." Henry V. Loeppert, Chicago industrialist and leading Methodist layman, declared, "It's like a fire in a hotel. We all rush for the exits. We grasp for the illusory security of *things* instead of the real security of the spirit."

What do we need?

"A leap of faith," said Reverend Claton S. Rice, of Seattle, Washington, president of the State Council of Churches. "The necessity to choose between two philosophies of life is forced upon us. One—materialism—leaves man with no hope except temporary ease of living, which may at any moment be taken from him. The other—faith—gives man absolute values despite uncertainty. His security, rather than being tied to temporary, ephemeral *things,* is anchored to belief in an ultimate favorable outcome for man."

Perhaps someday the *"leap" of faith* will no longer be necessary. Perhaps science will have carried us so far that we won't have to "leap" into dark and unknown territory; it will all be clearly illuminated for us, with perhaps a Bailey bridge to take us across.

Science, after all, is working wonders these days. There is an observatory near Johannesburg, South Africa, where the most remarkable photographs of the heavenly star systems have been taken, making them seem almost like next-door neighbors. But recently, one of the scientists connected with the observatory told me, the photos haven't been so good. It seems that dust from the nearby gold mines has been clouding up the view.

Same old trouble . . . gold dust getting in man's eyes again.

11

THE RELIGION OF "BUFFALO JOE"

Is nature God?

"Where will I find the buffaloes?" I called to some boys at the roadside.

"Straight ahead, one mile," one of them called back.

No, this was not the Bronx Zoo or a government reservation in Wyoming. It was old New England countryside in Connecticut some twenty miles east of New Haven. I was heading north on Route 81 after turning off the Boston Post Road at Clinton.

A couple of minutes later I spotted off in the distance on my left a huge, shaggy-maned creature contentedly cropping clover in a pasture and easily recognizable as that great American symbol which has all but vanished from our western plains as well as from our five-cent pieces. As I turned off the road and drove in toward the fenced-in pasture I could see five more buffaloes, looking quite fierce with their enormous shoulders and woolly faces. Grazing quite unconcernedly among them were a herd of slim and seraph-like deer.

The man I went up into Connecticut to see was Joseph Rollar, the only man I had ever heard of who raised buffaloes for a hobby. I found him bent over the engine of a tractor. When I apologized for being a bit late in finding the place, he rubbed his greasy hands in some dirt, clapped them together, and said, "All right. I'm not going anywhere."

We sat down on some field stone by the pasture fence.

"Com'ere Jimmy," Rollar called.

I was looking around to see whom he was calling when a crow came strutting up and perched on Rollar's knee. He patted the coal-black bird affectionately as it opened its yellow beak to him like a baby waiting to be fed. Rollar broke apart a piece of a hornets' nest which he had been saving for Jimmy and the crow began systematically to pluck the larvae out of the unbelievably intricate, honeycomb-like pattern of cells. Jimmy was enjoying himself thoroughly, plucking out each incipient hornet like a man working his fork around a plate of oysters.

"Just look at that work," Rollar said, pointing to the network of hexagonal combs in the nest. "See how regular they are. No architect could make them any better."

He turned to the crow. "Here, Jimmy, smoke a cigar."

Jimmy took Rollar's cigar in his mouth and strutted back and forth with it. "Try and get it from him," Rollar said to me. I tried but Jimmy held it fast in his long beak. Then Rollar called to him in a firm tone and Jimmy walked up with that kind of cakewalk that a crow has and surrendered the cigar back to his master.

"They say 'dumb animals,' " Rollar remarked with a bit of a rasp in his voice. "The more I'm around nature the more I see that the only dumb animals are human beings."

He looked across to the pasture where the buffaloes, the deer, a cow, and a horse were grazing and lolling. "They all get along fine," he said, "but look at the nations of the world today. Then ask yourself which animals are dumb."

Rollar's English setter, Sport, came moseying up, jealous of the attention Jimmy was getting.

"Watch this," Rollar said. He put Jimmy on Sport's back. The dog, begrudging the bird this limelight, lowered his hind legs, making a hill of his back so that Jimmy slid off. Finally, at his master's behest, Sport agreed to stand still and Jimmy preened happily on the dog's back. Everything was fine until Rollar patted Sport on the head and said, "Oh, what a nice dog." Now it was Jimmy's turn to be jealous. You should have seen him peck at Sport's ears! What would you call it—sibling rivalry?

Personally I always thought a crow was a mean bird. I've seen them around our own cornfield at home and couldn't imagine making a pet of one. In fact, I've even talked about getting rid of them, and a friend of mine from down south told me how he had killed a crow and hung it upside down in his cornfield as a warning to other crows (like an outlaw strung up on the edge of town).

And here was Jimmy. He was such an affectionate little fellow, strutting around with Rollar's cigar in his mouth or perching on Rollar's shoulder like a mariner's parrot. Sometimes, when Rollar dozed in his rocking chair in the evening, Jimmy would mistake his shoulder for a roost and go to sleep there himself—only to caw out his complaints irritably when Rollar got up to go to bed.

Once Rollar was up the road a few miles making hay when he looked around and saw Jimmy right there in the field beside him following every move. The crow had hitchhiked on his master's truck. It's nothing at all for him to ride into Clinton on Rollar's shoulder, but once in town Jimmy is always left in the car so he won't upset the villagers. Not that he'd hurt anybody. But he can be mischievous. Once he strutted up to Rollar's plate at dinner and started picking the noodles out of his noodle soup. And once when Rollar was working on his tractor he removed an oil plug and set it to one side—only to see the omnivorous Jimmy sneak up and swallow it.

A pair of squirrels in a chicken-wire house with a tree trunk inside it were giving us the eye as we talked. Not wanting any more sibling rivalry, Rollar walked over to them, went into the house with them, and sat on a box feeding them peanuts. "I got these little fellows in the woods when they were babies," he said. "I fed them with an eye dropper at first."

I wondered how they liked captivity. I couldn't imagine the squirrels that bound wildly over our hickory and apple trees being contented in a chicken-wire house.

"Oh, they go out when they want to. Two of them are out now," Rollar explained. He had four squirrels altogether, and they usually took turns going out to romp in the woods, two one day and two the next. Later I saw one of them come back in the evening. He came wearily home to the chicken-wire house like a commuter after a busy day and Rollar greeted him with his pick-me-up, a nice roasted peanut already shelled.

"Nature's all right if you give it a chance," Rollar mused as he walked toward the pasture to feed the deer. "People talk about 'mean' animals—I never saw a mean animal that didn't have a reason to be mean. People say a horse is vicious. N-o-o-o. That horse was mishandled." He asked rhetorically, "Right?" and then confirmed it himself with a cock of the head and a low, drawn-out "C-e-r-tainly."

"Nature's all right—it's only man that throws things out of balance," he observed, entering the pasture with a pailful of corn. He spread out the corn in handfuls, calling, "Come on, Dee Dee, come on, Dee Dee," and the deer came loping from the distance, bounding across the stream bed, moving with incredible ease and flow as though they were on ball bearings. They came right up to Rollar and ate at his feet.

He came back through the pasture fence, leaving them to their dinner—the tender and lovable little fawns, the gentle does, and the protective bucks with their long branching antlers. Deer are supposed to be timid, easily frightened. They run for dear life at the sound of a man's approach.

They didn't run from Rollar; they ran *to* him.

"Yep, it's only man that throws things out of balance," Rollar repeated as he came from the pasture. "Why I never spray my garden. N-o-o-o. People go drenching their gardens with sprays and kill millions of insects. Why do that? I just let the birds build their nests around my garden. They take care of it. S-u-r-e."

We walked over near the barn and sat down in some old wooden chairs that were scattered casually amid the grass and field stone.

"Nothing that is natural is sinful," Rollar remarked. . . .

Joseph Rollar once made a fortune in New York City and retired on it and lived a life of glittering leisure for five years, running around in a Pierce Arrow car—and then he gave it all up and came out to Clinton, Connecticut.

He was a builder in Jackson Heights during the big boom of the late twenties, and he retired with his pile, just getting under the wire before the big depression. He was only thirty-nine years old but had piled up, as he put it, "enough to make me feel fixed for the rest of my life."

But the life of glittering leisure, the money, and the Pierce Arrow left a big emptiness and as Rollar recalls the five years of retirement, from 1930 to 1935, he says, "They were the only years of my life I wasn't happy. Yes, I had that Pierce Arrow car and I just loafed around. But there's many a poor man who has nothing but money. S-u-r-e . . . C-e-r-tainly. Rest is rust. As long as a train is running every day the tracks are shiny."

So Rollar bought sixty acres and an old farmhouse and returned to nature with his wife Rose, his daughter, also named Rose, and his son George. George was only six at the time. Like most boys of six he was accustomed to saying, whenever he saw something he liked, "Daddy, buy me one of those." He said that one day when Rollar took his family to an auction at Nazareth, Pennsylvania.

Among the items for sale (you can expect anything at a small-town auction) were six buffaloes, put up for sale without prior announcement, probably from a zoo or circus that was going out of business.

"Daddy, buy me one of those," chirped little George.

Rollar, whose grandchildren still insist he never learned to say no, bought not one but two, two females, one of which had already been bred. Thus began the buffalo herd.

To them he added over the years ten European red deer, nineteen Mongolian pheasants, six golden pheasants, three wild turkeys, two peacocks, one milking cow, a pleasant black horse named "Old Smokey," four handsome palominos, and a pair of silver foxes. I watched him make the rounds of his personal menagerie, greeting each bird and beast as though it were a bosom pal.

"I just like animals. I'd be lonesome without them," he remarked. Then his face brightened—"I'm thinking of getting a couple of zebras!"

I pointed out to Rollar that a menagerie like his yields no income and must cost a whale of a lot to keep fed. "I spend about eighty dollars a month on grain alone," he replied. "But what's the difference. Contentment is riches."

He didn't mention the fact that his six buffaloes were among the fast-vanishing descendants of some 60,000,000 which once thundered over the plains. Conservationists should doff their hats to him. Still, it usually doesn't work that way. The world remembers "Buffalo Bill" Cody, who once killed 4,862 buffaloes in a single season, sixty-nine in one day. But will it remember "Buffalo Joe" Rollar?

Frankly, Rollar didn't care. He sat beside me in his bluejeans with high, hook-laced work shoes and a soiled khaki shirt. "Look at me," he said. "I walk around like a tramp. I like it that way. What do I care what people think. It's better to look like you have nothing and have a lot, than to look rich and owe everybody." He tweaked at his shaggy brown eyebrows, and his gray-blue eyes flashed—"Right? . . . C-e-r-tainly!"

When Rollar came to the farm he moved into the two-hundred-year-old farmhouse with its hand-hewn, tenon-and-mortised beams and pegged posts and plates. Over the years he fixed the house up and then sold it and a piece of land to go with it.

When he told me the price he sold it for I whistled. It was ridiculously low.

"But I got a good neighbor," he softly remarked.

He built another house for himself, a small, unimpressive one which was unpainted and looked like a sharecropper's house. Some rickety old rockers were on the front porch. The porch itself was built of posts and plates which Rollar hewed by hand out of cedar trees. Not to be outdone by the old pioneers he pegged them together too.

"I want it to look like a barn. I'm not much on appearances," he said. "Now that over there looks more like a house." He pointed to the barn.

In the barn, handsome in its white-painted clapboard, were the four palominos. They came trotting out at Rollar's call. He had another palomino but sold it to a carpenter in the town for a hundred dollars. It cost Rollar three hundred dollars. When I questioned his business acumen he explained, "He's a friend of mine. Does some work for me. That's the way it goes—one hand washes the other. You've got to be a friend to get a friend."

There is no heating system in Rollar's house, though the Connecticut winters blow cold. He burns nothing but the firewood he chops, burns it in the open fireplace and in the wood-burning stove in the kitchen.

"Why, when I lived in New York we used to have that steam heat and I'd always be catching cold," he said. "I don't catch a cold now. I used to wear winter underwear and catch cold. N-o-o-o. Not here. Wear the same winter and summer. Never catch cold"—he ran a hand over his weathered, red-brown face —"Get accustomed to it.

"People complain about the weather," he continued. "S-u-r-e. The man who's first to complain about the cold in winter is the first to complain about the heat in summer.

"When I was a boy I often wondered if we couldn't bottle up the heat of summer and use it in the winter. Then it dawned on me. We can do it by planting a tree."

So Rollar chops his wood, the "bottled" heat of summer, and burns it in his fireplace in winter. "I like to sit by the fire in the wintertime and look outside and watch the snow fall. I have my dog at my side. And I've got an old cowhide—I just like to curl up in it," he remarked.

Rollar got up from the old wooden chair and walked into the tool shed by the barn. I looked in after him and saw a big red and yellow juke box against the wall. He plugged it in.

"Some fellow sold this to me," he explained. "It's pretty good. I like to hear a little music while I work." The juke box started in on a Sousa march. "Sousa and waltzes are what I like best," he said. He had a line from the tool shed to the farmhouse and a loud-speaker sticking out of one of the farmhouse windows so the voice of the juke box would carry all the way to the deer and the buffaloes. Rollar didn't know if they liked music or not, but in case they did—there it was.

The juke box blared out incongruously from the tool shed, bathing the barn and pasture, and the bird and animal pens, with two-four and three-quarter time as Rollar and I approached the central reason for my coming to see him.

"God is nature," "Nature is God," so many people had said to me in my reportorial journey.

Rollar was the man to see about that. What was his philosophy? I wanted to find out. Here was a man who had done what so many have dreamed of doing. As Cedric Belfrage dreamed, he had gotten "away from it all." As Vincent Sheean dreamed, he had "renounced historical materialism." As Chinese sages of the past had dreamed, he was "cultivating his own garden."

What was the light he lived by?

"Nothing that is natural is sinful," Rollar reiterated. "If people only lived according to nature, there'd be less trouble in this world."

"And is that the first law with you?" I asked.

"It is *the* law," he replied. "When I was a boy my father told me, 'Do right and fear nothing.' I'm sixty-one now, and that still goes. *'Do right'*—that means do what nature intended you to do. And you'll fear nothing. *Nothing that is natural is sinful.* You only begin to fear when your conscience bothers you. Right? . . . C-e-r-tainly."

"But what about nature?" I asked. "Nature is pretty ruthless sometimes. What *is* the natural way—loving or killing?"

"Nature never kills for no reason. What it does is maintain the natural balance of living things in this world. If there get to be too many of a certain type of insect and they have to be brought back in balance—well, the birds take care of it. Everything balances out. If one species gets too strong, like, say, the prehistoric monsters, nature just balances them out of the picture. S-u-r-e, nature takes care of everything—it's only man that throws things out of balance. C-e-r-tainly."

"You mean the natural way—when all things are in balance—is for living things to love one another?" I asked.

Rollar went right on, "Why I even had three skunks once. You think I'd de-scent them? N-o-o-o. I left them just as nature made them. They had sixteen babies. I'd come right up to them and even take the kittens right from under them. Do you think they'd do anything? N-o-o-o.

"It's natural to be friendly. I don't care whether it's skunks or birds or people. Look at those deer and those buffaloes. There's your golden rule for you. They've both got horns, sharp ones—but they just do unto the other fellow what they'd like the other fellow to do unto them.

"If human beings only had the sense to do that! Why look at us—we're all *people,* just as nature made us. We can't even live at peace in our own pastures, let alone in the same pasture the way those animals do. The nations of the world could take a lesson from those deer and those buffaloes. Right? C-e-r-tainly."

I asked, "What about the different kinds of people in the world?"

"Just ignorance. We don't know them. They talk about people of different colors—now who are we to say about what nature has put on this earth? Nature shows no favoritism. It doesn't discriminate," Rollar replied. "Of all the causes of hatred, ignorance is the most powerful. You get to know any people, any kind of people, I don't care what nation or what color—and when you get to know them you like them."

He ran his fingers over his graying temples and looked off toward the woodland beyond the pasture—"There are no strangers in this world—just friends waiting to be met."

The juke box was still giving out with Sousa and waltzes, and as Rollar talked there would be an occasional quick clap as Sport, the English setter, did his part to keep nature in balance by catching flies in his trigger-like jaws. In the barnyard the palominos were nuzzling about the fence and cleaning up stray blades of hay.

My eye lingered on the two enormous haystacks beside the barn, covered with tarpaulin weighted with boards, looming like twin towers—the cathedral of the farm.

"How on earth did you get in all that hay?" I inquired.

"It didn't cost me a penny," Rollar replied. "It takes about fifty ton to get my family through a winter and I get it all free."

"How come?"

"Y'know these city people come out here nowadays. They buy a big place with lots of field and the grass keeps growing and they don't know what to do with it. I clean it up for them and get the hay free. Y-e-a-h. That's how it is nowadays. They don't realize how many quarts of milk or how many pounds of beef are in that field. N-o-o-o. They won't be bothered keeping a cow."

More out of pity than contempt, Rollar spoke of the generation of work dodgers which has taken over the earth. He talked about people chasing the will-o'-the-wisp of pleasure and seeking diversion and hanging out in taverns and becoming total strangers to the hard, honest work nature equipped them to do.

"You got to do a day's work to earn a night's rest," he said, walking to the well and drawing up a bucket of water. "W-h-y, I sleep like a sixteen-year-old. And nobody has to pull me out of bed in the morning. The birds in the trees, they wake me up, they're my alarm clock."

Of the late stayer-uppers and the cabaret hounds, he remarked, "A man who doesn't like his bed at night will surely like it in the morning."

He heaved the bucket of water down the spillway at the side of the well—"Work is the best medicine for the human body. Right? C-e-r-tainly."

He went right on talking—"The way I consider myself, I'm a common laborer, a piece of dust. Our real ancestors are Mother Nature and Father Time. Our real ancestors are dust—here." He picked up some soil and crumbled it in his hand.

"What we ought to do is have one day a year, a special holiday, y'know, like Christmas. Only on this day everybody would just look down a hole. That would remind them what the end of the journey of life is—back to dust."

I asked, "Do you have any fears or qualms about that, I mean about going back to dust some day?"

He gave a belly laugh—"Oh, hell no!"

"You have no fear of death?"

"N-o-o-o. Life is a circle. I've had my circle of life. I'm ready to fade away and let the young ones take over. It's just the same with a tree. The old ones die and go back into dust and the young ones grow out of that very same dust. I even call my grandchildren 'sprouts.' The old ones got to make room for them. I've lived my circle of life. Why fear? I'm willing to face the end of the circle. Sure. C-e-r-tainly."

Rollar stretched out on the ground near some of his flowers, and soon through the oak trees we could see one of his squirrels returning from a day out. It scampered down the oak nearest to us, stopped a second and thrust out its head as though wondering if the stranger, I, was to be trusted. Reassured by Rollar the squirrel came on down the tree and stopped by to take a peanut from its friend's hand on the way to its chicken-wire home.

"Nobody really *owns* anything," Rollar remarked. "Nobody can add anything to the earth, or take anything away. Even a man's children are only loaned to him. This nature we're talking about—this God—it's like it says to us, 'I'm putting this child in your care. I've searched the whole world for someone to care for it and I've chosen you. I make no guarantees. You may have the care of it for years and years, or only for a brief moment.' "

It was the first time Rollar had mentioned God.

I asked him point-blank, "Do you believe in God?"

"Nature really is my God," he replied. "There is *something*—we're not supposed to know who or what—that regulates everything. The duty of science is to unfold this. It has unfolded a lot already. If a man dead two hundred years ago came back to this earth and saw this electricity and television and—and even that juke box of mine, he'd get so scared he'd jump back in his grave.

"My religion is just this: there's something we don't understand, and that's what makes life beautiful. If you went fishing and you knew you'd bring home twelve fish every day, you'd get tired of it. C-e-r-tainly."

"Do you ever pray?" I asked.

"Prayer never enters my mind," Rollar answered. "A priest could wear his pants out kneeling down in prayers and the flowers wouldn't come up if it didn't rain."

"What do you think of formal religion?" I inquired.

"Religion is *inside* a person," he replied. "No man should take his religion from another. He should look for it in himself. That's the only place he'll find it. Right? . . . C-e-r-tainly."

On the basis of his answers, one could consider Rollar quite an unreligious man—unless you considered every day of his life a prayer and his whole existence a religion.

. . . It just struck me as I drove away from his place in the twilight that he had bought those first buffaloes of his in a little Pennsylvania town called *Nazareth*.

"Buffalo Joe" Rollar certainly wasn't the only one who had found God in nature. At the four corners of America I met people who looked to the wondrous, intricate, enigmatic, sometimes awesome, force of nature as God Himself. They had no need to seek further. Nature was God, and God nature. But no one epitomized that faith quite as Rollar did, and that is why I have told you his story.

Nature, even though it may not be one's total faith, has a way of creeping into the faith of nearly everyone. How can anyone who ever has planted a seed and watched life sprout from the ground be godless?

There is a sense of wonder just in looking into the blossom of the mountain laurel or watching the humble cornstalk grow from a tiny pebble of life into a tufted tower of green. How do hens know where to roost? What makes them place their eggs so considerately in the nests you set out for them? Who teaches the bluejay to fly? Do the cucumber vines take hold of weeds and fences with those magic fingers of theirs because of anything you could discern in the thin white seeds when you planted them? What turns a yellow blossom into a bright red tomato?

Many a city dweller who may have lost all track of God in the concrete deserts may find Him again in the green fields. How insensitive a man must be to see nature's wonder-working all around him and not be inspired!

It doesn't take a Grand Canyon or a Niagara Falls. When the painter Matisse was asked what inspired him, he said, "I grow artichokes. Every morning I go into the garden and watch those plants. I see the play of light and shade on the leaves and I discover new combinations of colors and fantastic patterns. I study them. They inspire me. Then I go back into the studio and paint."

A writer I know in Connecticut spends a great deal of his time nursing along a grove of fruit trees, pruning and spraying, and tending a vegetable patch with enthusiastic, loving care. An editor visited him and inquired about the amount of money he saved raising fruit and vegetables instead of buying them at the store. When the writer made a rough estimate, the editor laughed.

"Just think of how much more you could make if you used all that time at your typewriter writing!" he said.

The writer smiled and replied, "Then what would I have to write about?"

Closeness to nature becomes for many perhaps not a faith in itself, but a symbol of faith. It becomes a new yardstick for values. What does the materialistic value of a few beans matter, compared to the warm, inner feeling of having prepared the soil, put the seeds in their rows, watched the sprouts come up, weeded and cultivated, seen the pods form, and finally harvested the beans with your own hands? I remember a saying which the older folks used derisively when I was a boy. When they wanted to express total absence of value they'd say, "It's not worth a row of beans." I never realized how wrong they were until I raised a row of beans myself.

Psychiatrists speak of the "feeling of belonging." It is vital that human beings have this feeling; otherwise they drift into isolation and aloneness. Their withdrawal from life can become so acute that reality escapes them altogether, and one day a doctor may shake his head and write the diagnosis "schizophrenia." What is this but total detachment, the total absence of a feeling of belonging?

"We've gotten too far away from nature," an insurance man I met in South Carolina remarked. People everywhere expressed this feeling, time and again. "We never feel the grass under our feet," an Alabama merchant said. "We don't know one bird from another," said a nurse in Wisconsin. A physician in New York remarked, "If you ask a child where we get milk, he no longer says, 'From a cow'; he says, 'From a container.' "

All this is the gradual slipping away of the fundamental sense of belonging: the sense of belonging to nature. No wonder man feels alone. In the crowded cities the neon lights throw a screen across the sky so that he cannot see the stars at night. He knows what *dirt* is, but he is a stranger to *earth.* His feet beat against sterile cement. And the leaves of trees, when he is lucky enough to catch a glimpse of some, are sullied with the fumes of exhaust.

The poet Kahlil Gibran wrote of "life's yearning for itself." How can one feel that yearning unless he reaches out and at least touches the finger tips of nature?

A man who nurtures living things, the strawberries in a well-mulched patch, or even a few busybody chickens in a hen house he built himself, cannot escape a feeling of belonging. It comes to him subtly, as though by osmosis. He feels a responsibility for these living things; they depend upon him. He learns to know in the fathomless depths of himself a feeling of kinship with all life and of participation in its mysterious processes. He takes part in creation and feels himself a link in the great, maternal chain of life and new life. "Life's yearning for itself" begins, subtly, to become real and comprehensible to him. In the calm of evening, when the light of day takes its curtain call in the western sky, he can look upward and feel that he is a part of all this. He belongs to the universe.

General Courtney H. Hodges, whom I visited in San Antonio, Texas, where he was living in retirement, remarked, "Yes, I've turned to gardening. I plant zinnias and day lilies mostly. I feel a great sense of accomplishment when I see a green shoot come up." The old soldier, whom I had known when he was commander of the First Army in World War II, added, "I get the same kick out of it as I used to get from training raw troops into fine, effective soldiers."

The comparison shocked me a little. I couldn't help thinking how good it would be if all generals the world over could somehow turn to gardening. Perhaps that's why the visit with Hodges stuck in my mind. Psychiatrists talk of sublimation. Here was an old soldier getting the "same kick" out of raising flowers that he once got out of raising an army.

"I was taking a trek in the woods last fall and I saw some mountain laurel," Hodges continued. "I brought some seeds back and soaked them and planted them—and now look." He pointed to a seedling poking its head up in the garden. He beamed like a proud papa.

Hodges was living in a house of native field stone which he designed himself. It was in woodlands out at the fringe of San Antonio. Pointing to a well-cropped plot in front of the house, he explained, "I had some plants and shrubs in there too, but the deer come right up to the house and eat everything. I had to move my garden out back."

We strolled out in the garden and the general pointed with pride to each shoot poking up from the earth. He showed me his birdbath and the rock pool he had built. He pointed affectionately to the live oak, with its year-round green leaves. And he told me of his new friend, the cardinal, which likes to fly against its own reflection in the picture window and then slide down the pane.

"General Hodges," I wrote in my notebook, "has found *It* in nature, too."

In Kewanee, Illinois, I met Loyal M. Thompson, minister of the First Methodist Church. I first spotted him on a bench under a tree with a typewriter in front of him, batting away at it and looking off to the sky and the green fields.

"Whenever I feel tense I slip out here in the open and write nature poetry," he told me. "It releases the tensions. I actually feel mental pains like travail pains—I get rid of them by writing."

He showed me a snatch of free verse:

Beside a stream
I catch a gleam
Of sunlight filtering
Through the leaves,
While nature's mystic
Shuttle weaves
A mantle of
Remedial calm.

"When I am under great stress often I can get great healing just by a trek in the woods. I take in nature in all its broad sweep and put some of it down in my nature poems. This gives me release for days at a time," Reverend Thompson said.

Many another has found not only release from tension, but a more positive release of aggression in nature and, particularly, in wrestling with it as well as just taking it in. Ralph Waldo Emerson wrote:

". . . when surprised by company and kept in a chair for many hours, my heart sinks, my brow is clouded and I think I will run for Acton woods, and live with the squirrels henceforward. But my garden is nearer, and my good hoe, as it bites the ground, revenges my wrongs, and I have less lust to bite my enemies. I confess I work at first with a little venom, lay to a little unnecessary strength. But by smoothing the rough hillocks, I smooth my temper; by extracting the long roots of the piper-grass, I draw out my own splinters; and in a short time I can hear the bobolink's song and see the blessed deluge of light and color that rolls around me."

To some, nature remains a last refuge in an irritating world. The poet-adventurer Robert W. Service, fed up with the turn of life and civilization, said as he approached his seventy-eighth birthday, "I no longer believe in anything but nature. I feel very close to nature, which gives peace, happiness and tranquility. I would like to turn my back on the world and live with nature . . ."

Who hasn't felt the back-to-nature tug at sometime or other?

As I posed the question my thoughts turned at once to Henry David Thoreau and Walden Pond.

I decided to go there. The pond which Thoreau made immortal must be a shrine for lovers of nature, for people who have found faith in the great outdoors, I reasoned. So I set out for Massachusetts.

Well, I found it. It was a much larger pond than I expected, and there were businesslike signs along the highway establishing the fact that it now was a Massachusetts state reservation. It was right on a main highway; I had expected it to be tucked away in some sequestered woodland.

No matter. I parked my car and walked down a wooded hillside to the pond. I soon became aware that this shrine of Thoreau's lonely communion with nature had been turned into a beach. There was a stretch of sand at one end of the pond, backed up by bathhouses, and out in the waters of historic inspiration loomed a float and diving boards.

It was a cool day and no one was swimming. Some lifeguards were playing touch football on the sand.

I spotted two policemen sitting side by side on a low wall by the bathhouses, one chewing on a cigar. Certainly they would know a different side of Walden Pond, I thought; certainly they would feel its significance as something more than an up-to-date swimming hole; they would know about the devotees of Thoreau. I went up to the one with the cigar.

"I suppose a lot of people come here for inspiration," I began.

"Nope. Mostly for swimming," he replied.

"But what about the people who come to pay homage to Thoreau?" I pressed.

"We wouldn't know about that," he said.

I finally nailed down the fact that this *was* Walden Pond, as the signs said, and that Henry David Thoreau *had* come to live in a shack on the edge of it.

"You'll find the shack up around there," the policeman said, pointing toward a bend in the shore line off to the right. "It's about five hundred feet back in the woods, what's left of it. There's just the foundation."

Good. My hopes soared. Surely up along the shore line, up away from these bathhouses, I would find the Thoreau lovers. I started up a path toward the bend.

As I rounded it I spotted just ahead of me the kind of picture I had been looking for all along. Here was a young couple sitting on a blanket on the edge of Walden Pond. The woman was sitting up with a book in her hand, reading softly. The man leaned back pensively on one arm, looking out over the water. A few feet away, a baby played in the sand at the water's edge.

Thoreau lovers at last. I was sure the woman was reading aloud from *Walden, or Life in the Woods.* How many hundred miles had they come, I wondered, to be near the shrine of the naturalist-philosopher.

I walked up to them slowly. I thought I would break the ice with a simple question.

"Could you tell me where Thoreau's shack is?"

The man looked up with a start. The woman lowered her book, revealing the title *Corpse in the Closet*. She piped, "Who's shack?"

"Thoreau, you know, *Thoreau,*" I repeated.

The man shook his head.

The woman said, "Oh yeah, I've heard of that name somewhere. Wait——"

I waited.

"I know," she blurted. "It's up the pike I think. You just watch the signs along the road. You'll find it."

She thought "Thoreau's Shack" was a hamburger joint.

That was it. I didn't try to find any disciples of Thoreau at Walden Pond after that.

As I drove back through Massachusetts I thought again of Wordsworth: "Little we see in Nature that is ours; We have given our hearts away, a sordid boon!"

Yes, there were some "Buffalo Joes" in the world, and some Matisses and some Hodgeses and Thompsons, but there were a lot more who "For this, for everything" were "out of tune."

They stand in a garden and they see with unseeing eyes. If they live in the country, they fight with nature instead of living with it. Every fresh blade of grass that lifts its head through the sod of spring is but the unwelcome harbinger of a chore: it will grow some thirty-six inches during the summer and will have to be cut fifteen to twenty times.

The rare gift of faith that is in nature is lost upon them, for they have, in effect, resigned from nature. Since they no longer belong to it, it no longer belongs to them.

After I returned from Walden Pond I picked up the Sunday New York *Times* and in a book column written by J. Donald Adams this line fixed my eye: ". . . one feels, with a greater intensity than before, the extent of man's idiocy, and one thinks with stiffened resolution of his possession of a world too beautiful for him to live in by his present lights."

I set it down in my notebook and underscored it and thought again of "Buffalo Joe" Rollar, in whose book the only dumb animals are the human ones.

"Our fathers lived close to the earth and sky, and were not ridden by neuroses," Reverend George A. Buttrick, of New York, said at a Washington conference. "They learned thus that they and all men are pensioners of the universe."

That is, indeed, the lost idea.

". . . all men are pensioners of the universe."

The story is told of a Brahman priest in India who was sitting at the side of a water lily pond one evening watching the sun inch lower in the western sky. An American missionary approached him and took a seat beside him at the edge of the pond. The missionary started to talk and the Brahman priest listened attentively. The missionary talked all about his religion, its doctrines, the purity and verity of its theology, the logic of its philosophy, the beauty of its liturgy.

The Brahman priest listened. He did not change his expression. Thinking him unconvinced, the missionary started in again. This time he took the dialectical tack. He marshaled propositions and syllogisms, cited authority, interpreted history, drew conclusions.

Still the Brahman priest listened.

The sun now had dipped to the horizon and was saying farewell with a gentle wave of its golden kerchief. In the pond, the buds of night-blooming water lilies stood among the slit green fronds, their arms still folded about their shoulders, waiting to throw back their saris.

The missionary stood up a bit impatiently. He now took the persuasive tack. He began to explain God—in terms of his own religion. He told of the amazing miracles God had performed. He told of God's awe-inspiring works, of God's enormous power.

Now it was the Brahman priest who stood up.

He simply pointed to a night-blooming lily unfolding its petals, revealing the breath-taking pageant of color within it.

"Brahma," he said, and walked away.

12

ONE WEEK WITH GOD

From India, an Ashram

From everyone I had talked to so far—from the nature lovers and the farmers, from the miners and the steel workers, from the psychiatrists and the scientists, from the New York sophisticates and the villagers of Beaver Meadows, from the soldiers and the students, from men and women in a hundred walks of life—it was abundantly clear that most people today are reaching out for God. Many of them reach out in a vague way. But some are more direct. They simply pack up their suitcases and "go to see Him."

I went on such a trip with 208 men and women from all over America—people who journeyed by car, bus, train, and plane to the lake country of Wisconsin to spend seven days with God.

Many were professional people. There was a liberal sprinkling of doctors, psychologists, social workers, nurses, and teachers in the group. For they were visiting God in a new way, a way which fused the spiritual route of Western Christianity with the highly intellectual, rarefied route of the mystical East.

This week with God was called an "Ashram" (Ah-shrum).

The name and idea were borrowed from India, from the forest schools of Mahatma Gandhi, Rabindranath Tagore, and other luminaries of the East. From ancient times in India the followers, or *chelas,* of great men have journeyed to the forests and the hills, there to bask in the intellectual, spiritual, and mystical light of their leaders, or *gurus.*

"Why not a Christian Ashram with Christ as the *guru?*" wondered Dr. E. Stanley Jones, noted missionary to India, who had attended the Ashrams of both Gandhi and Tagore. He liked the word "Ashram," from the ancient Hindu *Asrama,* which, according to scholars, had two opposite meanings: "cessation of hard work," and "intensification of hard work." Dr. Jones took both meanings (cessation of ordinary, routine hard work; intensification of inner, spiritual hard work) and started a Christian Ashram in Sat Tal, India, in 1939. The next year he brought the idea home to America, and since then, quietly and without fanfare, he had held American Christian Ashrams each summer under sponsorship of the National Council of Churches.

The one I attended was at a onetime millionaires' country club, a pleasure dome of the twenties where fleshy men and flashy women had come with big bankrolls seeking something. To this fantastically lavish place, which now was the American Baptist Assembly, Green Lake, Wisconsin, folks of all denominations now had come to seek God.

They unpacked their suitcases and plunged straightway into what was called "the morning of the open heart." What better way to begin than by flinging the gates of their hearts wide open, telling why they had come, what they needed, what it was which nudged them out of their complacent niches back home and sent them to Wisconsin to call on God?

A good-looking, earnest woman rose to her feet and said, "I feel that I am very intolerant. I am forever assigning false motives to people. I don't want to be that way. I want to be a radiant, soul-winning Christian."

Her words floated softly through large, low Morehouse Hall,

which once had been a gambling casino and now was the central meeting hall of the Ashram. Dr. Jones had begun the morning of the open heart with the simple statement, "All of us have needs. If you act as though you had no needs, we've got your number. We are a fellowship of those in need. When this week is over, we'll all be different. This is an attempt to have God operate in all of us."

Spontaneously, without being called on and in no special order, the men and women—even some of the children—stood up and talked. Their sincerity was obvious and they were unashamed.

"I'm very tense, selfish and self-centered. I'm not giving my best because of fear," a plump, grayish-haired woman said. "I want to be free. I want to do what God wants me to do."

A young redheaded man with a crew cut stood up and said, "I need relief from a volatile temper and deep-seated selfishness." A youthful woman in the back row asked freedom from resentment. "I resent the fact that I resent," she said. "I want to feel kindlier toward people. I want to curb my tongue from talking too much." She was followed by an attractive, prematurely gray woman in a trim green suit, who said, "People don't like me. I'm domineering. I have a harsh tone to my voice. I want to love people. My need is to show them that I love them. I pray for it all the time."

In the center of the hall a small boy rose hesitantly. "I have a lot of troubles and I would like to turn them over to God," he began. "I have trouble getting along with my sister, that's one thing. I want popularity and I shouldn't want it, that's another—but I don't know what to do about it."

A young minister, glad to be away from it all in the fresh Wisconsin woodlands, spoke out, "I want freedom from resentments against my own parishioners. I'm always telling people how to go to heaven, but often I really want to point them in the other direction!"

A handsome man in his thirties said, "I need to surrender myself more completely to Christ. Then the disciplines of the Christian life will take care of themselves." An older woman followed him, "I want to be so filled with the Holy Spirit that I don't even have to think about my actions, that my life will be a Christian life automatically." A Negro man arose and said, "I am here for the purpose of saying 'yes' to the Lord. I want my life entirely surrendered to God. So far as I am concerned life is vain without Christ at the center."

They went on reciting their needs, spontaneously, without compulsion. None was more eloquent than a little woman with deep-set eyes and a soft, lined face. She spoke but three words—*"I need everything."*

At the conclusion of the morning of the open heart Dr. Jones told the members of the Ashram, "Now that we've looked *at* our problems, let's look *above* them. Every one of these problems has an open door upward."

The idea of the Ashram was to find the door, not simply the door to a specific problem but, essentially, the door to life. The Ashram was a concentrated one-week search for meaning.

"We have no time for a conference," said snowy-haired Dr. Jones, who managed to look like a young man at sixty-seven. "We ask only to be agents of God, to hear His voice through our voices, not to hear the 'wisdom' of men's voices. . . . We have come together to study the meaning of our coming together. Instead of trying to find an answer, let's *be* an answer. Let's be, in cameo, the Kingdom of God."

To live out their miniature of God's Kingdom, the Ashramites began by tearing down barriers. Since in God's sight all men are brothers, they were brothers at the Ashram. Without backslapping or maudlin emphasis, they simply called one another Brother George, Brother Henry, or Sister Martha, as the case might be, and Dr. Jones was Brother Stanley.

Next to fall was the barrier of race. Black or white, the Ashramites ate together, played together, prayed together. In some cases blacks and whites roomed together, sometimes not knowing about it until they opened the door and met their roommates —and certainly not caring. "We no longer see a person of a certain race," Dr. Jones remarked quietly. "We simply see a person for whom Christ died."

Barriers of class and cash dissolved completely. An executive bunked with a laborer, a society hostess with a shop girl. All titles were left at the gate, exchanged for "Brother" and "Sister" —to an Ashramite "the highest title in the universe," one of them told me, "because it puts you in God's family." Even barriers of brains went by the board. The Ashram made no distinction between "those who teach and those who are taught." Its motto: "Everybody will teach and everybody will be taught."

Finally the "barriers inside us" had to go. Dr. Jones told the Ashramites, "Elsewhere we're not free, we're not spontaneous, and we're not happy. We have masks on. Here, let's be 'supernaturally natural.' "

The assembly ground at Green Lake was a good place to be natural. It was, in fact, a fantastically good place for most any purpose. The Baptists, who owned it and allowed the Ashramites to use it, could themselves hardly believe the story of how it got into their hands and felt the only logical explanation was that God made the arrangements.

The 1050 acres with a two-and-a-half-mile frontage along Green Lake was originally the estate of millionaire Victor F. Lawson, onetime owner of the Chicago *Daily News* and president of the Associated Press. His wife Jessie, whom he met when they were singers in a church choir, was the prime mover in building up the estate from an original ten acres to one of the wonders of Wisconsin—at a cost of $8,000,000.

A dairy enthusiast, Jessie Lawson put in cow barns lined with white glazed brick specially shipped from Belgium, each one wrapped in white tissue paper, at thirty-five cents apiece. Each of her cows had printed name plates in glass-enclosed frames above their stalls. Once, because her Jerseys had to go over a hill to get to pasture she spent $45,000 on a tunnel to spare them the exertion. Her barn staff wore spotless white uniforms and if a neighboring farmer came by to bid on a calf, he invariably was stopped at the barn door by one of these attendants to have his shoes scraped lest he introduce germs.

Whether Jessie Lawson foresaw the eventual use to which her rustic realm would be put is doubtful, though the architecture certainly had a prophetic tang. She built her 280-foot Guernsey barn (now known as "The Abbey") with a huge Gothic window at one end flanked by twin silos which made it look like a hayseed version of Notre Dame. Her bull barn with its expensive hardwood paneling easily became one of the several lodges for delegates to religious functions, and the nearby silo was ideal as a prayer tower. The sheep barn, which she thoughtfully equipped with central heating, was extremely comfortable for winter delegates. And when rural ministers got together they couldn't have asked for a finer meeting place than what once was Mrs. Lawson's pine-paneled piggery.

After the death of the Lawsons (Jessie in 1914, Victor in 1925) their estate was sold to a Chicago realty firm. The shoot-the-works twenties were at their shootingest and "Lone Tree Farm," as the Lawsons had called it, was energetically converted into "The Lawsonia Country Club" complete with Hollywood swimming pool, swank Normandy-style hotel, excellent golf course, and diverse other accouterments including a gambling casino made out of Mr. Lawson's enormous garage.

This bubble burst with the depression, though the estate continued to function as a posh resort under tutelage of a Chicago bank until 1943. Then the block-long chauffeured cars which had spun playfolks up from Chicago and Milwaukee were stalled by the gas shortage and Lawsonia closed its doors.

The American Baptists stepped in and bought the estate for $300,000. In addition to the fabulous bargain (Mrs. Lawson had spent $300,000 for swamp drainage alone) they found the place eminently convertible to a religious assembly ground. A first official act was to rename the Lawsonia Hotel the "Roger Williams Inn" and remove slot machines from the basement.

"How the worldly, pleasure-loving people who flocked to Green Lake in the twenties would rub their eyes at the sight of what is going on there now!" exclaimed a brochure of the Baptists. Many felt it was more than fortuitous that Jessie Lawson built barns with church-like windows, that the real estate plungers fitted out a casino which, as "Morehouse Hall," was ideal for worship services, and that the whole thing was snapped up by the Baptists virtually for a hymn.

Said a young worker at the assembly, "God's ways sure are mysterious. He certainly took a long time getting this place ready for use in His service!"

The members of the Ashram, many of whom came by bus rather than chauffeured limousine, enjoyed—in their "supernaturally natural" way—all of the luxurious trappings. They swam in the Hollywood pool, played tennis, lolled on the hotel's rich terrace, went speedboating on the lake. That was part of the Ashram. "Piety set to music," Dr. Jones called it—"A gaiety that laughs at the rhythm of things." As a girl Ashramite put it, "Religion isn't something to go around crying about."

The Ashramites had their fun, but they never forgot Whom to thank for it. Their day began at 6 A.M. (Gandhi got his *chelas* up at 3:45). Immediately they went into "silent time." Without talking to anyone they emerged from the ex-luxury hotel, the ex-bull house, the ex-cow barn, and silently made their way to the Vesper Circle, an amphitheater by the side of the lake. There they sat on chairs and benches under the wide-eyed morning sky and slowly let a new day sink into them. Some read their Bibles. Some read inspirational tracts or poems. Some cupped their chins in their hands and sat motionless.

Often we talk of the great meditative and contemplative talents of the East. Our people, we say, don't have the art of meditation. But these mornings during the silent time, meditation was so palpable you could all but reach out and caress it. Contemplation was as manifest as the morning breeze. How creative the silence was! If you did nothing else you at least became aware how full a minute is. You learned, as if for the first time, how many different sounds the birds make. You looked at the flip-flopping aspen leaves down by the water and saw how much they looked like people clapping hands.

In the last minutes before 7:15 breakfast the silent time ended with a few people standing up and telling what came to them during the silence. One morning a woman said, "It came to me why I don't mind telling my age any more. When I was thirty I did mind because I didn't really know Christ then and I figured I had only so long to live—thirty years more, forty, fifty at the most. Now I know age doesn't matter because I have all eternity."

Another morning a young Negro rose and said, "I've been reading from Dr. Peter Marshall, the late chaplain of the United States Senate. This is what stuck with me: 'Where we are wrong, make us willing to change. And where we are right, make us easy to live with.' "

One woman said after a silent time late in the week, "Up to now I've been afraid I'd go back the same old gal as I came. Now I know I won't." She sat down with her face placid and relaxed but tilted a bit higher than before. A man said, "I feel about fifty pounds lighter—cleansed of pettiness."

At their "family meeting," the Ashram's form of self-government, the members decided to have a continuous prayer vigil with volunteers taking hourly stints so that someone would be talking to God twenty-four hours a day. A room in the hotel was set aside as a "prayer room" with a single chair in the center facing a white-covered altar on which an open Bible lay, framed by burning candles and vases of yellow snapdragons and daisies. At all hours Ashramites who had signed up for the prayer vigil came to the quiet little room. At two and three o'clock in the morning they padded along the woodland paths with their flashlights, some in dressing gowns, to keep their appointments with God.

There was a notebook in the prayer room for "prayer requests." One person wrote—"Send a revival, dear Lord, and let it begin in me." Another—"Please pray that I will say a great big 'yes' to God." Another—"Pray that I may be used by God to make a better world." Across one page was written in a large hand, "Please pray for a brilliant young doctor who is apparently going to pieces and turning to alcohol, drugs and women instead of to Christ."

The Ashram idea of prayer was not "the gimmes." People in this world work for their keep. At the Ashram everybody worked. For an hour each morning the men donned their dungarees and work shoes, the women their house dresses, and work was their worship. The women sewed layettes—panties, sacques, mittens, booties, wrappers—out of flannel for babies in Europe. They also scoured utensils in the kitchen, cleaned vegetables. The men, swinging picks and mattocks, heaving shovels, widened and filled a stretch of road near the lake front.

"Our goal in modern society is to get away from manual work," commented Dr. Jones, whose daily work assignment was policing the grounds with a nail stick and a sack flung over his shoulder. "We gain this workless leisure—then go to a psychiatrist and get occupational therapy!"

He added, "Here we would just as leave give up our worship period as give up our work. We are following a carpenter's son. We try to put our love into operation in our work. Work is love made manifest."

Mostly for laughs, the work period had a foreman known as "Pharaoh." He was James Henderson, vice-president and Chicago manager of the Wagner Baking Corporation, a flush-faced, booming-voiced man of sixty. He looked much more like a hard-hitting businessman, one of the dynamo type, than Christ's *chela* at an Ashram.

What brought him here? I wanted to know but was too busy swinging a pick into a shale ledge to interview Pharaoh during work time. Finally, in the playtime of the afternoon, I got him out on the lake in a speedboat. He told his story as the spray spurted by us and the hull of the *Pilgrim* slapped at the waters of Green Lake like one of Henderson's own pie makers patting dough.

"My father was an alcoholic. He died when he was thirty-six and I was seven, left on a farm in County Derry, Ireland," Henderson began. "My mother was left with the mortgages. I have never known such a faith in my life as that woman had. Through prayer, miracles were performed. Instead of going to the poorhouse she raised the money—and raised the family. Faith did it. Nothing but faith.

"I'm saturated with terrific faith in prayer. If I weren't I'd have to have my head examined. Mamma—my wife—and I have seen it work. Some years ago we almost lost Mamma. She was critically ill and it looked as though she wouldn't pull through. Prayer got us to the right specialist.

"Today, as a businessman, I believe in constant communion with God, a continual hookup with Him so that He's there to listen to you. I find I must pray always, not just when I'm in need. I pray all during the day. I have a 'quiet time' in my office at the end of the day. I am convinced that you can be a good businessman and a good Christian. It doesn't have to be dog eat dog. The wicked prosper like a green bay tree but soon they are cut off."

At the wheel of the *Pilgrim* was handsome, tanned Ken Brock, a photographers' model and—if you were looking for "types"—the last type in the world you would expect to find at an Ashram. On the outside Ken seemed to belong at a Hollywood cocktail party. But on the inside he was right at home.

"I'm not really pious," Ken remarked. "I'm just interested in God. I like to ask people how they feel about God just as casually as I might ask, 'Where do you buy your suits?' When I'm in Chicago I pray going to work on the elevated. I say, 'Thank you, God, for a wonderful day yesterday, for giving me the power to take whatever happens and to use it for a growing personality. What do you have in mind for me today, God?' "

Talking to God in the vernacular also was a penchant of twenty-year-old Larry Gavel, a Washington University student, whom I found sunning by the swimming pool with seventeen-year-old Jane Crandall, a fellow Ashramite from Missouri. "When I'm driving the tractor on the farm I enjoy talking with God. I joke. I laugh. I get a big kick out of it, and I'm sure God does," Larry said. "If it looks like rain I say, 'Well now, God, is it going to rain or isn't it? Can I make it once around the field again?' "

Once, planting soy beans, Larry had only two more rows to go when it started to sprinkle. "If it's all right with you, God, I'd like to finish this field," he requested. He made the two rows and had just reached the barn when it started to pour.

"Now, I think maybe God did hold it up a little, long as it didn't bother anyone," Larry opined with a twinkle.

Across the greensward, straddling a garden bench, alone, pecking away at his portable typewriter, I found my friend from Kewanee, Illinois, Reverend Loyal M. Thompson—the man who wrote nature poetry for release of worldly tensions.

"What are you writing this time?" I inquired.

He drew a slip of note paper from the machine:

When black oak, white oak, yellow pine,
Each one distinctly God's design,
Respond to breezes through the leaves
They waken sylvan melodies.

When black folk, yellow folk and white
Their voices in high hopes unite
They blend in one harmonious song
That wakens faith and makes us strong.

Reverend Thompson had come to the Ashram not only to find trees and flowers in their natural state, but people, too. At the Ashram, with its total elimination of the barrier of race, people lived together in the natural harmony Thompson loved so well.

His *"black folk"* stanza echoed later when I sat on the hotel terrace with Gladys Payne, a Negro schoolteacher from Washington, D.C. She told of the time a streetcar conductor in the nation's capital rasped at her, "You got no right on here, you nigger." At the Ashram one wasn't aware of any fundamental difference in Gladys Payne any more than the variously colored petunias in the urns at the Vesper Circle were fundamentally different, as creation goes. But Gladys Payne was no fool. She knew how deeply prejudice is rooted in the loam of conditioning. "The Christian attitude," she said, "is this: 'I know I'm prejudiced, but I'm sorry for it. And I'm doing my best to do something about it.' "

In her schoolroom she taught equations by the Golden Rule, phrasing it this way: "What you do to one side you must do to the other." She believed that went for prejudice, too. "I used to be resentful. I'd look for slights because I was a Negro," she declared. "But now God has shown me that understanding is a two-way street. I mustn't be too resentful, too bitter. I mustn't harbor too many hurts."

High up on Judson Tower, from which a neon cross shone at two hundred feet across Green Lake, I talked with Jean Freeman, a psychiatric social worker from a hospital in California. She had crossed half a continent by bus to attend the Ashram. Why? What did a psychiatric social worker want here, I wondered?

Miss Freeman explained, "I have a patient, a mental patient, who has been given everything. He has had every kind of treatment. But he doesn't get well. Now I am looking for faith. Perhaps that's what he needs."

"But would one patient mean so much to you?" I asked.

"One patient is every patient," she said with a gentleness that humbled me. "When treating people it is necessary really to care. In your mind you see them as well people and you want to make that vision come true. Medicine becomes love wrapped up in faith. Do you see why I have come to the Ashram?"

. . . All of them came for their reasons.

Stanly Zager, a drugstore owner from Washington, Iowa, came because he thought truth was the mainstay of mental health and God was the way to truth. He realized that after his mother drowned herself in the Iowa River twenty years ago. Now Zager was a director of the Iowa Society for Mental Health. "The Bible," he said, "is the greatest book on psychology ever written."

John Philip Koeller, a lean, rawboned raspberry grower from Oshkosh, Wisconsin, came because he was sure there was only one way to live. "That's to be born again in Christ," he said. "I myself was born again in 1893." He was over eighty years old.

A woman doctor came to the Ashram by way of autopsies. "Doing autopsies I became convinced that there is something more to man," she said. "A man is alive one minute and you are talking to him, and another minute he is a chunk of material on the table. I told other doctors, 'The soul is gone.' They laughed and said I was crazy. I don't think so."

P. Philipose Philip, an Indian taking his doctorate at the University of Chicago, came to the Ashram for "spiritual refreshment." Janet Aylor, a bookkeeper from Springfield, Illinois, came "to bring a look of approval to the face of God instead of always seeming to hear him say, 'You disappoint me.'" John Beed, a chemist-assistant at the Libbey-Owens-Ford Glass Company, wanted to "go back to the glass factory and help some of those fellows who aren't living fully to use the terrific power of God."

Several hours of each day were devoted to meetings—lectures, sermons, question-and-answer discussions—presided over by the Ashram faculty: Dr. Jones; Dr. John Biegeleisen, of Eden Theological Seminary, St. Louis; Margaret Applegarth, formerly of the World Council of Churches; Canon Quintin Warner, of London, Ontario; Anna Mow, of Bethany Biblical Seminary, Chicago; and the National Council of Churches' Harold H. McConnell, director of the Ashram.

These sessions set the formal tone. But the osmosis of ideas took place in the in-between times: at work and at play, in walks along the old Lawsonia bridle paths, climbs to the lookouts atop the stone water towers, in idle drifting in rowboats on the lake, or just lolling on the greensward in the sun. This was the "togetherness" of the Ashram, the group taking in one another's washing. I saw them—people who only last week were strangers—sitting about on the stone benches or on expensive settees in the rose-carpeted hotel corridors talking intimately about God and their problems.

"Isn't this what the psychiatrists call 'group therapy'?" I asked Dr. Jones.

"Of course it's group therapy," he replied. "They're submitting themselves to God and to the group. We'll use psychology, we'll use science—we'll use anything so long as it illuminates the face of Christ."

He paused, then added in a whisper, "Talk about emotional illness—I've never seen such swift and complete healings as take place right here."

Fear, I found, was a prevalent knot in which the Ashramites were tied. Most of them were afraid of something. "I've been more afraid of life than I have of death," a middle-aged woman told me. "I think I am even afraid of myself," said another. Anxieties, popular in our day, were perhaps more rampant in this group because they had faced up to them, brought them closer to the surface. Each morning after the silent time the group marched back to the hotel for breakfast singing the Ashram's theme song, "I Will Not Be Afraid." A typical stanza:

His arms are underneath me.
His arms are underneath me.
His hand upholds me,
His love enfolds me
So I'm not afraid.

This was the Ashram's therapy for fear. Turn your fears over to God. Surrender to Christ and let Him handle things. With Him at the center, with Him in control, what is there to fear? His arms are underneath you.

Mel Holtz, the Ashram's music director, a tanned young Rock Islander who looked like the hero of a movie western, explained, "That's why the psychology of Christianity appeals to me. God is always with you. It's a terrific thing always to have someone with you."

Twenty-two-year-old Dorothy Bell, putting her finger on a prime value of group therapy, said, "We're learning not to be overwhelmed by our fears and anxieties because we're learning that we aren't the only ones who have them, that others do too."

The Ashram sought, then, to smite fear at its heart: aloneness. Aloneness from God. Aloneness from others.

Emotional conflicts stemming from behavior formed another prominent pattern. Some men and women had problems related to integrity and honesty, some to selfishness and egocentricity, some to sex. One man asked for help in "curbing the abuse of a natural urge." Another said that prior to knowing God he had been an immoral man beneath the surface—"I had an immoral inside."

To these penitents, Dr. Jones hammered home his notion of Christian discipline as "not a whipping up of the will, but a surrendering of the will to God." The Ashram prescription was St. Augustine's "Love God and do as you please."

The first two words were the important ones, for in loving God one could only do good. All of one's natural urges would still remain, Dr. Jones acknowledged, "but they would be used in the service of God."

The keynote of the Ashram was *growth,* intensified, rapid growth squeezed into a week's time. People were to change at the Ashram. To the woman who said, "I'm about to jell into the kind of person I don't want to be," Dr. Jones replied, "The Ashram is an attempt to break up that jelling process."

He wanted to boot people out of ruts. "A rut," he said, "is a grave open at both ends."

To show they had crawled out of such graves the Ashramites got together at the week's end for a session known as "sharing." Here, in the once gay and frivolous casino of the Lawsonia Country Club, they told what seven days with God had done for them.

"I came here with lots of irritating little problems," said a schoolteacher. "Now I've forgotten what they were!"

A physician stood up and said, "Only twice in my professional career have I ever prayed with my patients. Now that I personally have felt prayer's power I am going to pray with all of them."

A Negro man announced with meaningful simplicity, "This has been the first week of my life in an unsegregated world. I have lost my resentment against white people."

A young husband said, "I came here needing to learn humility. I think I've learned it. I've learned that by submitting myself to the group I can have a better time, do a better job."

An energetic little woman in her fifties said, "I've been pushed out of my complacency. I've been disturbed, upset. I've been knocked out of my smugness and comfortableness. It's good for me!"

A bachelor remarked, "Here's what I'm taking home with me: When you try to cure hatred with love and it doesn't work—just double the dose!"

"I had been going after the Holy Spirit, too fast," said a young wife. "Now I see it was puppy love. I was throwing myself at God instead of reaching for His hand. Here, with others, I have learned how to reach. I have a new concept of 'we' and 'us.' "

A little old woman in a back row stood up. She said, "That partnership idea: It's not me alone or God alone—it's *us* working together. That's what gives me confidence. God and I can work things out."

As the 208 men and women piled into buses and autos to start the journey back to the four corners of America, I think that in each of them was a persistent echo of what that little old woman had said: *"God and I can work things out."*

13

MONDAY MORNING PAGANS

Where's God on weekdays?

The worst black eye which modern religion received at the hands of the hundreds of people I talked to was the oft-repeated charge, "Hypocrisy."

"Lots of these churchgoers—they'll put on a righteous pose on Sunday morning and do as they darned please the rest of the week," said a bus driver in Chicago.

"What good is lip service?" complained a housewife in Baltimore. "It doesn't do any good to talk holy if you don't act holy."

"You can't love your fellow man for a couple of hours Sunday morning and hate him the rest of the week," said a St. Louis lawyer.

People were fed up and disillusioned with Sunday morning religion. They didn't believe in a "Sunday-morning God." It was not enough to meet God once a week in His Sunday-go-to-meetin' clothes. They wanted living religion and a living God. They wanted God on weekdays too.

"No man can be worldly minded six days in the week and spiritually minded for an hour on Sunday. No man who is selfish, cynical, and superficial on his feet is ever a saint on his knees," declared Reverend Robert J. McCracken, of the Riverside Church in New York.

All right. No one really disputes that. But where do you find living religion and how do you live it?

I set this up as my reportorial assignment. I didn't want merely to hear talk about it, or platitudinous prescriptions, or exhortations. I wanted to see living religion *in action;* I wanted the story.

I went to a number of sources, as a reporter does, and asked the question, "Where? Where can I see religion live?" The best tip I got was from Dr. Roswell P. Barnes. He was the head of the Division of Christian Life and Work of the National Council of Churches. He said to me, "Go to the Wyalusing Valley."

I had to ask him to spell it out because I had never heard of the valley. When I got home I pulled an atlas off the shelf and located it on a map of Pennsylvania. The next day I was on the Black Diamond Express roaring through the Appalachian Mountains on my way there.

My first view of the valley was at twilight. It is a hidden valley, deep in the hinterland of Pennsylvania, with hemlock-sided mountains hovering over it and a hungry creek lapping its way through. The creek, the Wyalusing, from which the valley gets its name, is a tributary of the Susquehanna River. It cuts back into old Indian country, some of which remains as primeval as in the days when scouts in buckskin lay upon the jutting rocks and watched the Indians' birchbark canoes skim over the waters. The valley today is hardly more populated than it was then. I stayed for a time in three towns along the Wyalusing Creek and two over the hills, and not one of them had as many people in it as an average New York apartment house.

A minister from the valley, Reverend James M. Moffett, met me upriver, where I got off the train, and drove me into the valley. The twilight view was serene and beautiful. I felt the cares of some of the teeming cities I had recently visited slip away. As we approached Stevensville, the valley town where Reverend Moffett lived, we rounded a bend and five deer eyed us from the roadside, then bobbed away through the brush.

Reverend Moffett had three churches in the valley: the Stevensville Presbyterian Church, the Rushville Presbyterian Church, and the Camptown Community Church. Each of these towns had a population of around two hundred and could not afford a minister's exclusive services. Camptown (believed by some to be the town of Stephen Foster's "De Camptown Races") had brought Methodists, Presbyterians, and Baptists together in its Community Church. The pulpit was shared by Moffett and a young Methodist minister, Reverend William W. Reid. Reverend Reid also had churches at three other tiny towns.

Sunday was a busy day for these two preachers as they hurried through the valley and over the hills (Reid by jeep) to conduct three or four worship services. Reverend Reid, then twenty-seven, was fresh out of Yale Divinity School, having made a decision to go into religion instead of botany during long hours of contemplation in a German prisoner-of-war camp during World War II. Reverend Moffett, forty-five, was the son of a famous American missionary to Korea, Reverend Samuel Austin Moffett. His mother was a medical missionary and three of his four brothers were ministers. Once when he was offered a larger, better-paying pastorate, he replied, "No, I'll stay here in the valley. This is America."

To help feed his three growing youngsters on a rural minister's salary, Reverend Moffett raised and sold gladiolas. When I visited the valley he had the teenagers of Stevensville, Camptown, and Rushville raising them, too. They were raising ten thousand gladiolas on bits and pieces of land Reverend Moffett could "borrow" from the farmers and, with the proceeds, were going to send young folks to religious camp-conferences.

Lanky Jim Moffett was a familiar figure on the farms. When Miles "Mike" Haight's hen house burned down, the parson was on hand with the rest of the neighbors to cut timber for a new one. Or you might have found him chatting with Ben Sumner in the barn at milking time, or on Lacey Van de Mark's farm at silo filling.

On alternate Wednesday evenings he and Mrs. Moffett would be at the rook game at Rushville Community Hall. Mrs. Moffett could never forget the time, at one of these socials, when old Henry Atwater, a jokester, gave her dry mustard and water when she asked for ginger ale. But the big talk at the Community Hall was how Wright Griffin had carved a chunk out of the hillside with his bulldozer so farmers coming to church doings could have a place to park their cars.

In the valley, I found, it was hard to say exactly where religion left off and ordinary living began.

One afternoon I rode over the hills to Herrickville with Reverend Reid in his jeep. We stopped in to see Mrs. Eloise Welliver, a very religious woman. She told us how she happened to become religious. Here's what she said:

"I was very ambitious when I was younger. But I was thwarted at every turn and I became embittered. Finally I got down on my knees one day and said, 'Here I am, Lord. I've made a mess of my life. Here are the pieces.' That was eighteen years ago. I have had faith ever since. Whenever a doubt came, I simply remembered Jesus saying, 'Him that cometh to me I will in no wise cast out.' I just took Him at His word."

She continued. "God is my Father. I believe in Him as surely as I do in my earthly father. Though I have never seen Him, He has manifested Himself many times. When I came to the end of myself, God was there."

Many people, Mrs. Welliver opined, are "coming to the end of themselves" these days. That's why they're turning to God.

As we talked, in came Chauncey Lent, one of the neighbors. He had been out all day collecting wastepaper from farmhouse to farmhouse. Dog tired, he settled down in a chair.

"What's the paper for?" I asked.

"A drive we're having," he replied. "We're trying to raise money for the Herrick Township Volunteer Fire Company. Last year we bought a secondhand pumper from Pottsville for $350. Now we're trying to get up money for a firehouse to keep it in. We already bulldozed out a big pond. Got a good water supply and plenty of hose. It's all volunteer work, of course. We got to take care of folks."

Mrs. Welliver had her form of religion.

Chauncey had his.

Next day, Sunday, at the church in Rushville a visiting minister, Reverend Robert R. Smyrl, said in his sermon, "We can worship our God any time, any place. We do not need to face any direction. We do not need to be in any special building, nor need it be on any special day of the week. We can worship in the fields or on a mountain top, in the quiet of our room, or at busy noonday."

He said the church was really a "church family . . . and you folks in the valley know it because your church *is* a big family." Appropriately punctuating the sentence, baby Arnold LaRue piped up just then with a squeal from the front pew.

I thought of Reverend Smyrl's lines as I went choring the following day with farmer Benton Sumner in Stevensville. While his hired man was milking the seventeen hornless Holsteins in the barn Ben pulled ensilage down from the silo and carried a pail of it to each stall. He gave warm water to some young heifers and expertly eyed a new calf which had been born during the night and was still wet. He patted the hunting dogs, fed the hogs and the white leghorns, turned the sheep out of their shed, and tenderly tossed some grain and a forkful of hay to old Pete.

Pete was a horse well beyond his days of usefulness and expensive to feed, but Ben just wouldn't get rid of him. "Might as well take care of him in his old age," Ben said.

Then he tenderly examined a ewe which had been hurt by a frisky heifer and adjusted a bandage around its girth. Ben sent

Pearl, his collie, scampering after some sheep which had strayed too far and called some back himself, shouting, "Hy nanny! H-y-y-y nanny!"

Later his wife, Ruth, told me, "Ben will stay up all night with a ewe sometimes when she's lambing. Some of them have a pretty hard time. He's a regular midwife to them."

But Ben didn't go to church very often. Of course, he loved all those living things he took care of. And his farmhouse was warm with hospitality. And the neighbors knew that when anyone had trouble, Ben would turn up to help. Maybe that was what Reverend Smyrl meant when he said, "We can worship our God any time, any place"—even in a barn, or a manger.

Or maybe that's what Professor Harry C. Munro, of Texas Christian University, meant when he wrote, "Every task is as holy as the hands which do it and the heart which prompts it."

"Religion is a way of life here," remarked sixteen-year-old Janet Bates, who was tending the general store in Stevensville. She was one teenager who wasn't itching for the big city. Stevensville, which is just a turn in the road where a bridge crosses Wyalusing Creek—a post office, a general store, and an abandoned old mill—was good enough for her. "I like it here," she said, "because in Stevensville people *like each other.*"

She told about Oscar Aeppeli, who broke his leg, and how the other farmers got together and did his haying for him. And how, at silo-filling time, all the farmers helped each other just as the old New Englanders once did with their logrolling. And of the time one farmer's arthritis got so bad he had to sell his cows, and another farmer said, "If I just had the money—I'd buy them cows and give 'em back to him!"

It is said the heart of religion is love: *"A new commandment I give unto you, That ye love one another."* Reverend Moffett had a special definition of love. "It's love," he said, "when your neighbor has a hole in his shoe and *your* foot is cold."

The valley was full of that kind of feeling.

Bruce Dodge was sick once at harvest time, so sick he couldn't get in his potatoes. "First thing I knew," he related, "there was the sound of potatoes being dumped into my cellar." A dozen neighboring farmers had dug them for him—and also poured a concrete floor for one of his farm buildings that needed repair.

When Floyd Hitchcock's house burned down, the neighbors rounded up so much furniture and clothing to give him that he ended up with more than he had before.

John Graham was kicked by a cow and laid up for quite a while with a bad eye. The other farmers had a bee ("Everybody come ready to work, and bring your tools!") and they put in cattle-watering cups in the stalls of Graham's barn.

They had a bee for Henry Atwater once, too. He was in the hospital with blood poisoning. Ross Hibbard and some other farmers came over and planted his corn. Later they mended his fences and did his haying. When Henry's wife, Pearl, was sick, the farm wives had a housecleaning bee. They came over and cleaned her farmhouse from cellar to attic.

Most of the telephones in the valley were the old-fashioned kind: big boxes on the wall with mouthpieces that stuck way out and cranks on the side. They were party lines, anywhere from six to a dozen parties on a line. Your particular ring might be two shorts, a long, and a short, or some similar code.

"In an unfriendly town party lines like that would be awful. What gossip spreaders!" Reverend Moffett's wife remarked. "But in the valley, they're wonderful. In case of emergencies we can round up each other in no time."

I saw the system in operation the night I spent at Henry Atwater's. A teenager, Carleton Herman, was late getting home from a Rushville Church young people's meeting. He was supposed to pick up a truck at his grandmother's and drive it over a back road to Mike Haight's place, where he was working. The road was wet and dangerous that night, and soon Carleton's grandmother was on the phone fearing he had slid into the ditch where the sluice pipe goes under the road.

"Better get your boots on and go out there, Henry," said

Pearl Atwater. Henry and I started getting ready to head across the field to the sluice pipe.

The telephone kept ringing out its code numbers—but by now everybody was listening because they knew it must be an emergency with the phone ringing so much. In a dozen nearby farmhouses, neighbors prepared to go on a rescue expedition for Carleton Herman.

A few moments of silence. And then the jangle of the bell again. "Oh, thank God!" I heard Pearl whisper. She turned to us. "Never mind, Henry. Carleton's all right. He just ran out of gas!"

At the one-room post office in Stevensville, sixty-five-year-old Mabel Keeler, the postmistress, summed up the feeling of the valley in a single line. "The people pray to God—and they try to be human," she said.

"Do *you* pray?" I asked.

"Don't think I'd have ever come through with this leg if I didn't," she replied, pointing to a leg on which she had had a severe operation.

Prayer throughout the valley was a constant thing. I never sat down to a meal with those farm folk but what a prayer to God was offered. Young people's meetings began and closed with prayer. At a meeting at Mabel Van Guilder's house teenagers stood up in a circle holding hands, and each offered a prayer in rotation. When the Men's Fellowship Club of Camptown got together at Ed Kennedy's house fathers and sons bowed their heads and said prayers together.

"You never lose track of God here in the valley," Reverend Moffett said.

I knew, as I threaded my way back along the Wyalusing Creek, and then over the hills in Reverend Reid's jeep, and finally boarded the Black Diamond for New York, why Dr. Barnes had given me the tip he did. Religion lived, all right, in the Wyalusing Valley. God was a seven-day-a-week affair. There were no Monday-morning pagans.

I had been impressed, too, by the Camptown Community Church, where Methodists, Presbyterians, and Baptists worshiped together. Yet, as I looked out the train window, winding back home through the mountains, I realized this was typical of the Wyalusing Valley.

I remembered a story the valley folk had told me. It was of a farmer who drove to town with a load of grain and met a preacher when he got there.

"What is your denomination?" the preacher asked him.

"Well sir," replied the farmer, "thar's three roads leadin' to this town. Thar's the mountain road, and thar's the short cut, and thar's the swamp road. Now if you was goin' to buy my grain, would you ask which road I come by? Or would you want to know—how good is my grain?"

When Albert Schweitzer, the "great man's great man," came to the United States for the Goethe Bicentennial in 1949, admirers everywhere strove to see him or hear him, like followers of an Old Testament prophet hoping to touch the hem of a Godly man's garment. The physician, musician, writer, and philosopher, who had turned his back on worldly fame and gone to French Equatorial Africa to found a hospital for the natives, was a living legend. Among the thoughtful and the seeking and the groping, there already had sprung up a cult of Schweitzer lovers.

It was expected, then, that at each leg of Schweitzer's journey to the Goethe celebration in Colorado, groups of devotees would cluster around him.

In one city Schweitzer arrived by train and was met by a selected delegation of professors, doctors, public officials, and others of high standing among the great man's local admirers. They gathered ceremoniously on the station platform, each hoping to catch a few pearls of wisdom from the man who was a legend in his own lifetime.

Albert Schweitzer got off the train. As he exchanged brief

greetings with the delegation he glimpsed out of the corner of his eye an old woman further up the station platform trying to manage six or eight pieces of luggage. No porter was at hand.

"Excuse me, gentlemen," Schweitzer said. He left the circle of dignitaries and made his way to the old lady to help her with her luggage. Seeing him, the professors and doctors and public officials followed. They picked up all the luggage and, with Schweitzer in the lead toting a suitcase, they all made their way up the platform as porters for the old woman, who followed happily along.

Nothing Schweitzer could have said would have so crystallized his philosophy. Here greatness was summed up in humility. Here love was given action. Here Sunday-morning piety was given life on a weekday.

"What is the essence of Godliness?" I had asked Reverend D. Russell Hetsler, of the First Methodist Church in Brazil, Indiana. And he had replied, "Righteous love, justice and fair play: It is living that out in daily life by patience and kindness."

Schweitzer's "living out"—whether by the small act at the railway station or the big act of founding the hospital at Lambaréné—seemed to fit the definition.

We cannot all be Schweitzers. But there is not one of us who cannot, like the dignitaries on the station platform, pick up a suitcase and follow along.

See how a group of women did it in Rochester, New York. . . .

They called themselves the Young Married Women's Club. They belonged to the First Presbyterian Church and went to its services on Sundays, but they also managed to keep religion alive on the six days in between.

Once, for example, a woman in the community had twins and came home from the hospital to the small apartment in which she lived with her husband and two other children, one four and one a year and a half. Her husband was ill and hospitalized at the time, so that when she came home recuperating from childbirth with two pre-schoolers at home and two brand new twins, she really had her hands full.

The Young Married Women's Club promptly consulted its "benevolence list": the names of its members set down, each with a number, indicating the order in which they were to be called upon when a need arose. Half a dozen women who were next in order were telephoned.

One woman went over to the apartment of the beleaguered mother and did the housework for her. Another went out and did the grocery shopping. A third picked up the laundry and took it back to her own home and did it up. Another brought over baked goods. Another dressed and cared for the older children. The club president, Mrs. Elizabeth Gingrich, went in at nine in the morning and bathed the new babies, helped the mother make the formula—and then just stayed around and talked with her.

"I think she needed the talk as much as anything else," Mrs. Gingrich said. "A woman can become panicky under circumstances like that. Just being with her made her feel a lot more secure, not all alone."

I went over to Plymouth Avenue, to the apartment of a young couple named Peters. Hugh Peters was in the Royal Canadian Air Force and had been sent to Rochester to take some technical courses. When I visited their small, upstairs apartment Hugh and his wife, Beverley, proudly introduced me to their new little daughter, their first child, Suzanne, nine months old.

"Things could have been pretty difficult, and pretty lonely, when Suzanne was born—but they weren't," Mrs. Peters began.

She told how she found herself awaiting childbirth here in a country which was strange to her, without friends, without relatives.

". . . At least I thought I was without friends."

But word reached the Young Married Women's Club and the "benevolence list" quickly was tapped.

"Women came over and washed my dishes. They mopped the floors. They even brought in warm food at suppertime," Mrs.

Peters related. "I didn't have to prepare supper at all. Four women came in to do the work and help me with the baby, and four brought in food." She lifted Suzanne out of her play pen and, holding up the smiling child, said, "You can't imagine what it meant to me. Suzanne and I will never forget them."

When I had a chance to look over the "benevolence list" I saw that a new name had recently been added to the roster of those who stood ready to help others in need. It was a familiar name: "Mrs. Hugh Peters."

In addition to helping new mothers, the club had a "moving plan." There was difficulty, at the time, in getting vans and crews when a family moved from one house to another, so the Young Married Women's Club refurbished a good old American tradition. As in the days of logrolling, they simply got together on moving day with whatever cars, trucks, or trailers they could muster and all pitched in.

"We can move a family in jig time—and save them quite a bit of money, too," Mrs. Gingrich remarked.

Of course, the deeds of the women of Rochester are rarely heard of outside the circle of the grateful beneficiaries. But this too seemed to be of the essence of living religion. Schweitzer did not help the old woman at the railway station for a headline.

Perhaps these deeds are heard of somewhere. . . .

Certainly they are heard of in the hearts of the doers.

In Towanda, Pennsylvania, in an institution for the aged known as Jennings' Nursing Home, I met Aldona Buntinas. She was twenty-three, a girl with sandy hair and green eyes, wearing the blue polka-dot uniform and white apron of a nurse's aid. She could not speak very good English.

Aldona was a living example of living religion.

In the roster of the two billion people in the world Aldona's name would be followed by two letters: "DP". She was one of the millions whose lives were caught between the upper and the nether millstones of war.

Remember 1939, when the name "Memel" so frequently figured in the news of Hitler's saber rattlings? Aldona was there. She was a little girl in Memel, or Klaipeda, as it was known in Lithuanian. She and her family were simple people, wanting nothing more than to live and let live. But they were geographically unlucky.

The Germans came in and took over their village. At first the Germans made all the people German citizens, but later they relented and gave the people a chance to decide for themselves what allegiance to hold. Aldona's family chose to be Lithuanian citizens, just as they had been before.

By 1941 the conquerors had become more stern. They confiscated all the property of those who had not become Germans. Then they gave them twenty-four hours to decide whether to be expatriated to Germany or go to a concentration camp. Aldona and her family went to East Prussia.

They stayed for three years before the wild waves of war engulfed them there. Then they migrated to South Germany, where the Third Reich put them to work as farm laborers. From there they were transported to Bavaria. Aldona's father was separated from the family then. She didn't know where he went or what became of him.

In 1948, with the war over but the world still busy sifting out the human debris, Aldona, her mother Trude, her sister Gilma, and her brothers Ramunas, Martinas, and Gervydas, were given tags and sent to a displaced-persons camp. For two years they were shuffled about, from one camp to another to another.

It was a long night for the Buntinas family. It seemed that day would never come. . . .

But just at that time in Towanda, Pennsylvania, a young minister, Reverend Thomas F. Luce, was talking to his young adults' group at the First Presbyterian Church about displaced persons. They were going over some literature, full of legalistic terms and carefully placed commas, telling how and under what conditions displaced persons could be brought to this country.

It boiled down to this: One would have to guarantee that the

DP would have a home that would not displace an American, a job that would not displace an American, and transportation from the port of entry.

The young adults looked at each other. "Well, why not?" their expressions seemed to say. They got busy. Within a fortnight they had found two apartments, one house, and a large tenant house in the country suitable for four families, and in no case would a single American be displaced. They got promises of jobs—in restaurants, factories, private homes. Reverend Luce and his wife said one DP could stay at their home and help with the housework. The transportation money was raised, too.

Within a year twenty displaced persons had been brought to Towanda.

Aldona Buntinas was one of them.

She was working as a nurse's aid, studying English in spare time in a special class the church people had organized.

Gratitude sparkled in her eyes when I spoke with her. But more than that, her very being in Towanda was a kind of halo about the heads of a group of young adults who had made religion live.

Not long ago a church was moved from one side of the road to the other in my home town of Westport, Connecticut. It was jacked up on enormous timbers and in quite an operation with cables and winches—and engineers buzzing about like busy bees—the entire church building was trundled out into the Boston Post Road, moved down the road a bit, and then reinstalled on the other side. It was quite a feat.

On a morning of the week when the church was to be moved, after long preparation, I happened to be in a snack bar across the street. There the church stood, jacked up and poised to go. Its path was laid out with timbers, cutting diagonally across the Post Road to the new location on the same side as the snack bar. It was to be moved the following Sunday.

The counterman brought me an order of waffles and we both

looked for a moment at the church sitting up on its stilts, ready to go. I joshed to the counterman:

"Well, next Sunday you won't have to go to church. The church will come to you."

The counterman returned to the counter. Clearing some dirty dishes, he rejoined:

"I never go to church anyway, so what's the difference. Say, if I ever went to church, they wouldn't have to move it. It would fall down!"

The incident stuck because it was typical of so many. On every leg of the journey I met people who didn't go to church or temple and more or less joked, or even bragged, about it. They weren't villains, and most of them weren't irreligious. When I probed a bit I found that they hadn't lost the church quite so much as the church had lost them. Here are typical remarks which turned up in my notebook:

"The same old stuff every Sunday. How much can a man take?"

"It's just bad showmanship. They'll lose their audience."

"Same old hymns, same old sermons."

"No relation to life, that's the trouble. If you want a crowd on Sunday morning, I say—don't duck the issue, get down to earth."

"I go to church once a year just to check up. It's always same as 'twas last year, so I don't go again till next year."

I wondered why this had to be. Religion is man's basic relationship, the tie between him and all that is unknown, mysterious, infinite, mystical. It deals with the source of the greatest of all human powers: the power of belief. We know to what ends belief has moved men. It has supplied the drive behind exploration and invention, has given men the will to conquer the jungle and tame the wilderness, has given them the courage to live and to fight to live, and likewise the courage to die—for what they believe in.

What has happened to this dynamic?

"Religion ought to be luminous and colorful," Reverend Samuel Henry Prince of King's University, Halifax, Nova Scotia, said on a visit to New York. "Instead, it is too often tarnished and gray. It has lost its earlier spiritual glow. Its hymns are pitched to a minor key. Like all old institutions it has experienced the blight of the backward look."

The job of the church, he insisted, was to recapture its "lost radiance." It must become "the protagonist of more than a glorified etiquette or a social code of bourgeois respectability."

For this it needs leadership. One clergyman was frank to say, "It is no secret that we have a lot of inferior men in the ministry. By and large, our best people go into law, medicine, the sciences, and the business world. After all, the rewards of the ministry are low—sometimes almost starvation low—and what are the prospects? You have to live in a goldfish bowl. You have to walk as if on eggshells, for fear of injuring someone's delicate sensibilities. And you have to duck constantly, lest the ax of the trustees and elders descend upon you."

I knew just what he meant. I had met in my travels quite enough men of the cloth who were not only swathed in the cloth but mummified in it. I had met young ministers, priests, and rabbis who desperately wanted to restore religion's "lost radiance" but were hamstrung at every turn. If it wasn't the higher-ups in the church organization they were afraid of, it was their local board, and if it wasn't the local board, it was the local busybodies and the local gossips.

I also knew what a sizable number of unqualified men got into the ministry in the first place. At a New York seminary I sat in with a discussion group which dealt honestly and openly with "motivations for the ministry." No punches were pulled. The incidence of effeminacy and even overt or latent homosexuality among seminary candidates was frankly discussed.

The seminaries are becoming more alert to the need for selection. They are weeding out the candidates who are impelled to the ministry by guilt complexes or by neurotic piety or by a masochistic sense of martyrdom. They are looking for mentally healthy individuals capable of seeing and feeling the virility of religion and taking up its challenge with courage and spunk.

There always have been, of course, a nucleus of first-rate religious leaders; otherwise religion as we know it in the churches and temples might have died long ago. One could not ask for more brilliant, more dynamic leaders of their creeds than Protestantism's Ralph W. Sockman, Catholicism's Fulton J. Sheen, and Judaism's Barnett R. Brickner. The trouble is that we do not have more of their caliber.

One may hope that with people turning to the churches in a war-shadowed atomic age, and with higher enrollments in the seminaries than ever before, religion will make good the opportunity to shine again.

Much of it is up to the men in the pulpit, and they know it. There are some heartening signs that the word "sermon" may someday no longer be synonymous with dull, long-winded, repetitious, and soporific.

In Elizabeth, New Jersey, the members of the Madison Avenue Presbyterian Church came to their pews one Sunday morning and instead of hearing the customary sermon they were handed questionnaires. Their thirty-year-old minister, Reverend Charles Brackbill, Jr., wanted to know what they thought of his sermons. "Go ahead," he told them, "be ruthlessly honest."

There were thirty-eight questions, including:

"Are the sermons too long?"

"Are they understandable?"

"Are there disturbing mannerisms?"

"Should a sermon be about modern times and living?"

"Is the voice: graveyard, singsong, monotone, belligerent, harsh?"

When the young minister tallied the answers he found, among other things, that twenty per cent of his flock thought the sermons were too long, sixteen per cent said they didn't understand them, one person regarded "chin pulling" as a disturbing mannerism, sixty-four per cent wanted sermons on modern times and living, two persons thought Reverend Brackbill's voice was "graveyard," two "belligerent," and the rest that it "fit the subject matter."

But more important than the questions and the percentages was the fact that a clergyman realized that you can't keep your show on the road if you've lost your audience.

"We go on preaching year after year thinking we are getting our point across. I think some of us are kidding ourselves," the young minister declared. "There are five million sermons preached in the United States every year. That's a lot of sermons. The big question is—what comes from all this?"

There is terrific competition for people's time, for the attention of their eyes and ears, he pointed out. The old preachments don't stand a chance against radio and TV.

"Today's sermon must talk cold turkey," Reverend Brackbill insisted. "You can no longer scare people into religion or out of false ideas."

In Biggs, California, the fact that a modern minister need not create that old, uncomfortable "holier-than-thou" feeling was illustrated by thirty-four-year-old Reverend Arthur R. Kirk, pastor of the Community Church. He won the world's championship award—of the Burlington, Wisconsin, Liar's Club! But not a bit embarrassed by it, the young minister declared, "I've always felt that Christianity is a full, enjoyable way of life. I try to impart that feeling in the relaxed informality of jokes and stories."

The gem for which Reverend Kirk was proclaimed the world's champion liar was this:

"A man living west of town tried to raise watermelons this summer. He had very bad luck. The soil was too rich. The watermelon vines grew so fast that they wore the watermelons out dragging them along on the ground.

"One of the boys from town went out one night to swipe a melon. He got the melon all right, but the vines were growing so fast that warm night that the boy had to be taken to the hospital. Before he could break the melon off the vine, it had dragged him half a mile and he was in bad shape."

When Leon Brink, the president of the board of the Community Church, was asked what he thought of the "honor" the pastor had brought home, he replied:

"I think he deserves a raise in salary. We have a minister with a broader than usual viewpoint. After all, he was just bragging about our northern California soil, and anything you can say about that is just the simple truth, and that's no lie."

A minister who can have that kind of relationship with his people is in far better position to lead them than a stiff and distant master of the righteous pose, or a pulpit policeman who uses every Sunday morning to bawl his people out.

We no longer live in the Puritan era. Our minds are not centered upon fire and brimstone in some other world, but on saving our own world from fire and brimstone here and now. It was all very well for the devil-hounding Texan, J. Frank Norris, to preach of hell, hell, and more hell in the nineteen twenties. It was a different era. Once Norris preached for a whole week on this, his favorite subject, until, as one of his listeners said, "You could hear the wails of the damned and smell the smoke of their torment."

I did not find in month after month of reportorial leg work throughout the United States that this was the kind of religion people wanted. I found that they wanted something to hold on to, not something from which to recoil in fear. They wanted a faith that gave meaning and direction to living. Their heart hunger was for a steady glow of truth in the heavens which would not be blotted out by anything, even an atomic mushroom.

That is the "lost radiance" they want back.

"How are you going to get it?" I asked a minister in a New England town. "Certainly not by getting the people to sing hymns and put quarters in the plate."

"Certainly not," he agreed. "A lot of what we call 'religion' is just window dressing. Take some folks—they think that if they don't drink, smoke, or cuss, they're religious. Well, Hitler didn't do any of those things. Some others feel that if they go to church and sing hymns and say the responses on Sunday they are automatically religious. Let's get it straight. Going to church and singing hymns, and all that, are merely the way a religious man can *express* his religion if he feels like it. It doesn't make him religious. A man can be deeply religious without ever going near a church. And he can be pagan and empty though he's never missed a Sunday in twenty years."

The minister and I sat down on a couple of tree stumps in the shade of the steeple of his church. We had a long talk. And I wrote most of it down because I thought he came close to spelling out the kind of new radiance people were groping for.

"People won't come to church at all if they ask for bread and are handed a stone," he said. "We've got to fill their *real needs.* I may be wrong, and I've made lots of mistakes, but I'm taking a stab at it here in the parish."

"Just how?" I asked.

"Take our Young Couples Club," he replied. "It's not just a prissy group to drink tea and gab on Friday evenings. It's a serious group where the problems of marriage are threshed out. We can see the frightful divorce rate, and we're worried about it. Our young couples get frank aid in marital adjustment—and we don't dodge the sex issue either.

"For the teenagers we have talks on preparation for marriage, on courting, on necking and petting. We don't pull our punches. These are vital problems in the lives of young people. Talk about delinquency and promiscuity! Why talk about it? We're trying to *do something* about it!

"Mental health is another big problem. Can the church sit back and dodge it? Not the living church. In our parish we have two doctors and two psychiatrists who work with the church. When I find a parishioner in trouble—tied up in mental knots or full of inner conflicts—I have to decide whether I, the minister, can handle it or whether one of the doctors or psychiatrists should be called in.

"Sometimes the doctors and psychiatrists will send patients to me—people who are all right physically and mentally but sick spiritually, people who don't believe in anything. See, we work as a team: the mind doctor, the body doctor, and the soul doctor."

The minister paced on the grass for a moment. He looked up at the serene, white steeple of the church.

"Of course I give sermons on Sunday," he continued. "I try to deal with some of the things that bother people where they live. I had one sermon, for example, on the high cost of living and what people could do to help keep prices from running away. I talk a good deal about what Congress is doing, and the United Nations, and how we are going to prevent another war.

"Sometimes when you come into our church on Sunday you'll find petitions on the table to sign and send to Congress. We put the names and addresses of our senators and congressmen in the church bulletin so people can write to them. You see, religion isn't up on a cloud. When you believe in something and know where you're going you can get awfully busy with things right under foot."

"There's a lot more to it than preaching on Sunday and handling ceremonies when people get married and have babies," I commented.

"Sometimes I have to step in when people *aren't married* and have babies," the minister went on. "There was a fine young couple—they wanted to marry but the circumstances were all against it. The girl became pregnant. They were panicky, without anyone to turn to. So they came to me."

"Wasn't it too late—by then?" I asked.

"I don't believe in the words 'too late,'" he replied. "I went to the parents of the girl and talked with them first. Then I talked with the parents of the boy. Then I got all four parents together. And we looked upon these young people as human beings who fell into error, not as fiends or ghouls or willful sinners. We agreed that they ought to be allowed to get married; they had every right to get married. And so they did—and happily.

"You may wonder about the community. How could we save these young folks from a life of condemnation and ostracism? Well, we got the problem discussed in our local paper—not the problem of these particular young people, but the problem of youth in general, of boys and girls of marriageable age who want to marry but are blocked by circumstances. They're not demons, you know. They're just caught between the natural urges and desires God gave them and the economic and social blockades to marriage.

"Townsfolk began to understand that. The newspaper got about fifty letters. Only one pointed the finger of condemnation. All the rest admitted it was a problem for *all* society, including the smug married folks, to see that young people are given the natural opportunity to marry when they're ready to.

"Then there's the alcoholic. Every pastor in the country has a bit of that problem. About a million and a half men in the country are alcoholics, and the women are catching up to them fast. Sure, I know that a lot of ministers are reading the riot act to them and making them pledge never to touch another drop. But that's not helping them. That's kicking a man when he's down.

"I say it's up to every minister, priest, and rabbi in the country to study up on alcoholism. They've got to know that you can't say 'stop' to it any more than you can say 'stop' to scarlet fever. The Yale University studies have shown us what makes an alcoholic—the feelings of inadequacy and lack of self-esteem that make escape necessary for these people. You've got to get in there with them and work on their faith, their self-esteem and their whole past history if you want to help them get well.

"You see, that's what I mean by *living religion*. I'd rather see a pastor reading the Yale studies on alcoholism than half the ecclesiastical literature that comes across his desk!"

The minister lit a cigarette and puffed rapidly a few times. "Lots of pastors act like little tin gods," he went on, "because they're afraid they'll get bounced out by the trustees if they don't. I say it's dead wrong. I say if a clergyman can help his people by having a smoke or a drink with them, then more power to him. The best parish work in all history was done by One who was called a 'wine bibber and a friend of sinners.' His name was Jesus. And He said that it is not what goes into a man that counts—it is that which comes out of him."

I repeated the line as I wrote it down—*"that which comes out of him."*

"Sure, we've all got to rebuild from within," the minister concluded as he walked to the church to close the windows for the night. "All great revolutions start with revolutions inside ourselves. All great changes and great growth in the world come from within. Think of the prehistoric animals. They had their armor on the outside—that's why they're in museums today. But man lives on, and will continue to live on, because his armor—his strength—is on the inside."

This parson of a small New England town was an example, a shining one, of a leader who could make religion live. But where was the leadership of the entire, organized church? I set out to look for it and the first finding was a bitter disappointment.

I found Jim Crowism.

If there is one word which crops up more than any other at religious gatherings, one word which the church orators work to the bone, that word is "brotherhood." We are, of course, all brothers under God. We all recognize, of course, the "fatherhood of God and the brotherhood of man." We know that God loves us all equally. We love each other, too. But on Sunday morning, let's not have any brothers who happen to be Negroes in the pew next to us!

In the South I met a woman who considered herself a devout Christian, and in nearly every sense of the word she was. But when it came to having the Negro children of God in the same church with her she ardently said no. Her reasons were: 1. The Negroes have their own churches. 2. The races shouldn't mix. 3. It's better that way.

How often the same arguments have been used to keep the Negroes out of "white" hotels, out of "white" restaurants, out of "white" schools, out of "white" theaters, and, when they finally return to the Father, out of "white" cemeteries.

The pattern of Jim Crowism in our churches is spotty. There are, of course, some inter-racial churches. And there are some where the color line is drawn like a chain across the portals of God's house. But the prevalent pattern is not as forthright as either of these; it is the pattern of the gentlemen's agreement. A Negro family is not "barred" from membership in the white church, it is simply "discouraged." A very reasonable elder or a sweet-voiced matron of the congregation simply explains that, after all, it would be awkward to be just one Negro family among all those white people. And there'd be the problem of the socials and the dances. And then the young people. . . . "Well, after all, you do have your own church. Wouldn't you be much happier there? Yes, we knew you'd understand. . . . It's better that way."

If God were the wrathful Jehovah man thought Him to be in an earlier day, just how would He illumine the hypocrisy of such a scene? With a bolt of lightning, perhaps, as in *Finian's Rainbow?*

But no, He is a loving God and patiently allows enlightenment to sink into us, in such measure as we are grown up enough to absorb it.

We absorb it slowly indeed.

"There is more Jim Crowism in America at eleven o'clock on Sunday morning than at any other time," charged a speaker at the Baptist World Alliance in Cleveland.

In the same city Mrs. Hoke Dickinson, wife of the minister of the Franklin Circle Church, told the Sisterhood of the Euclid Avenue Temple: "After listening to hundreds of pronouncements on brotherhood, I have a right to expect that the church lead in the battle to outlaw segregation. Instead, the church has made Jim Crowism respectable. . . .

"It saddens me immeasurably that the church—that institution serving organized religion—has failed to lead out in this area. Organized labor and organized sports have been far more successful, it seems to me, in breaking down prejudices and in recognizing individuals on the basis of merit than has organized religion. The Brooklyn Dodgers and, I'm proud to say, the Cleveland Indians have made a tremendous contribution toward making discrimination unpopular."

The Dodgers and the Indians, yes, but what about those Sunday-morning teams, the Deacons and the Elders?

The little town of Staffordville, Connecticut, with a population of less than a thousand, caused somewhat of a sensation in 1950 by offering the pastorate of the Staffordville Congregational Church, which is in a white parish, to a Negro minister. The minister, Reverend Roland T. Heacock, accepted. "NEGRO MINISTER STARTS WORK IN WHITE CHURCH" proclaimed a headline in the New York *Herald Tribune*.

But when Reverend Heacock stepped to the pulpit for his first Sunday service he looked out over the white faces of his flock and said:

"It is a sad commentary on the state of democracy and Christianity that, when an obscure, untalented Negro minister takes over the pastorate of a tiny rural Connecticut church, it is big news. Why should it be big news?

"Why shouldn't we human beings just accept one another regardless of the color of our skin or our eyes, if we are decent and worthy? And why is not the Christian religion in the forefront practicing this simple, elemental precept we so loudly proclaim—the worth and dignity of human personality?

"The plain truth is that the Christian church should hang its head in shame at its snobbery, racism, and class consciousness."

I went on looking for living religion in the organized church. Though this first finding was a bitter disappointment, there were heartening discoveries later on—even on the subject of Jim Crowism.

I found the National Council of Churches waging a valiant fight for racial equality, even though it occasionally got a black eye for doing it. Because the National Council (and its predecessor, the Federal Council) included Negro denominations in its membership, the Ku Klux Klan came rushing out with charges that the Council was "pro-Communist."

Dr. Samuel McCrea Cavert, general secretary of the council, evenly replied:

"The Council is an inter-racial body, including four Negro denominations in its membership on a basis of equality and fellowship. For thirty years it has carried on a program in behalf of inter-racial understanding and co-operation, equal opportunity for men and women of all races, and the full protection of the rights of every citizen regardless of race, color, or national origin. To the Ku Klux Klan this seems to be a 'pro-Communist program' but the Council regards it as simply the effort to practice Christianity in daily life."

On many other fronts I found the National Council of Churches breathing life into religion—practicing what it preached.

I went to the sugar beet fields of Colorado and the strawberry farms of Michigan and found one of the organization's member agencies, the Home Missions Council, doing a tireless job of improving the lot of migrant workers. Its field staff was ranging up and down the country following the crops as the migrants do, working to get them better housing, better medical care, better education for their children. I'll never forget one Home Missions worker, Reverend Ellis Marshburn, with whom I barnstormed through the migrant camps of Michigan,

Illinois, and Minnesota. Some of the time he had his wife and children in the car. We covered hundreds of miles. But rough roads and itinerant living and low pay didn't matter, not so long as he could help bring a better life to the Mexicans and Negroes and other folks who worked in the fields.

I found, too, that the National Council was doing a living, breathing job in mental health. Through its commission on pastoral services and its commission on religion and health, it was helping pastors everywhere to deal more effectively with the emotional as well as the spiritual problems of their flocks. It was not sitting back. With skilled leaders such as Reverend Seward Hiltner and his successor, Reverend Otis Rice, it was sending out a constant stream of enlightenment. It was educating the clergy to be more skilled, more effective in dealing with sickness, bereavement, parent-child problems, marital crises.

Again, in the council's department of the church and economic life I found realism and the living out of Christian ethics. And again—no punches pulled.

"The hunger of any man anywhere becomes the concern of Christian men everywhere. . . . We must not assume that either governmental control or the automatic operation of any economic system can take the place of the conviction and action of Christian people working for justice in a free society," declared the council after a conference on the church and economic life in Detroit.

In a Labor Day message it set down an economic creed: "We must declare unremitting war on poverty, ignorance, greed, and prejudice. . . . Every person has a calling to serve God unselfishly in some useful occupation. All Christians are equally called to honor God daily in love to their neighbors through their different vocations. Every useful occupation, be it that of wage earner, businessman, or minister, can be an expression of a person's will to serve God and his fellowman. . . . Jesus left us no blueprint for a social system, but he gave us the law of love by which the whole of our life is to be measured."

When I looked in on the department of the church and economic life it was busily engrossed in research. With aid from the Rockefeller Foundation, it was doing a several years' study on "the role of ethics in economic life." Quite a project; too often in the past the church had been content to deal with ethics only on Sunday and leave economic life to its own devices the rest of the week. Now one of the National Council's objectives was to find out how spiritual principles could be applied to the mundane business of money-making.

Religion need not inhabit an ivory tower. The National Council of Churches was, for me, the living proof of that. I remember the constituting convention in Cleveland when the old Federal Council became the National Council in 1950. It was a long convention and I filled up several notebooks, but one page of notes I flagged with a string of stars on top. It was a bit from a speech by Ambassador Francis B. Sayre, U. S. Representative in the United Nations Trusteeship Council:

"Certainly no true and sincere Christian can believe that Christ was an escapist. He faced life foursquare. He plunged into the very thick of its hard realities; He faced the evil of it with His eyes wide open. He did not seek, like some religious leaders, to withdraw from life's intensities. . . . Instead he taught Christians to heal the sick, to feed the hungry, to live more vividly. The whole of His teaching was an insistence that men and women should meet life realistically, seeing and fighting its evil without flinching. 'I have come that they might have life and have it more abundantly.' Christianity offers a workable pattern of life, applicable to *all* human activities."

And *applicable*—I would like to add—*seven days a week.*

14

MATURE FAITH

A God to seek

The search for God led to many places, to many people. One person I shall never forget was a little old lady named Mary Tusch, and one place, her "Hangar" in Berkeley, California. It was her home, really, but it was known as her "Hangar" to the most famous aviators in the world because she had become, over the years, their guardian angel. She was "Mother Tusch" to thousands of airmen from Billy Mitchell to Jimmy Doolittle.

This little old lady, who was born on Christmas Day in 1876, held out a shiny silver dollar and smiled as she pressed it into my hand. I felt a bit like an interloper, for I knew that Mother Tusch's famous silver dollars customarily went to people like Doolittle, or "Hap" Arnold, or to young bucks who fly for the Air Force.

"That's all right," she said. "You can use it too. You're flying someplace . . . We all are."

She squeezed my fingers around it and said a little prayer. Then she lifted her eyes to meet mine and added, "Remember this one thing—remember it above everything else. If you ever get into trouble, take the silver dollar in your hand just like you've got it now—and *read the instructions.*"

Instructions on a silver dollar?

I looked into the palm of my hand and there were the *instructions* looking up at me. Four simple words:

"In God We Trust."

Not long ago, on a more formal occasion, Mother Tusch had pressed a silver dollar into the hand of General Hoyt S. Vandenberg, Chief of Staff of the United States Air Force. Accepting the presentation he had said, "Mother, I deeply appreciate this, coming as it does from the most beloved lady of the air service. I'll never part with it. I'll put it away——"

And she had interrupted, "Oh no, you won't *put it away.* You'll keep it right with you—on your person, at all times."

And the general had docilely agreed.

Mary Tusch, at her "Hangar" in Berkeley, had given away nearly seven hundred silver dollars. Her little white cottage on Union Street, all but surrounded by the mushrooming University of California, had become—unofficially—an aviators' shrine. Old-timers of the days of daring transatlantic tries and wooden struts and open cockpits came in whenever they were within landing distance of Berkeley. And fledgling airmen from the training bases, full of the mysteries of radar and automatic pilots and supersonic flight in jets, wandered in timidly to see what to them was a living legend—the Mother of Fliers, the little old lady with wings.

I found Mother Tusch in the very last days of the "Hangar." A rush of circumstances which strongly tested her own faith crowded in upon her shortly afterward. . . .

There she was in the little white cottage with the porch entrance on the side. She was among her souvenirs: a strut from the famous Kitty Hawk, the cap Admiral Byrd wore in Little America, a piece of fabric from the venerable NC-4 (which flew the Atlantic in 1919), the propeller of an ancient Jenny that crossed San Francisco Bay in 1912, a flying jacket the Prince of Wales wore when he flew over the German lines in World War I, the famous insignia of "The Swoose," sole survivor of an intrepid B-17 group in the Philippines in World War II. . . .

And on—and on, through the hallway, the living room, and the sitting room of Mother Tusch's home. The walls were plastered ceiling high with pictures, medals, propellers, air instruments, and trophies captured from the Germans in two wars such as field telephones and spike-topped helmets.

The living-room walls, above the molding, were reserved for signatures. Back in 1917 a spunky University of California track star who was training for the Air Corps climbed up on a couch and wrote his name, "Charley Anderson," high up on the wallpaper. Mary Tusch, whose home hadn't yet become a hangar, took a dim view of Charley's autograph. She said it would wreck her wallpaper.

Indeed it did. As wallpaper, the strip above the molding wasn't worth much when I saw it. But, as history, it was virtually priceless. Stretching out in all directions from Charley Anderson's name, in closely packed profusion all around the room, were the signatures of the men who had made aviation: the famous, the near famous, and the unheard of. For thirty-three years they had been coming to the "Hangar" to scrawl their names on the wall and to hear the quiet blessings of the mother eagle of them all. Among those who helped wreck the wallpaper were Mitchell, Doolittle, Arnold, Byrd, Smith, Wilkins, Bennett, Pangborn, Balchen, Rickenbacker and—a name written in a softer, more delicate hand—Amelia Earhart.

But Mother Tusch meant a great deal more to her fliers than simply a house full of relics. During World War II, the boys of the 305th Bombardment Group named one of their planes the "Mother Tusch." Jimmy Doolittle, commanding the Eighth Air Force, heard of it and wrote to the little lady in Berkeley, "I am sure the plane will *do good,* as you have done."

The good which Mother Tusch did was, in the main, to give faith to people who dare the skies. Many an air pioneer and many a fighter for freedom took out her silver dollar somewhere in a lonely heaven, unwrapped the waxed paper that kept it shiny, and read the instructions—"In God We Trust."

Mother Tusch looked up at me through eyes of infinite softness, beneath the ringlets of her graying hair, and she quietly said, "You know—there are no atheists in cockpits."

It was the simple faith she gave them—not a belief in magic, but a peaceful attunement to God and life—that brought fliers flocking to the Berkeley shrine. It wasn't that they thought a prayer would bring you home safe and sound every time. But they learned from the little old lady that the power of *believing* is stronger than any aileron, or prop, or tail fin. As one of her fledglings said haltingly, wringing a flying cap in his hands, "I dunno, when you *believe* like Mother Tusch does, your hands just seem to make the flaps and props do the right thing."

To a fraternity of men in probably the most risky business of all, Mary Tusch had given grown-up faith. Fliers often are superstitious. They stick "lucky chewing gum" on the cockpit doors. They carry "lucky rings" up with them. They wind "lucky scarves" about their necks, make "lucky signs" to their buddies as they take off. Mother Tusch substituted belief in God, not magical reliance upon some charm or talisman but a deep-down belief in the ultimate purpose and the ultimate good of life no matter how things turn out. In place of wooing luck she offered them an abiding confidence. For earthly demands or guarantees, she substituted a mature kind of faith. She simply said to them, in the words of her silver dollars, "Trust God."

And she trusted God herself.

Not long after I saw her, the septuagenarian lady suffered a cerebral hemorrhage. It left her unable to walk or to talk. And to complicate matters, time was running out for the "Hangar." The University of California, which had grown and spread until it pocketed the little white cottage, needed the site desperately. The Smithsonian Institution in Washington, which had sent its air curator, Paul E. Garber, to Berkeley to look over the

"Hangar," liked it well enough but found itself unable to incorporate the entire cottage in the institution's National Air Museum. And with Mother Tusch so seriously ill, her daughter, Irene, found it impossible to keep the "Hangar" going alone.

It was clearly a time to unwrap a silver dollar and read the instructions.

Mother Tusch didn't need to, though, for the instructions had for a long time been written in her heart. And perhaps written there, too, was the line in which she surely believed: "All things work together for good to them that love God."

The next time I got in touch with Mother Tusch she was no longer in Berkeley. The "Hangar" had been taken over by the University and was awaiting demolition to make room for a building. But handsomely arranged in a large case under glass were the best of the little old lady's mementoes. They were labeled "The Mother Tusch Collection" and they were just where she had always wished in her heart they would be—in the Smithsonian Institution in Washington.

Mother Tusch herself was living quietly in the nation's capital, taking life easy in her seventy-seventh year. She still had occasional visits from her aviators, and, in the contemplative calm of her own zenith of life, she often sat feeding God's aviators, the birds, at a little feeding station near her window. She read the Bible often and never let a meal pass without the saying of Grace. In church, or even while watching a service on television, she'd bow her gentle, gray head and, as her son-in-law remarked, "She seemed *actually to receive* the blessing of the benediction."

Her son-in-law, by the way, was a brand new addition to the family. He had just married Mother Tusch's daughter, Irene. His name: Paul E. Garber, air curator of the Smithsonian.

"All things work together for good. . . ."

It was in Paul and Irene's house that the little old lady was living. She had given her entire collection to the people of the United States as a gift. What was not in the glass case at the Smithsonian was carefully packed away for posterity. Even the "wrecked" wallpaper of the "Hangar," with all its signatures, had been saved. By evening a gentle smile would cross Mary Tusch's face as she watched while her daughter, Irene, worked over the sheets of wallpaper to restore signatures which had faded a little.

One day a silver dollar came in the mail. It was from a new young man of the Air Force who had heard of Mother Tusch and wanted her to bless it. She did. But in the past Mother Tusch had bought all the silver dollars herself, tithing her small income to do so. She had shined them up and taken each one to a minister, a priest, and a rabbi to have a simple prayer read over them before giving them away to her boys.

"When my boys are up there in the sky, I want them to have something to hold onto," the little old lady with wings had told me. "I want them to see 'In God We Trust' shining up at them. No other nation in the world has that slogan. We Americans are carrying it around with us—in our pockets—every day of the year. How many of us ever stop to read it?"

Her soft eyes looked straight into mine as she added, "I don't want my boys to look for God far away, in some never-never land. God is right with them—in the palms of their hands."

Mother Tusch had a way of expressing her faith, a special way of expressing a faith which was especially hers. Most of the people I met were special, each in his own way. One trouble with formal religion, I began to realize, was that it often tries to pour all people into a single mold. They do not fit.

The erroneous belief that we can make them fit a single mold is responsible for all sorts of religious rivalries and collisions, to say nothing of intolerance. What is intolerance but an insistence that the other fellow believe and express his belief just as I do?

"Freedom is the first prerequisite of faith," Rabbi Hirsch E. L. Freund, of the Synagogue Council of America, said to me. "God reminds us of this in the first of the Ten Commandments—

'I am the Lord thy God, which have brought thee out of the land of Egypt, out of the house of bondage.' He reminds us that we must first be free if we want to find God."

Mature faith is a broad meadow. There is space for all and no need to crowd. I found, on my reportorial journey, many people who found their religions within the hallowed walls of churches and temples, but I also found many whose sanctum was a garden, or some rock-bound coast, or the twilight, or the tumult of a mass of people, or the silence of a private room.

A mechanic told me he could express his faith best right in his garage doing his chores, pumping grease into a chassis. A young woman said she could talk to God only at a holy shrine. I wondered what difference it made so long as each had faith. And as the journey lengthened and I had dug a great deal and seen many people and gathered many facts, I found myself respecting faith in any garb.

There was John Buck, Jr., a lean-faced youth of twenty-four with deep, earnest eyes. I met him in a factory in Detroit. When I asked him, "What do you believe in?" he replied:

"I believe God is everything. People forget about God these days. They shouldn't. If a person prays in earnest things seem to be brighter, the world seems to be brighter. I find that people who believe in God get further."

The young man looked hard across the table where we were sitting. "I wouldn't think of neglecting God," he continued. "Some people have time for everything—working, eating, recreation—but no time for God. Why not just ten minutes a day? Is that too much to give to God? Why not ten minutes in good, solemn, deep prayer?"

This was one kind of religion. I asked Buck how he came by it, and he told me it originated in his childhood—out of a "miracle."

He was just eight when it happened, he related. In his room in the little mining village where his father worked there were two statues. They stood upon his dresser, plaster figurines, brightly colored, one of Jesus and one of the Virgin Mary.

One day the boy was playing in his room and light was streaming in the window bathing the two statues. The boy looked up. His eyes opened wide. His heart began to race. There, upon the dresser top, the statue of the Virgin began to walk toward him. He rubbed his eyes, looked again. Now from the heart of the statue of Jesus bright red drops of blood began to trickle.

The boy pulled himself together and leaped to the dresser. There were the statues, just as they had been before. He searched the dresser doily, but there was no blood on it.

Buck didn't represent the incident to me as a bona fide miracle, to be entered in the annals of supernatural events. He simply told me the story, acknowledging that he was just a child at the time and that, even now, he could not explain it and didn't fully understand it. Its importance to him was that a powerful faith had sprung from it. And that, regardless of the "miracle," was very real indeed.

I followed the trail of Buck's "miracle" to the little Pennsylvania mining town where it had occurred sixteen years before. I went to the home of Buck's father, John, and his mother, Mary. And there, before me, were the two figurines. Mary Buck held them in her hands. They were two sacred statuettes of the kind you might see in any religious-goods store, though these were a bit worn with the years.

John and Mary Buck knew all about the "miracle." John, Jr., had told them at the time. They knew the statues meant a great deal to him, even though he was a man now and off working in Detroit.

"I'm going to give them to John when he gets married," Mary Buck said, holding the statues to her bosom.

I had planned to ask the family if they believed the "miracle" really happened. But when I sat with them in their living room the question seemed superfluous. Their faith, and young John's, went far beyond the validity or invalidity of the incident.

Young John himself had said, "Some people think this is baloney."

But there was no baloney about the faith of the Buck family.

Mary Buck in her little gray house with lace curtains, in her flowered cotton dress, said to me, "I believe in God and I'll always believe in God. That's the way it is. I believe in my church. And I believe in prayer."

"Why do you pray?" I asked her.

"Prayer makes me feel better when I am in difficulty," she replied.

"Why not just take a sedative?" I pressed.

"That would be temporary, artificial," she answered, not thrown for a moment. "Prayer is permanent."

I could see that John Buck, Jr., had carried much with him when he left the little mining town to work in the big factory in Detroit. His spiritual luggage had been well packed.

Buck's was one kind of religion and one kind of "miracle." I encountered another in the mining town where he grew up: the religion and the "miracle" of Olin Kuncelman. Kuncelman was working at a conveyor belt, bringing coal up to the surface in a shiny black stream.

Once, he told me, while he was working on the tipple his foot got caught in the heavy chain of the "car haul." The chain, used to haul coal cars up on the tipple, weighed some two thousand pounds. It began to coil back with Kuncelman's foot tangled in it, dragging him over the rails and ties.

His body finally wedged into a small opening where the chain went downward, and there he lay with the excruciating torture of that enormous chain tugging at him, trying to pull him apart.

"I thought I was a goner," Kuncelman related. "I even hoped the chain might pull my foot off altogether, so I could at least get out alive."

He would have died of the rending and the agony. But at that moment three men just happened to be returning from lunch, crossing the yard by the tipple. They just happened by *at that moment*. They spotted him and rushed to the rescue.

In concluding the story, Kuncelman summed up his particular religion:

"God is there to help you at the right time."

"But couldn't it have been just a coincidence," I asked skeptically.

"Well, then," Kuncelman retorted with an arching of the eyebrows, *"who arranged it?"*

Everywhere, in every corner of America, I found people with their special pillars of faith.

"The place to find God is in God's house—in church," said one.

"I haven't been to church in years, but I live my religion daily," said another.

"I don't believe in *getting* religion. I believe in *doing* religion," said a third.

From a fourth came this terse capsule of faith: "I believe in prayer and conscience. Prayer is me talking to God. Conscience is God talking to me."

The pattern of freedom of faith was never more clearly etched than during my visit to Fort Sam Houston, in Texas. Here was an aggregation of Americans, men and women, from all sections of the country and all walks of life.

The headquarters commandant, Lieutenant Colonel William F. Kernan, was a regular churchgoer, never missed if he could help it. One of the WAC contingent, Private Evalyn Gurganus, said the church people knew "more about God" than she did and she'd take it from them. Aviation Cadet Lieutenant Gordon Walls, at nearby Randolph Air Force Base, made a practice of saying the rosary with a group of other cadets in the barracks every night at 8:30.

But then there was Private William Dickens, Jr., "When I want to pray I go out to a hill on Castorville Road, twenty miles from the fort," he told me. "There's a cross on the hill. I go up there with a Bible. I want to be alone with God—I don't want other people watching me. I talk out loud when I talk to God."

"What do you talk about?" I asked.

"First I explain my troubles," he replied. "Then I ask for a little help in ironing things out. I figure if God's got a few extra things in his bag up there, well, He sure could afford to throw a few my way.

"I pray for people to love one another and to see smiles on people's faces. I never forget to thank Him either. . . . I don't open the Bible. I just take it up there like a badge to show I'm on God's side. I tell God I may not live up to it all the time, but I'll try.

"When I go up on the hill it's 5:30 or 6 A.M. It's just breaking dawn. The dew is still out. It's a little cold up there—shoot, that doesn't make any difference. The sun is just coming up. It paints its own picture."

Private Dickens had made that hill into his own personal sanctuary.

WAC Sergeant Ethel Kulhanek had a personal sanctuary, too, a very big one—the sky. She had learned aviation and taken out a private pilot's license.

"Only when flying do I get the feeling of being cleansed," she told me. "Everything is so clean, so free. I look at the clouds and I can see the faces of people I know and the faces of fairy-tale characters. I feel so cleansed when I come down. Everything seems right. It's like being in another world. . . . The chaplains say that's my form of church. The sky is my cathedral."

The cathedral of WAC Lieutenant Marjorie Wightman was the New Mexican mesa. "In Albuquerque," she told me, "I used to get up in the morning and go riding out on the mesa. The mountains would be purple in the distance. In winter there'd be snow on top of the red and purple peaks. I'd be loping along and suddenly draw up my horse and just sit back and look. I'd lose myself. I'd lose all concept of time. How did I feel? I felt a surge of gratitude just for being there, just for being part of it all."

Each of these, and each of hundreds of others I talked to, had his own approach to God. I could see how important freedom is; how it is, in fact, a cornerstone of faith. God did not stamp us like robots out of a die. He gave us, prime among His gifts, individuality. In the faith which binds us to our Creator and our universe, it would seem He wants us to be free and individual too.

I found a rule for faith across the length and breadth of America as one can find it in the heart and vitals of democracy itself. It was a simple one:

To each his own.

I found, too, that this is a time for faith. Some eras seem to have gone along pretty well without it: the humanistic era of the late nineteenth and early twentieth century, for example. Man seemed quite a self-sufficient package then. To use the words of Mrs. Welliver of the Wyalusing Valley, man hadn't yet come "to the end of himself." He seems to have reached that terminus now and, to his credit, seems to be aware of it.

We are on the threshold of some sort of renaissance of belief, some sort of resurgence and reshaping of man's alliance with the infinite. There is a yearning for this, a great wish which showed itself everywhere my journalistic safari took me: a wish to stop flapping in the uncertain gusts of doubt and cynicism and to sail steadily before a strong wind. In the prayer room of the Green Lake Ashram someone had written in the open notebook, "Send a revival, dear Lord, and let it begin in me."

Statistically, the revival may be said to be under way. Church memberships have risen steadily since 1940, rising at a rate more than twice that of the population increase. The 1940's and World War II seem to have been the turning point. Cynicism was the mood of the twenties, apathy the mood of the thirties, and a growing, groping search for faith the mood of the forties and fifties.

In the decade of the forties, church membership in the United States increased thirty-four per cent, while the population increased only fifteen per cent. A total of 22,000,000 new members flocked to the churches and temples during the forties, as against only 5,000,000 new members during the thirties.

Growth continued into the fifties, with an increase of two per cent during 1951, while the population increased 1.7 per cent. By 1952 church membership in the United States stood at an all time high of 88,673,005. This meant that fifty-eight per cent of the entire population, or nearly three out of five Americans, had come into the fold of church membership. Of these, the major group was the Protestants with 52,162,432, second the Roman Catholics with 29,241,580, and third the Jews with 5,000,000.

"There is statistical evidence," declared Dr. Benson Y. Landis, editor of the Yearbook of American Churches, "that the people of the United States turned to the churches in a period of war, international crisis and the atomic age to a much greater extent than during either the depression years or the relatively prosperous years of the Nineteen Twenties."

It was understandable that Protestantism's Reverend Ralph W. Sockman should say, "Never since the first century have conditions been so ripe for a new Apostolic Age."

But frequently in my travels someone would buttonhole me with the question, "If we're all children of one God, why can't we have one religion?" It was a hard one to answer. Religion, formal religion at least, seemed to be mocking its own lofty ideals by setting up sects and denominations, with all their hot rivalries and jealousies and contentions.

"You go downtown in your own city," one man said, "and you look on one corner and you see a Presbyterian church and you say to yourself, 'I guess that's the way to God.' Then you look across the street and there's a Catholic church. 'Wait a minute now,' you say to yourself. 'I guess maybe this is the way to God.' Well, on the third corner you see a Jewish temple, and on the fourth a Methodist church, or Lutheran, or Episcopalian, or something else. So in the end you say to yourself, 'Well, if these professionals can't agree among themselves, what's there in it for me?' "

Fragmentation certainly has been a characteristic of formal religion. Ministers tell the story of one sect calling itself the "Church of God," from which a dissenting group split off to call itself the "*True* Church of God," from which, in turn, a rebel fragment split off to call itself the "*Only* True Church of God."

Protestantism seems to have been hardest hit by fragmentation, having more than two hundred denominations, from big ones like the Methodists, with close to nine million members, to tiny sects like the Primitive Friends, which at a recent count had a flock of thirteen. Some denominations have been separated by liturgy, some by theology, some by geography, and some by hardly more than a thread—as was almost literally the case when one sect of Mennonites separated from another over whether coats should have hooks and eyes or buttons.

Between 1900 and 1936, twenty-nine Protestant denominations buried their differences and merged into thirteen denominations. But during the same period seventy-six *new* denominations were formed. One discouraged church official remarked, "If we had a united church tomorrow a new sect would start up the very next day."

Add to this the more fundamental cleavages among the Protestant, Catholic, and Jewish religions, and then throw in the differences among Mohammedans and Hindus and Buddhists, and you have the potpourri which baffles the average man. Are they all the flocks of the same shepherd, the children of the same God? Then why don't they get together?

The best answer I found came from a rural minister in a small New England town. "Why don't they get together? Because they're not really different!" he said.

"Not different?" I questioned.

"No, not fundamentally different," he went on. "Only the window dressings are different. Take you, yourself. You can wear lots of different clothes but they do not make you any different inside. If you were going skiing, you'd wear snow togs, if you were going to play tennis, you'd wear white ducks, if you were going to a masquerade, you might dress up like a scarecrow. But it would be the same *you* inside. There's only one *you*."

I asked him how that applied to religion.

"We have a *uni*-verse, not a *duo*-verse, or a *tri*-verse, or a *quadri*-verse," he replied. "*Uni* means one. The universe is all one, and the infinite forces in it are all one, and the religious truth that links us to the infinite, or to God, is *all one*. Buddhism, Hinduism, Mohammedanism, Judaism, and Christianity—they all have one thing in common which gives them the right to be called religions. That is: they reach out toward the realm of truth."

What are the various religions, then, but ascending paths winding upward along the many sides of a mountain, each filled with parties of climbers hoping to reach the very same summit? Since there is but one God, does not every upward path lead to Him? Isn't every upward path a path of faith?

The famous psychiatrist and philosopher, Dr. Carl G. Jung, found no difficulty in more or less absorbing all religions. "The idea of an all-powerful Being is present everywhere, if not consciously recognized, then unconsciously accepted," he once remarked. To relate himself to this Being, Jung drew upon a whole assortment of formal faiths including Catholicism, Hinduism, Taoism, and Zen Buddhism.

The incipient renaissance of belief in our time has much of this broad searching in it. It is no narrow crowding into the cells of denominationalism. These cells are too confining for man's needs when time seems to be running out. Struggling for spiritual life in a storm-tossed sea, he is reaching out for a life preserver and he is not primarily concerned with the label on it.

When Dr. M. Willard Lampe, director of the School of Religion at the University of Iowa, spoke of the religious resurgence among college students. He said, "It doesn't take the form of a mass movement. It is more on an individual basis. Young people are searching for a philosophy of life that can give an inner peace and security against the outward confusion and turmoil of the times."

So we must not be misled by the statistics. Yes, the church memberships have been rising swiftly. It is to be expected that in times when the need for faith is strongly felt people will turn first to the churches and temples. But will they stay? We do not know yet whether formal religion will fill the need, whether it will be sufficiently alive and growing and dynamic, or whether it will be shriveled by the "blight of the backward look."

Will formal religion offer the mature faith for which people are groping? Will it help Dr. Lampe's students find their "philosophy of life"? Will it give to the hundreds of men and women I talked to, and to millions more, the "something to hold on to," the "direction in life," the "sense of meaning" which they are seeking?

Fear and superstition will, of course, fill a lot of pews. After a train wreck on the Long Island Railroad a clergyman in one of the nearby towns said to his assistant, "We'll probably have three hundred for the Sunday service." The usual attendance was two hundred but he knew the wreck had scared a lot of people. But he didn't know how badly it had scared them. The attendance that Sunday was nearly five hundred.

Tragedy sends people to the churches. Disaster sends them to the churches. War sends them to the churches. But these things do not keep them there. Two weeks after the train wreck the attendance at the Long Island service was back to two hundred again.

"Emotional infantilism" was the term used by Reverend Harold L. Bowman, of the First Presbyterian Church in Chicago, for the kind of religion which rests upon suggestibility and fear. It was, he said, for people "who want to live all their lives in a kind of cosmic bassinet." Along comes war, or the atom, or simply the reality of life itself, and the bassinet tips over. Belief spills out of it along with the believer.

People today are seeking, not emotional infantilism, but mature faith.

"Faith," said the philosopher Josiah Royce, "is the discovery of a Reality that enables one to face anything that can happen to one in the universe."

Is such faith possible? Let me give you an example of it. . . .

November of 1950 was a perilous time for American missionaries in Red China. There were imprisonments, street incidents, vilification and abuse, and hovering over it all was the constant threat of what each uncertain tomorrow might bring. "Now we are in the midst of a rabble-rousing campaign that makes the earlier anti-American weeks look pale and respectable," wrote a young missionary couple, Sam and Bet Moffett, to their friends in the United States.

There was the feeling of living in a closing trap. But, wrote the Moffetts, "we faced and accepted the possibility of concentration camp when we stayed on two years ago.

"The pendulum swings back and forth from light to dark. At the moment the news from Tibet and of Chinese troops in Korea seems to be swinging us back toward pessimism," they reported. " 'Things are very tight,' our Chinese friends tell us. But only a short view can make Christians pessimistic."

And they concluded, "In the long view, what is the swinging pendulum but the very arm of God, and where better to live than at the end of the pendulum, for there, whether it be light or dark, we are in the hollow of His hand."

. . . Weren't Sam and Bet Moffett the embodiments of Royce's definition? Hadn't they discovered "a Reality that enables one to face anything"?

We talk a great deal about *security* these days. Security is virtually the cornerstone of our thinking in mental health, in problems of behavior, in inter-personal relationships. The psychologists and social scientists have melted all the major human needs down to this essential nugget.

Give a man security and you give him the gift of gifts, for then he is safe and nothing can touch him. Conversely, he is a bundle of fear and anxiety, lacking confidence in both himself and his world, if *insecurity* envelops him. Security has become the *sine qua non* of inner health and equilibrium in our world.

But actually it is nothing new. It is just a new label. For man always has been a wanderer in a strange place, not knowing where he came from or where he was going, able only to make a fleeting and fragmentary acquaintance with his surroundings and never able to answer the questions which bothered him most.

Insecurity is the natural state of man.

But so is security.

Just as God endowed man with the capacity to fear, so He endowed him with the capacity to conquer fear. Just as He created him ignorant of the infinite, surrounded by the unknowable, so He created him capable of trust. "Trust God . . . nor be afraid," wrote Browning.

What is security, anyway, but trust? If I trust a boat, I feel secure sailing in it. If I trust a bridge, I feel secure crossing it. If I trust a ladder, I feel secure climbing it. If I trust the universe, I feel secure living in it.

Trust is the answer to the unknowable. How often we demonstrate this in our daily lives. If there is something we cannot adequately explain to a small child, we tell him what we can, and we expect him to trust us on the rest. If we do not know exactly what the doctor is doing, we trust him. In business, we say in the face of the inexplicable, "Trust me, it will be all right." We tell a friend a secret and say, "It's all right, I trust you."

What is mature faith but man's willingness to say to the very essence of reality, to God, "I trust You"?

This is the ultimate security. Psychiatry aims to help a man become secure within himself. Faith aims to make him secure within his universe. The Bible's way of saying it is in the words of Job, "Though He slay me, yet will I trust in Him." Thousands of years later Royce speaks of "a Reality that enables one to face anything that can happen to one in the universe." Security does not change.

From the security of faith stems the ability to risk. There is no venture without it. Declared Reverend George A. Buttrick, of New York, "No venture can move an inch without a prior act of faith, for faith is life's thrust into an always hidden future."

Think of it. Life would be cut and dried if we knew all the answers. A businessman would know just how many refrigerators he could sell next year. A playwright would know just how long his play would run on Broadway. A mother would know just how her children would grow up. It would be like living backwards, into the past instead of into the future. But since it is not like that, since every breath we take and every move we make sends us coursing into the future, we are constantly risking and venturing.

Faith gives us the venturesome spirit, for the only thing which makes gross uncertainty tolerable is the underlying trust that all will be well, that *no matter what happens* all will be well.

A man I met in Missouri said, "If I didn't have faith, I'd go out and commit suicide."

The nadir of faith is, indeed, suicide. It may be actual suicide, or a living suicide in which the spirit of a person dies though his body keeps going through the motions. It is, in any case, the denial of life, for life accepts the unknown and the unknowable and extends to them full faith and credit. Reverend Robert J. McCracken, of New York, succinctly put it: "Faith is betting one's life that there is a God."

In addition to security, faith also provides miracles. Or perhaps I should say it provides the ability to recognize a miracle when you see one.

I do not mean a miracle like the parting of the Red Sea. I mean the miracles of our time, which occur by the dozens every day and which are, to those who recognize them, wondrous and spectacular.

Take the miracle of Edwin Barber, a young research chemist

in Newport, Delaware. He had lost his right eye in a laboratory accident. When I sat down to talk with Barber's wife, Ora, it was not to get the story of some supernatural restoration of his eyesight. It was to hear about another kind of miracle. . . .

"Ed lost his eye, but he found his soul," said Ora Barber.

I asked what she meant.

"We used to live an aimless, empty life before the accident," she went on. "We used to flit around like so many others, always chasing after something. All our friends knew was 'go'—stay up to all hours, restless, chasing.

"Life is better now. After the accident, what a relief it was to start over. We could just take a deep breath and start all over."

Edwin and Ora Barber were seeking now the solid things of life, the real joys, the verities. They were loving life more than ever before, finding satisfactions they had never dreamed of. They were happy.

Ora concluded, "Sometimes God chooses to test your faith the hard way. If you stand up to it, He will stand behind you. . . . Ed and I wouldn't trade back for anything."

I suppose anyone would call it a miracle if a man could see an optical chart with a blinded eye. But if he could see life——?

In Villa Park, Illinois, there was Dorothy Bell, a young career woman who worked in Chicago. She had recently come by a conviction of faith when I saw her. She was ebullient about it. "In the last two months so much has happened. So many of my ideas have changed," she said.

Again I asked what she meant.

"Before—I was so confused," she explained. "I didn't know any peace. I didn't know joy. I was in turmoil. I used to walk alone at night and cry out to God. . . . Now, I think He has answered me. I know what it's like to be happy. I know joy and peace. And the inner turmoil is gone. In its place there is faith in God and the world. I can hardly describe what it's done for me."

Worked a miracle—perhaps?

Then there was the woman in Independence, Iowa, who was depressed and wanted to kill herself. A minister-psychiatrist, Reverend Walter P. Bell, helped her to find faith—mature faith—and when I saw her she was whole again, a vibrant woman living creatively and doing valuable work for her community.

If, through faith, a broken arm had been made whole, everyone would shout, "Miraculous!" Was it less miraculous that a broken spirit was made whole?

I call these things miracles because they fit the definition: they transcend the known laws of nature. They occur, but we do not know how.

Faith may not change the weather, but it can change our view of the weather. Our own inner attunement, or lack of it, makes a gray day sunny or a sunny day gray. The very same set of circumstances may seem dismal and hopeless, or sanguine and bright, depending upon the faith inside us. The people we know may seem friendly, they may seem to like us; or they may seem hostile and they may seem to hate us—depending upon our faith in God's love. Life, our very same life without a single circumstance altered, may seem horrible or wonderful—depending upon our faith in God's works.

So when you get to the ultimate reality, faith can work many miracles. You just have to recognize a miracle when you see one.

Faith sometimes comes the hard way. Sometimes it takes what a woman in Boston called "an awfully hard knock." When life deals out a bad blow and we are knocked flat, the awareness that life is worth living on any terms comes overwhelmingly upon us. We reach upward from this new, enforced humility and beg God's pardon for being so cocksure, for taking so much for granted, and we find that a door of faith is opening in our hearts.

After the devastation of Hiroshima one of the first structures to be raised up out of the ghastly plain was a little shack. A lone man lived in it, and outside it he hung a simple sign, "Love thy neighbor."

Faith also may come through the simple act of saying yes. I

do not mean mouthing the word. I mean saying yes inside yourself. Psychiatrists often speak of "saying yes to life." Alcoholics Anonymous' first principle is the acknowledgment of one's own helplessness. Mrs. Welliver spoke of "coming to the end of yourself." The doctor-writer A. J. Cronin said, ". . . I lost my superiority and this, though I was not then aware of it, is the first step to finding God."

It is all the same. It is affirmation.

At the end of a long journey, this, I believe, is the light toward which the men and women of our time are groping. It is the bread of their heart hunger. It is the safe port of their drifting skiff.

It is a simple affirmation, based upon a simple truth: God loves you, otherwise He would not have made you.

INDEX